As Women of Faith

As Women of Faith

Talks Selected from the BYU Women's Conferences

Edited by Mary E. Stovall and Carol Cornwall Madsen

Marjorie P. Hinckley • Neal A. Maxwell

Marion D. Hanks • A. D. Sorensen

Donna Lee Bowen Barnes • Suzanne Evertsen Lundquist

Eugene England • Janath R. Cannon

Jill Mulvay Derr • Ann N. Madsen

Carlfred Broderick • Shari E. Pack

Signe Hale Gillum • Ida Smith

Stephen J. Bahr • Kay P. Edwards

Deseret Book Company
Salt Lake City, Utah

©1989 Deseret Book Company
All rights reserved
Printed in the United States of America

No part of this book may be reproduced in any
form or by any means without permission in writing
from the publisher, Deseret Book Company,
P.O. Box 30178, Salt Lake City, Utah 84130.
Deseret Book is a registered trademark of
Deseret Book Company.

First printing March 1989

Library of Congress Cataloging-in-Publication Data

As women of faith.

 Includes bibliographies and index.
 1. Women, Mormon—Religious life—Congresses.
I. Stovall, Mary Elizabeth, 1951-   . II. Madsen,
Carol Cornwall, 1930-   .   III. Brigham Young Univer-
sity.
BX8641.A8   1989   248.8'43   88-33569
ISBN 0-87579-200-6

Contents

Contents

*I*n the summer of 1984 the Brigham Young University Women's Conference moved from its home in the associated students' women's office to sponsorship by the university president, Jeffrey R. Holland. President Holland's original charter to the interdisciplinary planning committee expressed his hope that the conference be "a rich experience for women—young and old, married and single, mothers and daughters— . . . [in] a conference content full of intellectual stimulation, cultural enrichment, and spiritual affirmation." The committee has sought to fulfill that charge and has constantly struggled to address issues of vital concern to all of us—women and men—in a manner that unites the best scholarship and rigorous thinking with faith, spiritual insight, and, as appropriate, comfort and healing.

That perspective makes the BYU Women's Conference unique among women's conferences, university or otherwise, and offers us manifold advantages in devising solutions that are truly transforming because they strike at the roots of problems facing women, not just at symptoms. Solutions, we submit, can best be found by bringing to bear *both* scholarship and faith, a synergistic union that enhances each. Indeed, the gospel, intelligently understood, provides the answer. As Professor A. D. Sorensen of the BYU political science department says in his essay from the 1987 conference, "The only way we can finally escape the sins of inequality [between men and women] is to embrace the order of life required by divine love—to become a Zion society. The kingdom can be built up in no other way."

The second major principle behind our planning is the belief that women's issues are in reality human issues, issues of relationships, which can be solved only with all of us— women and men—working side by side. Certainly, we as Latter-day Saints know that we must learn to truly understand each other, to become one as husbands and wives, since exaltation can only be achieved jointly. That same understanding must be extended to all our sisters and brothers. We must see each other with new eyes and learn new patterns of interaction based on our enhanced vision of divine potential. Thus, we have invited and encouraged men to participate in the conferences as both attenders and presenters. We simply cannot solve the problems facing women without involving the other half of the human race.

And, as men and women need each other, so do women need their sisters. Each of us will experience over our lifetime physical pain, emotional anguish, heartache, grief, even betrayal in one form or another. If we attempt to deny the problem or to cover it with a facade of forced sweetness and light, we imperil both ourselves and each other—ourselves because we deny the healing that can result from the love, strength, and insights of true friends, and each other because people then assume we *are* our facades and feel even more isolated with *their* problems. We must be honest with each other—about our hurts, fears, even doubts, as well as our hopes and joys—and we must be strengths and safe harbors to each other in pain and happiness as we offer not judgment but love.

In this collection of essays from the 1985, 1986, and 1987 conferences, we have assembled presentations that address some common themes and that exemplify intellectual rigor expressed with love and support. Many of these papers require us to think deeply and even to rethink certain assumptions, to see issues in a fresher light, to examine how well our behavior expresses our ideals; others offer sustenance, renewal, and comfort in our trials. Readers should not, however, expect to find dictatorial prescriptions for what someone believes constitutes "the perfect Mormon woman." The essays, we trust, will not leave us with more burdens—with prescribed ways of thinking and feeling and yet more lists of things we "should" be doing and about which we will feel guilty but which may not be what the Lord wants us individually to be doing after all. The conferences, and these essays, never intended to provide the "ultimate handout" that promises to fix our lives and fill them with unending bliss if we will just follow its ten easy steps. We cannot reduce life to such simplistic formulas, nor do these authors attempt to do so. But they do offer personal insights and honest testimony from which we can derive perspective and understanding of our own experiences.

The first section of this volume, "Strengthening Faith," discusses the nature of faith and faithfulness and the meaning of both in our lives. In the keynote address from the 1986 women's conference, Marjorie P. Hinckley describes, with loving supportiveness, the diversity in the lives of faithful Latter-day Saint women and challenges us to offer each other true sisterhood despite that diversity. Elder Neal A. Maxwell explicates some of the "strategic challenges" to developing faith and discusses opportunities for building it, while reminding us that we are the creators of current history in the kingdom and, thus, we must make of our history "days never to be forgotten."

Essays in the second section, "Building Relationships with Self, Others, and God," address the nature of our identities as daughters and sons of God and how our understanding who God is and who we are should transform all our attitudes and actions toward each other. Elder Marion D. Hanks stresses the importance of realizing God's "equality of esteem" for all His children and of coming to know God and Christ through prayer, the scriptures, and the temple. A. D. Sorensen agrees that divine love, which is the order of the celestial kingdom, is no respecter of persons and that the earthly kingdom must reflect that same heavenly order. He reminds us that we cannot "continue living as the world does." Donna Lee Bowen Barnes elucidates the universal search for order and argues that it is only by conforming to the divine order that we gain both temporal and divine happiness. In an exegesis of the scriptures discussing Adam and Eve, Suzanne Evertsen Lundquist shows how negative misreadings have influenced relations of equality between men and women and how deeper readings of the texts contravene such notions. We cannot, however, offer only intellectual assent. Eugene England asserts that eternal marriages can be built on no foundation other than the acceptance of female and male equality before God and then describes many of the challenges entailed in becoming truly one as husbands and wives. Janath R. Cannon and Jill Mulvay Derr expand the vision from marital union to unity with our diverse and individual sisters and brothers in the kingdom and offer case studies from the history of Relief Society on resolving differences. Finally, Ann N. Madsen offers suggestions, personal experiences, and insight from her extensive knowledge of the scriptures on how to grow closer to God.

The third section, "Struggling with Adversity," opens with a profound and deeply sensitive essay by Carlfred Broderick on possible reasons why we suffer and how we can endure in faith and hope without becoming embittered by tragedy. Personal essays by Shari E. Pack and Signe Hale Gillum movingly share their own trials and struggles and their endurance and coping in faith and love.

The essays in the final section, "Understanding Our World," offer the perspective of both research and experience in illuminating vital aspects of personal, family, and community dynamics. Ida Smith challenges us to broaden our definition of *home* to include the community so that we become influences for righteousness there. Summarizing the sociological research on the effects of family structure on family dynamics, Stephen J. Bahr explodes some persistent myths and discusses the implications of empirical research for how we structure our own families. The final essay by Kay P. Edwards explains how our values affect our attitudes toward money and offers practical suggestions for reducing family conflict over allocating monetary resources by reaching mutually beneficial compromises.

We would like to thank our associates in the Women's Research Institute: Jeri Lyn Gill, who cheerfully spent hours in the library checking quotations and citations as well as proofing copy, and Diane Nielsen, whose superb computer skills facilitated the production of the manuscript.

This volume is another in a series of collected talks on a variety of subjects from the BYU Women's Conferences. We

hope that these essays will offer enhanced visions of our identity and of the meaning of the gospel as well as comfort, hope,
insight, testimony, inspiration, and strength in our quests to
follow the Master.

Mary E. Stovall and
Carol Cornwall Madsen

STRENGTHENING FAITH

Sisters, we are all in this together.... We need to lock arms and help build the kingdom so that it will roll forth and fill the whole earth.

— MARJORIE P. HINCKLEY

Building the Kingdom from a
Firm Foundation

MARJORIE P. HINCKLEY

*W*e are in a time when the winds of adversity and sophisticated criticism and bitter attack have become the order of the day. It therefore becomes the exciting responsibility of those of us who have inherited a firm foundation from the faithful ones who preceded us to build the kingdom, while others may wear out their lives trying to destroy it.

Like many of you, I grew up in a family where there was a firm foundation of faith. And so my love for my Savior began at an early age. Hanging on our bedroom wall when I was a child was a very large print of a famous painting of the boy Jesus teaching the wise men in the temple. Mother had positioned the picture so that the first thing our eyes saw when we awakened each morning was the beautiful face of Jesus. I was grown and long gone from the home before I realized what a profound effect this had had on my life.

My love and appreciation for the Savior took on a new dimension when we visited the Holy Land. We arrived in Nazareth at noon. The main street was narrow and uphill, crowded with merchants selling their wares, everything from fish from the Sea of Galilee to nylons. The noise was deafening. School-children were on their way home for lunch. At the bottom of the street was a very large camel. A group of children were

Marjorie Pay Hinckley, homemaker, civic leader, and long-time Church worker, has traveled extensively throughout the world with her husband, President Gordon B. Hinckley. In her travels she has spoken at regional and stake conferences, mission seminars and conferences, and in the dedicatory services of twenty temples. An ardent genealogist and temple patron, she has taught and presided in the Primary, Young Women, and Relief Society organizations. She and President Hinckley have five children, twenty-six grandchildren, and one great-grandchild.

gathered around it, chattering with excitement. Two boys about nine years of age were making their way up the street, one walking backwards as they threw a ball back and forth. "Was this the way it was when Jesus was a boy?" I asked myself. "Did he go home for lunch and stop to look at the camel and throw a ball with his friends?" I began to understand more fully that even though He was divine, omnipotent, the Prince of Peace, the King of Glory, He also was mortal. He lived on the same earth we live on. He had to overcome even as you and I. He had to discipline Himself to get up in the morning and do His chores. He had to study and learn to get along with His peers and learn obedience. My love for Him knows no bounds.

But even though my love for the Savior and my faith in Him are deep and satisfying, I believe what President Harold B. Lee once said in addressing a large group of Young Adults at a fireside in the Salt Lake Tabernacle. He talked of testimony, and what he said applies also to faith:

"The testimony we have today will not be our testimony of tomorrow. Our testimony is either going to grow and grow until it becomes as the brightness of the sun, or it is going to diminish to nothing, depending on what we do about it."[1]

While traveling with President and Sister Lee, I heard him say many times to the missionaries that a testimony must be reborn every day. This can happen in many, many ways. Sometimes it is as miraculous as the dedication of a beautiful temple in Freiburg, Germany, or in Korea, or as small as a sunset, or a verse of scripture that touches a tender spot. But mostly it comes from living the gospel. Jesus said in John 7:17: "If any man will do his will, he shall know of the doctrine."

Now when we develop this firm foundation of faith, what do we do with it? The following answer from President Spencer W. Kimball has become a well-known favorite: "We had full equality as [our Father's] spirit children. . . . Within those great assurances, however, our roles and assignments differ."[2] So your way of strengthening your faith and building the kingdom is different from my way because our roles and assignments are different. Some of us are married; some are not. Some of us have children and grandchildren and even great-grandchildren. Some have none. Some are widowed, some divorced. Some are affluent. Some live on the edge of poverty. Some are students; others have full-time careers. Some are full-time homemakers.

It is the mothers of young children I would like to address first. These are golden years for you. These are years when you will probably do the most important work of your lives. Don't wish away your years of caring for small children. Life is what happens to you while you are making other plans. This is a time of great opportunity for you to build the kingdom. When you teach children to love their Heavenly Father, you have done one of the greatest things you will ever do. If you can be a full-time homemaker, be grateful. If not, you must do what is best for you. I for one have never felt a need to apologize for my role as a full-time homemaker.

These are busy, busy days for you. I have seen women in all kinds of circumstances — Chinese women working on road repairs, European women working in the fields, Asian women sweeping streets — but it is my opinion that American women, especially Mormon women, are among the hardest working women in the world. They plant gardens and bottle the produce; they sew and bargain shop. They go on the heart fund drive. They take dinners to new mothers and the sick in their neighborhoods. They take care of aged parents. They climb Mount Timpanogos with Cub Scouts, go to Little League games, sit on the piano bench while Jennie practices, do temple work, and worry about getting their journals up-to-date. My heart bursts with pride when I see them come into church on Sunday, some as early as 8:30 in the morning, their children all clean and shiny, their arms loaded with supplies, as they head for classes where they teach other women's children. They scrub their houses with little or no domestic help and then try to be the glamour girl in their husband's life when he arrives home at night. But remember, my dear young friends, that you are now doing the work that God intended you to do. Be grateful for the opportunity.

My concern for you is that you are trying to cover all the bases at one time. You cannot be everything to everyone all the time. Sister Belle S. Spafford, in her parting words to the Relief Society sisters in the Tabernacle some years ago, said:

"The average woman today, I believe, would do well to appraise her interests, evaluate the activities in which she is engaged, and then take steps to simplify her life, putting things of first importance first, placing emphasis where the rewards will be greatest and most enduring, and ridding herself of the less rewarding activities.

"The endless enticements and demands of life today require that we determine priorities in allocating our time and energies if we are to live happy, poised, productive lives."[3]

This does not mean, however, that you should have nothing in your hands but a broom and a dustpan and nothing in your head but laundry procedures and economical casseroles. Be creative. Reach out and embrace the things this wonderful world has to offer. I met a mother in Florida who was taking a class in, of all things, bird watching. It was exciting to walk through Cypress Gardens with her and share her enthusiasm for the birds that abound there. To her children a sparrow will never again be just a sparrow.

The danger and challenge is that much of what we do does not have eternal consequences. Much of the time we are running to and fro and spinning our wheels. And much of what we do is for the wrong reasons. When my neighbor had a son in grade school, the PTA was raising money by having a cookie sale once a week during the noon hour. The students paid a nickel for a cookie. Each class had a turn to furnish the cookies. It came my neighbor's turn to send a dozen cookies to school with her Ronald. The day preceding was a hectic day. No time for baking cookies. But how could she not send homemade cookies? What kind of mother would they think she was? It was after midnight when she took the cookies out of the oven. The next morning she proudly sent Ronald to school with a dozen homemade, beautifully decorated cookies. When Ronald came home from school that day she asked, "Well, did you buy a cookie at noon?" "Yeah," he responded, "but by the time I got to the table all the store-bought cookies were gone. I had to buy a homemade one."

I love the scripture from Doctrine and Covenants 10:4: "Do not run faster or labor more than you have strength." Choose carefully each day that which you will do and that which you will not do, and the Lord will bless you to accomplish the important things that have eternal consequences. Let me tell you of two women who have done this under some difficult circumstances.

Ann is a single parent, a divorcée. While some divorcées feel that there is no place for them in this society, and especially in the Church environment, Ann has kept her eye on the big picture and moved steadily forward. It has not been easy, especially when her children were young. It was a challenge to provide both physically and spiritually for her two sons and one daughter, but she taught them well. Now both her sons and her daughter have filled missions. Ann went back to the University of Utah to increase her education and her earning power. While she was in school she took care of an unfortunate woman who was practically housebound. This job gave her some much needed money, while she also performed a loving service. And, believe it or not, during this time she was the Relief Society president in a large, family-oriented ward. She ran that organization as if she had nothing else in the world to do.

At the end of her next to last quarter in school, the grant that made it possible for her to attend school ran out. Her recently returned missionary son said, "Don't worry, Mom; we'll get you through." The dean called her in. He had gone over her record and had concluded that her work had been so outstanding that the university would waive the student teaching requirement and the rest of her class work and make her eligible for graduation with the upcoming June graduating class. The Lord blessed her because she learned early to eliminate the unnecessary and do the things that had eternal consequences. She operated from a firm foundation of faith. In so doing she blessed her children and helped to build the kingdom.

Another women who looked toward the eternal consequences of her actions was Francie. As a child Francie suffered

7

embarrassment when she walked out of a lighted area into the dark because she often walked into a light pole or stepped into a hole or ran into objects that she could not see because she suffered from night blindness.

She loved the outdoors and spent the summers of her early childhood in Rico, Colorado, a mining town in the beautiful Colorado Rockies. The summer after the fourth grade she was walking around the small town one evening with some friends. The girls were looking up and talking about the stars. Francie wondered why she could not see them.

By age sixteen or seventeen she found that she could not see many things at night. The doctors were puzzled, and though she felt some frustration, she compensated for her problem in various ways. One was to simply avoid going places she didn't know well at night, even some places in the house, or she would find a friend to use as a guide. Her frustrations were mounting, but perhaps it was fortunate that she did not know what was ahead of her.

At the end of high school she began to set her goals with incredible drive and faith for one so young. In three years she graduated from BYU with honors, the first young woman to graduate in youth leadership with an outdoor emphasis. She had more than once completed the BYU survival trips in the rugged desert and had proved to herself that if she capitalized on what she had and did not give in to her limitations, she could do anything.

Upon graduation she served a mission to Italy and was known as the "sergeant" because she worked so hard and encouraged others to do the same. While on her mission she found that she could no longer read the small print in the scripture footnotes. Immediately upon her return home she was diagnosed by the family ophthalmologist as having retinitis pigmentosa, an irreversible disease of the retina, which would eventually lead to total blindness.

This upsetting news did not stop her. Once again she packed her bags and left home, this time for Michigan State University in Lansing where she completed her master's degree in educational curriculum and then continued to do all the course work for her Ph.D.

While in Michigan, she met her husband, and now they have four lovely children. At this writing, she is legally blind. She is employed part-time at the University of Michigan as an academic adviser.

She pursues her church work with vigor, is a Cub Scout leader, and serves in the Primary presidency, and always she is a missionary. She has taught in the women's organizations by having a friend record the lessons from the manual on tape to which she listens and stores up the information in her mind. She works as a volunteer in the school her children attend. They go as a family to community activities, lectures, and museums. By necessity she has chosen carefully that which she will do and has concentrated on those things that have eternal consequences.

"The scriptures give me comfort and direction in the things that are most important to do," she says. "I have learned to work with what I have rather than what I don't have. I have strong feelings about my good heritage with noble ancestors who worked hard to do the things they felt were right. Their good qualities are something I can capitalize on. I have a spiritual heritage from my Heavenly Father. I have felt His divine guidance and have received blessings that are beyond measure and sometimes beyond what I deserve."

We are talking here about faith and building the kingdom from a firm foundation. May I say to Francie, "You, Francie, *are doing it* and sweeping us all onto a higher plane in the process. We are learning from you about courage and faith and building the kingdom."

And now a word to women who, for various reasons, are part-time or full-time career women. Today is your day, sisters. Never have there been so many doors open to women. It was not too long ago when, according to a report made by the University of Utah, more than half the women graduated in six majors: elementary education, English, home economics, sociology, history, and nursing.

These are very worthy pursuits. But the opportunities are

widening, and more and more we see women getting law degrees, medical degrees, MBA's, degrees in computer science, and even degrees in electrical engineering. What a tremendous contribution they are making in the business world. Our women bring to the corporate world a firm but soft touch. Hardly realizing it, they bring a special quality of friendship, flexibility, love, and understanding to the professional environment. They are making this a better place for all of us, as their faith and integrity and their understanding of right and wrong flavor everything they do.

And now to my peers. On my seventieth birthday I repeated to myself all day long something I heard Stephen L Richards's wife say when she was in her nineties. She said, "Oh, to be seventy again! You can do anything when you are seventy." Now a few more seasons have slipped away and it is even better, for now I can brag about being the same age as President Ronald Reagan. One woman who turned seventy-five on President Reagan's seventy-fifth birthday said, "If President Reagan is anything like me, he must go into the Oval Office on occasion and say, 'Now what did I come in here for?' "

Contrary to rumor, these *are* golden years, if you have a measure of good health. At this age, my dear contemporaries, we no longer have to compete with anyone. We don't have to prove anything—we just have to enjoy it all. How many of you have told your children how wonderful it is to be this age?

In 1985 Sister Camilla Kimball addressed the Women's Conference at BYU. She was ninety years old at the time and still going strong, perhaps not physically, but certainly spiritually and mentally. She inspired us all with her continuing drive to learn and her ability to make us all reach beyond our inclinations. And later, at age ninety-two, she took up oil painting.

There is so much we can do to be an influence, perhaps not in ways we have once known, but in many other ways. Last year in the Upland Terrace School in the Granite School District, which three of my grandchildren attend, grandparents gave the equivalent of two hundred hours of volunteer service.

Who can measure the worth of a grandmotherly or grandfatherly influence in the classroom!

You will appreciate a letter written to Ann Landers that appeared in the newspaper some time ago. "Dear Ann Landers," it began. "I am a twenty-two-year-old graduate student who would like to express my admiration for some people who have taught me more than all the books I ever read." If you are over seventy, you can take this personally:

"Dear Older American, I want you to know how much you have improved the quality of my life. Today I was driving down the street. You were sauntering uptown, your white hair shining in the sun, a smile on your face. You waved when I went by, though you had no idea who I was.

"On my first job as a cashier, I was nervous and scared. The line was long and everyone was impatient. You let the others go first because you didn't mind waiting. When your turn came you said: 'Take your time. My, but you have pretty eyes.' I could have kissed you.

"You say, 'Have a nice day,' in the elevator and talk about the weather. I can tell by your gnarled hands that you've done a lot of hard work and I admire that.

"You have an aura of calmness that so many of my generation will never know in their mad rush for money and status. Thanks, Older American, for being there."

So if we are too tired to go mountain climbing with the grandchildren, it's all right. We can still reach out and lift someone.

Sisters, we are all in this together. We need each other. Oh, how we need each other. Those of us who are old need you who are young. And, hopefully, you who are young need some of us who are old. It is a sociological fact that women need women. We need deep and satisfying and loyal friendships with each other. These friendships are a necessary source of sustenance. We need to renew our faith every day. We need to lock arms and help build the kingdom so that it will roll forth and fill the whole earth.

May I close with these words attributed to Lucy Mack Smith:

Let us "watch over one another . . . that we may all sit down in heaven together."[4]

Notes

1. Harold B. Lee, *Stand Ye in Holy Places: Selected Sermons and Writings of President Harold B. Lee* (Salt Lake City, Utah: Deseret Book Co., 1984), p. 91.
2. Spencer W. Kimball, "The Role of Righteous Women," *Ensign*, Nov. 1979, p. 102.
3. Belle S. Spafford, "The Wonderful World of Women," *A Woman's Reach* (Salt Lake City: Deseret Book Co., 1974), p. 23.
4. Minutes of the Female Relief Society of Nauvoo, 24 Mar. 1842, Archives of The Church of Jesus Christ of Latter-day Saints, Salt Lake City, Utah.

Women of Faith

ELDER NEAL A. MAXWELL

I have a ministry which I feel inadequate to perform. I regularly watch my wife, Colleen, in the circle of her ministry which is wide and deep as she moves about her rounds quietly. It is not uncommon for me to be starting a meal and find that she is fasting — sometimes for someone I hardly know who is ill or has a sick wife or for whomever. I am not offended but happy when she gets the promptings that come to us in our mutual roles as neighbors and parents.

It was a year or so ago that she said, "You really ought to go see Pearl Lence; it is her birthday." Earlier I had been Pearl's home teacher for a few years. Pearl is now over ninety. But it had been a long, hard day, and I said, "Oh, honey, I am just so tired." Colleen said, "I think you ought to go." So I went.

Pearl came to the doorway after I rang the bell. When she opened it and saw who it was she said, "I prayed to Heavenly Father that you would come today, and the Spirit told me you would come." I am grateful that such signals come. I don't worry about which of us they come through, as we strive to serve as parents and neighbors.

If I fail otherwise in these thoughts, I desire to salute and to encourage the faithful women of the Church. Previously, I have paid public and deserved tribute, describing them as "the

Elder Neal A. Maxwell, member of the Quorum of the Twelve Apostles, previously served in the presidency of the First Quorum of the Seventy, as assistant to the Quorum of the Twelve, and as commissioner of education for the Church Educational System. He received a master's degree from the University of Utah, where he was executive vice-president of the University, and holds four honorary degrees from Utah institutions of higher learning. In 1973 he was named Public Administrator of the Year by the Institute of Government Service at BYU. He is the author of several articles on politics and government and numerous LDS books. He and his wife, Colleen, have four children and seventeen grandchildren.

women of God." Happily, their numbers increase, for there has been, and is now taking place, by both birth and conversion, a significant infusion of such sisters into the kingdom. These saintly sisters have been sent by God to share in performing significant tasks which I will reference later.

Unquestionably, as brothers and sisters, we share alike both blessings and challenges. We share in a single system of salvation. We strive to walk the same straight and narrow path. We read the same scriptures. We frequent the same holy temples of God, participating in their holy ordinances. We partake of the same sacrament and share spiritual gifts. We are called to serve and are released from serving in the kingdom of God by the same divine authority. We depend upon the same atonement for immortality and upon obeying the same commandments for eternal life. We are to cultivate the same celestial attributes and to develop the same righteous reflexes.

There are other shared realities, too, however. For example, as women are more and more *in* the world, the tendency, as with men, will be, alas, for some women to become more *of* the world. Unless they are women of faith, this process will inexorably occur. A father-prophet's reproving, tender words to an erring child would be no less instructive had they been, "But this was no excuse for thee, my daughter." (See Alma 39:4.)

For us all, whatever one's roles, assignments, or achievements, any move away from Christ is a move toward unhappiness and emptiness. The praise and applause of the world may, for the moment, muffle the grim sounds of such movement—but the distance will still be there, and the consequences. There are no immunities because of gender, as sin isolates the individual and destroys the tastebuds of the soul. Hence, the laughter of the world is really loneliness trying to reassure itself, whether the hollow laughter is masculine or feminine.

The strategic challenges to sustain faith are likewise the same for us all; the only variations are tactical. Jesus taught how temptation, persecution (also, intriguingly, fear of persecution), tribulation, and the cares of the world draw us away from Him. (Matthew 13:21; Luke 8:13–14; D&C 40:2.)

Into those broad but debilitating categories the tactical challenges fit. For instance, the cares and anxieties of the world include being unduly anxious about receiving the praise and honors of the world. Fear of persecution includes the unwillingness to bear the mocking and scorning of the world.

Temptation includes the lure of more worldly life-styles. For some, the straight and narrow path seems to be too confining; hence, such seek a little more room to commit "a little sin," to "lie a little" — to do a little more merrymaking. After all, they reason, for conforming a little bit to the fashion of the world, God will only "beat us with a few stripes." (2 Nephi 28:8.)

Shared, too, is the matter of to whom we look for leadership. Meridian-day Saints, like Mary and Dorcas, did not, for instance, look for guidance or satisfaction from the prestigious Sanhedrin, the Sadducees, the Pharisees, Herod, Caiaphas, Pilate — or even regal Rome and its Caesars, whose impressive days of power spanned centuries. Instead, these and other saintly sisters viewed things with the eye of faith and thereby saw "things as they really are." (Jacob 4:13.) They had the precious perspective of the gospel.

It is no different in our day. Faith cannot be placed safely in the arm of flesh (D&C 1:19), nor happiness derived from "the things of the flesh" (Romans 8:5). For all the faithful, therefore, the ultimate and most demanding goal is that which was stated unmistakably three times in holy writ:

"Be ye therefore perfect, even as your Father which is in heaven is perfect." (Matthew 5:48.)

"Therefore, I would that ye should be perfect even as I, or your Father who is in heaven is perfect." (3 Nephi 12:48.)

"What manner of men [and women] ought ye to be? Verily I say unto you, even as I am." (3 Nephi 27:27.)

Indeed, for brothers and sisters alike, to be truly about our Heavenly Father's business consists in striving to become like His Only Begotten Son. His cardinal qualities include love, mercy, meekness, purity, patience, and spiritual submissiveness. Being portable, these qualities, insofar as we have developed them, will rise with us in the resurrection, when so little else will.

Given this, our grand objective, it is vital to inventory and ponder some of our challenges and our opportunities, which exist side by side like the wheat and tares, for it will be in that setting that we are to strive to emulate the Master.

Since you live in a time of prophecies in fulfillment, rather than simply prophecies under anticipatory discussion, this sampling may suffice. I stress that whatever our roles or the sector of our service, we can contemplate the tapestry of our time, seeing divine design and pattern whatever our season of life or circumstance.

Jesus foresaw the last days, when "because iniquity shall abound, the love of many shall wax cold." (Matthew 24:12.) This coarsening is spreading in our time. Paul said the incontinent among us would be "fierce, despisers of those that are good." (2 Timothy 3:3.) This coarsening will, alas, include some of the women of the world, not just the men. For me, seeing the language of the locker spread to the living room or kitchen under the guise of emancipation and sophistication is sad indeed. I never liked it in the locker room, because its sounds diminished and degraded all who spoke and listened.

As some of the people of the world become more coarse and more hard, there will be a lessening of the collective capacity to love. Pathetically, this diminution of love will occur in a world in which, already, there is not enough love to go around. The women of God who play nurturing roles in families and neighborhoods will thus become increasingly prized even as the coarsening feeds on itself, spilling its harsh and multiple consequences out upon society.

This foretold resentment of righteousness, this hardening with its inconsistent regard for human life, and this desensitizing will make of the human environment a slum, however adorned it may be by creature comforts. Such increasing iniquity will not only bring the coldness Jesus prophesied, but also devastating despair. This, too, was foretold by one of His

prophets who said, "Despair cometh because of iniquity."
(Moroni 10:22.)

Technology ensures that people in one nation will feel the
pains and difficulties and perplexities of those in another, il-
lustrating, in part, how another of Jesus' prophecies will be
fulfilled: the nations of the earth shall be in distress, "with
perplexity." (Luke 21:25.) The distress of nations — whether
reflecting failures in coping with famine, or international debt,
disease, or arms control — will be very real. The seeming human
inability to solve these perplexing problems will attest to the
faulty, secular premises on which proposed solutions are
based. The vision of the world is forever amiss, looking "beyond the mark." (Jacob 4:14.) The women of faith will thus
have to cope with these generalized circumstances (and also
with some added challenges) precisely because they are genuine believers.

How genuine believers will be viewed by some is portrayed
in the remarkable vision given to Lehi and then to Nephi.
Therein we are treated to imagery involving a great and spacious building and its multitudes; it represents the "pride of
the world" and "the world and the wisdom thereof." (1 Nephi
11:35–36.) The inhabitants of the great and spacious building
are strangely preoccupied with Church members, pointing fin-
gers of scorn and mocking members of the Church who seek
to cling to the iron rod. (1 Nephi 8.) Some who have clung to
the rod, alas, become ashamed, not for any objective reason,
but "because of those that [are] scoffing at them." (1 Nephi
8:28.)

This mocking and scorning of the Church and the things
we hold sacred will persist. It was all foreseen, however, but
so was the eventual joyous triumph of those who cling faithfully
to the iron rod. (Mormon 8:21–22.)

An angel also told Nephi that though members of the growing Church would be scattered upon all the face of the earth,
their dominions would be comparatively small. (1 Nephi
14:14.) Why comparatively small? Because, said the angel, of
the wickedness of this planet. (V. 12.)

Furthermore, the Saints of God will go through a sifting

and winnowing process (D&C 112:25; 1 Peter 4:17) but will reach a point in their spiritual development when the faithful will be "armed with righteousness and with the power of God in great glory" (1 Nephi 14:14). Obviously, a substantial portion of that great group of emerging Saints will be composed of the women of faith, just as sisters were co-builders of the singular city of Enoch.

Sister scriptorians will savor this particular prophecy and will personally profit from its fulfillment:

"I beheld other books, which came forth by the power of the Lamb . . . unto the convincing of the Gentiles and the remnant of the seed of my brethren, and also the Jews . . . that the records of the prophets and of the twelve apostles of the Lamb are true.

" . . . These last records . . . shall establish the truth of the first, which are of the twelve apostles of the Lamb, and shall make known the plain and precious things which have been taken away from them; and shall make known to all kindreds, tongues, and people, that the Lamb of God is the Son of the Eternal Father, and the Savior of the world." (1 Nephi 13:39–40.)

The Holy Bible and these "other books" of scripture will, in your time, combine in a powerful witness that Jesus is the Christ, not merely a Plato in Palestine nor a Socrates in Samaria! The latter-day scriptures have also brought back certain plain and precious things which had been lost and have established the truth of the Holy Bible, especially its apostolic witness about Jesus Christ and the reality of resurrection. All of this is in fulfillment of the prophecy of Peter about those who engage in "denying the Lord that bought them." (2 Peter 2:1.) No wonder President Spencer W. Kimball spoke about the need for appreciating and using sister scriptorians in our time.

Saintly sisters will pass through the times of which this sampling of prophecies is at least representative and will come to know, even more deeply, the truth of Paul's declaration: "Who shall separate us from the love of Christ? shall tribulation, or distress, or persecution, or famine, or nakedness, or peril, or sword?" (Romans 8:35.)

The quiet certitude of our sisters will see them through these tempestuous times and prepare them and theirs for things joyous and glorious, such as Jesus' triumphal return in power and glory.

On Patmos, after the "Amen" ended Jesus' declarative words about His eventual return, John pleadingly added, "Even so, come, Lord Jesus." (Revelation 22:20.) Before the Saints of the latter days are through, they, too, will pray without ceasing for Jesus to "come quickly." Indeed, the very shortening of the time before His Son's coming will be an act of mercy on the Father's part.

Meanwhile, women of faith will have moments and even seasons when they cannot explain what is happening to them or around them. Yet as with Nephi of old, they will say, "I know that [God] loveth his children; nevertheless, I do not know the meaning of all things." (1 Nephi 11:17.)

Time and time again, they will see the sobering truth of this saying with regard to this life: "The only way to go is through; there is no around." Being strong and hardy, these saintly sisters will replicate the experiences of their pioneer forebears, who, in the crossing of the plains, after burying their dead, resolutely picked up their handcarts and headed west.

It will not surprise me if, later, someone observes how so much of what the Church and its people will achieve in the last days of the last dispensation will be attributable to the spiritual superiority of Latter-day Saint women when compared with the women of the world.

Latter-day Saint women, who are full of faith, will steadfastly display quiet goodness like that of Dorcas:

"Now there was at Joppa a certain disciple named Tabitha, which by interpretation is called Dorcas: this woman was full of good works and almsdeeds which she did." (Acts 9:36.)

Faithful sisters will be spiritually submissive, like marvelous Mary of old. Entrusted with impending duties which she could not then fully comprehend, nevertheless Mary said, "Behold the handmaid of the Lord; be it unto me according to thy word." (Luke 1:38.)

Sisters of faith will have no difficulty believing in the word of God as it comes from His servants:

"And Ammon said unto her: Believest thou this? And she said unto him: I have had no witness save thy word, and the word of our servants; nevertheless I believe that it shall be according as thou hast said." (Alma 19:9.)

Such believing capacity is a spiritual gift: "To others it is given to believe on their words, that they also might have eternal life if they continue faithful." (D&C 46:14.)

The women of God will also gladly spread His good news as witnesses:

"And many of the Samaritans of that city believed on [Jesus] for the saying of the woman, which testified, He told me all that ever I did." (John 4:39.)

Yet saintly sisters will be understandably anxious for family and others to attain their own full, firsthand witness:

"And said unto the woman, Now we believe, not because of thy saying: for we have heard him ourselves, and know that this is indeed the Christ, the Saviour of the world." (John 4:42.)

Our sisters will come to have greater and greater personal appreciation for the Savior's blessed benefactions, especially how "he suffereth the pains . . . of every living creature, both men, women, and children, who belong to the family of Adam." (2 Nephi 9:21.)

In the midst of these things, our sisters will make it possible for others to experience love at home and in a neighborhood in a cold world. In effect, they will thus be portable and persuasive preachments — sparkling sermons for all seasons. They will not, in the words of Paul, unduly "mind earthly things." (Philippians 3:19.) Instead, women of faith will come to have "the mind of Christ." (1 Corinthians 2:16.) Since the women of faith are members of Heavenly Father's proven congregation of saints, as God has revealed, they and the faithful men of the Church will become both "pure" and "tried." (D&C 100:16; 136:31.)

Saintly sisters are usually the first to understand that in this life we live not by days but by deeds, not by seasons but by service. They will likewise have no difficulty realizing that God chose them before this world was. President Kimball put it well:

"Remember, in the world before we came here, faithful women were given certain assignments while faithful men were foreordained to certain priesthood tasks. While we do not now remember the particulars, this does not alter the glorious reality of what we once agreed to. You are accountable for those things which long ago were expected of you just as are those we sustain as prophets and apostles!"[1]

They have a view of life in which mortality is seen not as linear but as experiential, not chronological so much as developmental. Hence, the high need for faith and patience as the sculpturing of souls proceeds. (Mosiah 23:21.)

Such sisters have the capacity to cope with seeming routine and repetition, doing the chores of family life and the work of the kingdom with minimal muttering. This capacity to keep moving forward simultaneously develops another capacity: to "endure . . . well" to the end of one's mortal life. (D&C 121:8.)

Righteous women are less demanding of the Lord with regard to life. Being less demanding, they are able to give more abundantly without any concern for credit or without regard for recognition.

Worldly women, however, want to fashion a selfish future while ignoring the harsh lessons of the past. They also want happiness without righteousness. Like their male counterparts, these women of the world seek "for that which ye could not obtain; . . . for happiness in doing iniquity." (Helaman 13:38; see also Alma 41:11.) As Mormon observed of another sad group, these women of the world suffer "the sorrowing of the damned" because they fail to learn fully that we cannot "take happiness in sin." (Mormon 2:13.)

In contrast, the women of light, being idealists without illusions, know that happiness can be obtained only in the context of righteousness and selflessness; the women of light are not blind to the lessons of spiritual history. Paul wrote to the faithful Saints, demarking the time since their spiritual conversion as being that "after ye were illuminated" (Hebrews 10:32), meaning, of course, since the light of the gospel and

21

the gift of the Holy Ghost had lighted up their lives and behavior. There is a luminosity that goes with gospel gladness, a spiritual radiance. It is an almost physical thing. It is to be seen in the faces of the women of faith.

Since the light of Christ lights everyone who comes into this world (D&C 93:2; John 1:9), that spark, which some call conscience, is still present in the lives of many women and men of all races, nations, creeds, and cultures. The women of the Church will enhance that intrinsic illumination by sharing with others the full light of the gospel of Jesus Christ. Our sisters will be the means of bringing into the fold many who seek to come in out of the cold. They will be your friends forever and call your names blessed.

Unsurprisingly, the women of Christ, like Him whom they follow, will—especially in today's world—give more love than they receive; they will offer more truth than is accepted. But no matter!

Our sisters will also have increasing appreciation of and a spiritual appetite for the things of the holy temple. Should we be surprised that these spirit daughters of our Heavenly Father would feel so at home—indeed would tarry there longer—in His holy house? As they encounter the profound truths and ordinances of the temple, today's women of faith will do as Mary did when confronted with things she could not then fully understand: "But Mary kept all these things, and pondered them in her heart." (Luke 2:19.) Temple truths, some scattered in the scriptures, are like pulsating flames of fire for those who have eyes to see.

So much will depend on how the women of the Church treat the sacred things of God. Said President Brigham Young: "If [a mother treats] lightly the things of God, it is more than likely her children will be inclined to do the same."[2]

Men of faith and women of faith are, of course, alike in their developing spiritual submissiveness, in their unconditional trust of God. They do not ask for advance explanations or even reassurances. It was so not only with Mary but also with three special young men who entered their fiery furnace knowing "our God . . . is able to deliver us from the burning fiery furnace. . . . *But if not,* be it known unto thee, O king, that we will not serve thy gods." (Daniel 3:17–18; italics added.)

Those three little words "but if not" convey so very much. Just as valiant were the three virgins noted in the book of Abraham who actually were sacrificed because they, too, refused to worship false gods. (Abraham 1:11.)

Opposition will come; it will be clever. There will be casualties. Still, nothing can separate this people and our righteous women from the love of Christ and from bringing to pass the fulfillment of all that is to be done in this dispensation in preparation for His second coming.

A word about casualties, since the reasons for falling away are similar, whether among men or among women. My sample of a few adult male friends who have fallen away is large enough to generalize somewhat, though these observations apply differently. For some, imperfections in Church members and leaders, past or present, became a cover for withdrawal into looser life-styles. Another factor was becoming thoroughly fascinated and preoccupied with the professional cares, the reinforcing rewards, and praise of the world. Withering followed scorching, "because they had no deepness of earth." (Matthew 13:5.) Developing selfish expectations of life in the kingdom was present. All of this handful were and are proud, and they cultivated their doubts instead of their faith. The sample is small, but the results, though not surprising, are very sad. Happily, some of these have now made their way back.

But, to return to the shared work of the Lord:

In furthering the establishment of the kingdom of God on the earth, certain specific things — both sobering and exciting — need to occur, involving both brothers and sisters alike. For instance, in Book of Mormon times when the Church was more fully established, this condition meant more converts to be sure, but it also meant that members themselves were "awakened to a remembrance of their duty." (Alma 4:3.) Members checked their pride and began to be more humble and more prayerful. Think of how many casualties were prevented! Alma referred to this as their "victory over the devil." (Alma 16:21.) One of the happy outcomes of this was that the "word of God [was preached] in its purity in all the land, and the Lord [poured] out his blessings upon the people." (Alma 16:21.)

I mention these ancient circumstances because they indicate what must happen in the Church today. The Lord has indicated that Zion must "increase in beauty and in holiness" and that "her stakes must be strengthened," obvious references to spiritual growth. (D&C 82:14.) Zion's borders are also to be enlarged, indicating numerical growth. Likewise, we are instructed about how the Lord's army must "become very great" — another numerical indication. Yet that same army is to become "sanctified." (D&C 105:31.) Thus, there must be, cheek by jowl, both numerical and spiritual growth in the Church.

Remember what Nephi saw? In the latter days, the covenant people of the Lord would be scattered upon all the face of the earth; they would be "armed with righteousness and with the power of God in great glory." (1 Nephi 14:14.) Though the dominions of the growing Church will still remain comparatively small in the burgeoning human family, this comparatively small size will be so because of the wickedness in the world. (V. 12.) In the building of the pure in heart, Zion and the stakes of Zion are not only convenient administrative entities in the Church but also spiritual sanctuaries, places for "a defense, and for a refuge from the storm." (D&C 115:6.)

Thus is the shared work which lies before us, and the sisters of faith will play such a large part in accomplishing it. Therefore, while talking about other challenges and opportunities and about the tactical challenges that go with roles, assignments, and concerns — real and needed as these discussions may be — we should place all of these things in the larger spiritual and scriptural context. Besides, like it or not, the women of faith are placed in history. These days are your days in the history of the kingdom, and you must make of them days never to be forgotten.

The summational wisdom attributed to eighteenth-century British clergyman William Law applies to all: "If you have not chosen the Kingdom of God first, it will in the end make no difference what you have chosen instead," because, as Moroni said, "the eternal purposes of the Lord shall roll on, until all his promises shall be fulfilled." (Mormon 8:22.)

Notes

1. Spencer W. Kimball, "The Role of Righteous Women," *Ensign*, Nov. 1979, p. 102.
2. Brigham Young, discourse of 8 Oct. 1876, in *Journal of Discourses*, 26 vols. (Liverpool: Latter-day Saints Book Depot, 1853–86), 18:263.

BUILDING RELATIONSHIPS WITH SELF, OTHERS, AND GOD

Resolving differences does not necessarily mean dissolving them. It is possible to move forward . . . without perfect harmony if we steer by what we have in common rather than by our differences. . . . True unity can be achieved only through patience and understanding.

—JANATH R. CANNON AND JILL MULVAY DERR

Equality of Esteem

ELDER MARION D. HANKS

I will say to you as I begin that I remember no assignment that has seemed more important to me or has been given more sincere attention. In preparation, I have had the great blessing of reading talks given at previous BYU Women's Conferences and much of scripture and Church history relating to women.

We here have much about which to smile. I am highly conscious that behind our smiles there are deep and diverse and often complex and painful realities. Human life is like that, and we learn sooner or later that jolly greetings and a pat on the cheek will not resolve much that must be individually confronted, worked out, and, with such assistance as one may discover, either lived with or resolved in the best way we can. Yet all of us have much about which to rejoice and be glad in this free and fruitful land.

I sat with Elder Richard L. Evans once long ago and heard him repeat the story of the lad who had come home from school with a report card that was worrisome to his father. He was no longer first in the class; he was second. "Second," said

Elder Marion D. Hanks has served as executive director of the Priest-hood Department of the Church and as a member of the First Quorum of the Seventy. He has also served as president of the British Mission, Church administrator in Southeast Asia/Philippines, and president of the Salt Lake Temple. He has been a member of the President's Citizens Advisory Committee on Children and Youth and the President's Council on Physical Fitness and Sports, receiving in 1978 the Distinguished Service Award of that council. He has served on the National Executive Board of the Boy Scouts of America, receiving all of the special scouting awards, including an honorary National Eagle Scout Award. He holds a J.D. degree from the University of Utah as well as honorary degrees from several other institutions of higher learning. He and his wife, Maxine, are the parents of four daughters and one son.

the father; "who is first?" "Mary Smith," said the sad boy. "Mary Smith! You mean a mere girl is first, and you are second?" He said, "Dad, girls aren't so *mere* any more."

Women are getting a lot of media attention lately. News stories in the recent past have included something about the woman mayor of a major city in Florida and of seventy-five courageous Soviet women striking in the cause of Jewish emigration from Russia. There was also a story of a woman judge who was robbed on the streets of Philadelphia, attracting little attention from some who might have defended her but, interestingly, wide attention from those who thought it an act of appropriate retribution for her to suffer this affliction since she is a judge and thus, in their feeble minds, responsible for the troubles of those with whom she had had to deal as an instrument of justice. Then recently we have seen pictures and read stories about the Reagan ladies, whose squabble over a family book briefly simplified their husband's and father's life by pushing him off the front page.

Another news item may be more instructive than any mentioned thus far. A professor addressing a Women's Week meeting at the University of Utah saluted the gains made in recent years for women and minorities in equality of rights and opportunity, though, she said, the largest results have yet to be accomplished. Then she spoke of an *"equality of esteem,* which is an unwritten moral equality . . . and still beyond the grasp of most women and minorities."[1]

Equality of Esteem

Whatever our reaction to the events of the last few years, the testing and contesting, the shouting and pouting, the insistence to take sides on the question of equality, all of us can very likely respond with sympathy and appreciation to that interesting phrase, "equality of esteem." That is surely an appropriate way to characterize the attitude of Almighty God to all of His children. In His loving Father's heart there is truly "equality of esteem." Indeed, He specifically declared, "Behold, the Lord esteemeth all flesh in one." (1 Nephi 17:35.)

There is added to that statement through the prophet the

declaration, "He [or she] that is righteous is favored of God." That some are favored doesn't, of course, reflect on His love for all of us or on our value in His eyes and heart, but it does express the expanded opportunities that are the natural consequence of learning and obeying the law and thus enjoying the blessings that are predicated on that law. Through His prophet, the Lord said, "If it so be that the children of men keep the commandments of God he doth nourish them, and strengthen them, and provide means whereby they can accomplish the thing which he has commanded them." (1 Nephi 17:3.)

As the youngest child in a large, one-parent family in my growing-up years, I understand perhaps as well as most what some of the problems associated with sustaining life on a low level of subsistence are. Some of the feminist furor of recent years has been understandable to me from that base of experience. Necessity and our mother's character and faith and her determination to remain independent as a family after our father died motivated all of us to work and contribute. Earlier, during a long period of financial stress, she had employed her special domestic skills to make jellies and jams, which our father had sold from door to door. She sewed and served others and provided a haven for many needful people who came to our home seeking counsel and comfort.

One of my earliest philosophical meanderings began as I pulled my little red wagon with the Relief Society president's distribution of welfare goods. That was the welfare program in those days for the Church, to deliver commodities to the home of the Relief Society president, who then distributed them. As I did that, being the delivery agent, I on occasion was caused to muse, "If we are not poor, who is?" But we never tasted the food. It was for the poor. And all of us worked almost from childhood, all of us together attempting to survive and to do it with the good cheer that constantly reflected Mother's view of life.

Not long ago I spoke at the funeral of a great lady who had known me literally from the day of my birth. I said at that service that it seemed strange to me that anyone should ever

31

question whether women of Sister Anderson's quality were equal to men. She, with Sister Reynolds and Sister Neal and my mother and others like them, were a real presence in my life. Most were widowed, with families, none lacking anything on the score of knowledge and intelligence, all able and kind and gracious and good and representative of everything wholesome and holy, in my mind. Circumstances were difficult for my mother, but everything I experienced with her and my three sweet sisters strengthened my admiration for women. My own wife and four choice daughters have enhanced my capacity for respect for special daughters of God, as did my wife's mother and other choice individuals who have influenced my life and added to my gratitude for the refining and uplifting quality of wonderful women.

Of course, woman differs from woman, as man differs from man. Our experiences in living in Europe and Asia and traveling continually across the world have emphasized for us the great varieties of circumstances, cultures, language, families, education, sophistication, political situation, economics, talents, and opportunities for growth and development. There is much similarity among this great group here today, but there is also significant diversity. I assume that a large number of you are married and in traditional families. Some are divorced or widowed; some are the heads of single-parent families; others not yet married.

In recognition of that diversity, let me read a few paragraphs from something I wrote that was published a time ago, dealing particularly with single women. Some of the special problems for the single woman who is a faithful believer in the gospel of Jesus Christ are reflected in these brief extracts from choice Latter-day Saint women of various circumstances:

" 'Being 32 and not married has some aspects of pain known only to the single Mormon woman. As I begin to write this I am crying. My dreams seem so unattainable. But the dreams are not unusual or grandiose. They seem so simple in my mind. I hunger to be happily married. Where do I go with these dreams? . . .

" 'Maybe it is this need to "be lovable" that becomes the

pain inside us. In the mind of society there must be a reason when one is not married. What is the flaw in me?' "

A widow writes:

" 'It is better for us, I think, than for the divorced or never married. We have loved and been loved, and though we become desperately lonely for the one who has gone, yet we feel married still, and still loved as we continue to love.' "

A divorced woman writes:

" 'Divorced Mormons often become alienated from the Church entirely. For those who cling vigorously to the source of blessings rather than cutting themselves off, there is yet the sometimes present problem of uneasy fellow members who regard divorced people as having something wrong with them, perhaps something contagious, like a disease, and who do not know how to act with such a one who may be innocent of any wrongdoing, even victimized.' "

To these sobering comments is added one from what to me was an unexpected source: a lovely, faithful Latter-day Saint who married out of the Church and who had hopes for a future she no longer feels will come to pass. She writes about a particular kind of singleness:

" 'I have always been a member of the Church and was active (did not miss a meeting, held three jobs at a time, etc.) up to the very day of my marriage. I married a Catholic. (Go ahead and wince. I am still kind of shocked at myself at such an incredible, complete flip!) With this in mind, I thought I would mention that one version of the single woman in the Church is the woman who married a nonmember. You know — the woman who really believed that all those faith-promoting stories on conversion would happen to her. They have not. They may not. She is no longer the unattached sister. Her hardcore non-believer is very real and loving, but not Golden Question material after all. She is alone. Sitting. Sensitive. Weeping (inside). Never wanting to give up hope; never seeing it either. It can be psychologically devastating to realize that you are now numbered among the inactive. You are still somebody's ward project. You are downing the percentages in all the books. Still, you have a testimony. You certainly think about the Church all the time. If you have ever practiced love, charity, humility, and studied the gospel in your home, it has been these married years — alone.' "

And two sentences from another sum up these candid statements:

" 'The Church is not only family-oriented, but it is also couple-oriented. One who lives the life of the gospel, being a single adult, must be content with these feelings and battle to be happy in spite of them.' "[2]

Offspring of God

The traditional, anticipated role of woman in the Church is as a partner in marriage, as wife, mother, homemaker, the heart of a family. This will forever be so. The Church will continue to emphasize the importance of home and family and of the role of parents in that setting. Motherhood will always be regarded as the highest blessing and privilege of the daughters of God. Emphasis will be given to the important nature of the home and the vital meaning of the family in preserving and building a constructive and worthwhile society. Temple marriage will continue to be a lofty objective for members of the Church. Preparation for that kind of marriage will be strongly counseled. Instructions and encouragement will be provided to help qualify people for that holy experience. But all of this must not and will not be done insensitively and without tender consciousness that there are many wonderful women (and men) in the society and in the Church, like those from whom we have quoted, who have not experienced or do not now enjoy the blessings of marriage and family in the traditional way. They are "fellow-citizens with the saints, and of the household of God" (Ephesians 2:19), entitled to every blessing and every opportunity in the kingdom on the same basis as everyone else — that is, individual desire, willingness, capacity, and worthiness.

From an unidentified author come these four lines relating to a bullfight, which are perhaps applicable to the circumstances of those to whom we have referred:

The experts ranked in serried rows
Fill the enormous plaza full.
But only one is there who knows
And he's the one who fights the bull.

Every woman is special, a *somebody* of intrinsic worth who
has been a somebody for a very long time, indeed, forever.
Every daughter of God, born of divine heritage in the spirit
before this world was formed, enters mortality already a special,
eternal person. Each has proved herself in demanding periods
of trial, has chosen the right course and pursued it with faith
and courage, and comes here with credentials earned in action
elsewhere. Every girl, every woman, is a somebody apart and
aside from anyone else, husband or family or otherwise. If she
is privileged to enjoy fruitful family association in this world,
happy marriage, motherhood, then she is favored indeed and
through obedience to the laws of God qualifies for eternal
creative union and all the other choice blessings promised for
every faithful child of God who desires them and is willing to
receive them.

If the anticipated timetable for establishing a base for those
blessings is delayed in this world, or disrupted, the promises
still pertain. "All that God hath" can be hers if she desires it
and lives for it.

On a plaque on the wall of my office is this choice statement:
"To believe in God is to know that all the rules will be fair
and that there will be wonderful surprises."

Eternal life — life with God, life of divine quality, creative
progressive life, the life of exaltation — is a loving life shared
with dear ones. The ultimate enjoyment of this life is a consequence of individual choice in accepting, through obedience
to His commandments, the invitation of the Lord to be with
Him and other loved ones everlastingly. The path to earthly
and eternal happiness always leads from the individual and
the way each uses her agency. The prophet Lehi taught that
God's children "are free according to the flesh; and all things
are given them which are expedient. . . . And they are free to

choose liberty and eternal life, through [Christ], or to choose captivity and death." (2 Nephi 2:27.)

It is important to know how the Lord feels and who we are to Him. Socrates said, "The ignorance which causes vice and immorality is not ignorance of moral principles or laws but an ignorance of self, an ignorance of who we really are."

God is our Father; He loves us; He desires for us everlasting joy. We may be confused when we are young, as Lucifer was — he who "knew not the mind of [his Father]" (Moses 4:6), who did not want men to follow the plan God presented for our mortal experience and ultimate maturity. Lucifer wanted to "destroy the agency of man." (Moses 3:4.) He wanted to conduct us on a safe, round-trip journey, not one soul to be lost — and not one soul any better for having made the trip. Why? Because growth and maturing are processes involving opposition and free agency, contending forces between which we must choose.

Failure, futility, frustration, loss of self-respect because our conscience cannot approve what we have just done or decided, or long ago did or decided — these are elements of normalcy, but they are meant to be overcome as we mature in our capacity to understand what God really wants and how much He wants it. In our life before mortality He permitted Lucifer to tell his story and mislead a host of our Father's beloved children. In this world there is "opposition in all things" and freedom to choose.

For parents who suffer through destructive decisions made by beloved children this should be comforting. God understands, and He believes enough in the importance of our eternal growth not to shield us from the experiences of mortal life which we came here to undertake. Perhaps we did not foresee every detail, but all of us understood in principle. This is what is at the heart of it all.

In the wonderful musical *Fiddler on the Roof,* Tevye explains that the strength of their beleaguered lives is possible because "Everyone knows who he is and what God wants him to do."

What is mankind? Who are we? Is it so vital that we know? Ah, yes! The apostle Paul taught the Romans: "The Spirit itself

beareth witness with our spirit, that we are the children of
God: and if children, then heirs; heirs of God, and joint-heirs
with Christ." (Romans 8:16–17.) His testimony to the men of
Athens on Mars Hill is that we are all the "offspring of God."
(Acts 17:29.)

I humbly confirm with you today, then, what your nature
is and who you are. You are unique in personality, in pattern
special. You belong here on God's earth and in this time. The
Book of Mormon and Bible both declare in specific language
that the earth was created for us and that it may be our eternal
home. "Behold, the Lord hath created the earth that it should
be inhabited; and he hath created his children that they should
possess it." (1 Nephi 17:36.) Isaiah, seven hundred years before
the coming of Christ, taught that God formed the earth to be
inhabited. (Isaiah 45:18.) And in the dispensation of the fulness
of times it is written: "The poor and the meek of the earth
shall inherit it. . . . That bodies who are of the celestial kingdom
may possess it forever and ever." (D&C 88:17, 20.)

Someone to Love

The very essence of our natures is perhaps best expressed
when we are following the Savior's example of service. This
was forcefully emphasized for me in the last several weeks of
stake conference visits, during which I had two of the tender
experiences of my lifetime. On a Saturday recently I stood on
the steps of a stake center and listened to a lovely lady whose
husband had been killed a few months before. She had a large
family of little children. I told her about herself and who she
is and what she can do. I didn't pretend it would be easy; it
wasn't for my mother or any other in like condition. She said
something I shall never forget: "Brother Hanks, we miss him
terribly. We miss his taking care of us. We miss his love. But
you know," she said reflectively, *"I think even more we miss
having him to take care of; we miss having him to love."*

A week later I listened to a man speak of his wife who had
suffered painfully over a long year of terrible illness before
her death. He said, "I don't seem to think as much now about
all those happy years with the children, of the wonderful com-

ing together, of the passion, the union, her beauty, and all the sweetness of all our many married years, as I do about that one last year we had together. I think especially of the time when I was kneeling at her feet to put on her shoes for her when she couldn't do it for herself. I looked up," he said, "into those beautiful eyes filled with tears and filled with love and appreciation. I thank God that through all the pain and anguish she suffered during that heartbreaking year, I could take care of her and serve her and comfort her and help her know how much I truly love her. That picture is the one I wake up in the night with — my kneeling at her feet, putting on her shoes, and looking up and seeing those dear eyes brimming with gratitude and love."

Women in Scripture

In the scriptures we learn of the sacred roles of Mother Eve and of Mary. We may know less about Hannah, noble wife who was unable for a time to bear children. Through her humility and faith and prayers, ultimately she was blessed with that privilege. Bringing forth a son, she prepared him for a prophetic calling, schooled him and taught him and loved him and prayed with him, and helped him to get ready to hearken to the voice of God when He spoke. Samuel became a mighty prophet.

Abigail saved her family and friends through wise and courageous counsel to an irate David bent on violence and vengeance. The words of David to her when he had turned from his angry course are instructive: "Blessed be the Lord God of Israel, which sent thee this day to meet me: and blessed be thy advice, and blessed be thou, which hast kept me this day from coming to shed blood, and from avenging myself with mine own hand." (1 Samuel 25:32–33.)

Abigail is described in the scripture as "a woman of good understanding, and of a beautiful countenance." (V. 3.) She represents the civilizing, refining, gentling influence of choice daughters of God.

Esther saved a whole people. Orphaned, brought up by a cousin, she undertook a very dangerous mission to the king in behalf of her people. To them, with her life on the line, she sent this message, "Fast ye for me, and neither eat nor drink three days, night or day: I also and my maidens will fast likewise; and so will I go . . . and if I perish, I perish." (Esther 4:16.)

In the Book of Mormon we meet an unnamed queen and learn the story of her love and faith, which reflects the unselfish service rendered by many noble women. Lamoni, Lamanite king, was taught by Ammon and touched by the Spirit and was overcome as if he were dead. He thus lay for two days and two nights, and his servants were about to take his body and lay it in a sepulchre. But his wife, the queen, had great faith in the power of Ammon, a servant of God. She sent for him, keeping vigil by the side of her husband. The words she spoke to Ammon were pertinent to the circumstance: "Some say that he is not dead, but others say that he is dead and that he stinketh, and that he ought to be placed in the sepulchre; but as for myself, to me he doth not stink." (Alma 19:5.)

It is recorded that "she watched over the bed of her husband, from that time even until . . . the morrow." (V. 11.) The king arose as Ammon declared he would, "and as he arose, he stretched forth his hand unto the woman, and said: Blessed be the name of God, and blessed art thou." (V. 12.)

There are many other examples, but could there be a lovelier tribute to a woman than this from her grateful husband: "Blessed be the name of God, and blessed art thou"?

What do we learn from these scriptures? Again, the importance of women in motherhood and home, and leading children to leadership and contribution; gently bringing wisdom and refinement to rough men; influencing events through wise judgment and courageous action; expressing the intuitive intelligence and faithfulness of a pure woman; serving as agent of God in prayer and healing and stilling contentions; comforting, inspiring, teaching, and bringing music and beauty and art into the congregations, as did Emma, who was invited to put together a hymnal of sacred songs which, said the Lord, are "prayer[s] unto me." (D&C 25:12.)

Our Father's Will

How does one live with integrity and self-esteem? Is it in frantic flailing for a perfection we won't find on this earth? Is it seeking to do anything and everything to meet all the standards everybody else seems to set for us, to give the faultless performance they seem to demand of us?

The apostle Paul prayed for an Israel who had, he said, "a zeal of God, but not according to knowledge." (Romans 10:2.) They had the zeal but not the understanding. Their purposes were proper—they wanted to please God; they wanted the comforting assurance of His approval but thought they could accomplish this through a punctilious preoccupation with their own perfection. Like Lucifer, they did "not understand" the mind of the Father. "For they being ignorant of God's righteousness, and going about to establish their own righteousness, have not submitted themselves unto the righteousness of God." (Romans 10:3.)

We may set up stern standards for ourselves or others—or struggle with standards set up by others for us—and then judge ourselves or others harshly for failing to meet them when they may have little reference to the true qualities of fidelity that constitute God's plan for us.

In the Doctrine and Covenants are these words concerning the "best gifts," which we are to earnestly seek: "For verily I say unto you, they are given for the benefit of those who love me and keep all my commandments, *and him that seeketh so to do.*" (D&C 46:9; italics added.)

How real and how comforting—as He is real and full of compassion and loving kindness!

We do not always remember that He understands, that He loves, that we are esteemed in His sight equally with all others. Our hope lies in learning to submit ourselves to the will of the Father, learning to accept His forgiveness and affection, to look to Him and His unfailing love with confidence. For this purpose Christ came into the world, as He clearly explained. (3 Nephi 27:13; John 4:34; 5:30.)

We are here to learn the lesson, also, that we are here to

do the will of the Father. And how do we discover His will? How do we find Him? Pascal gave us a line: "You would not seek me had you not found me." God is closer than we know, more truly concerned for us than we understand. And the best in us is better than we know and reaches out and up, seeking Him.

We worry about our faith: does He really exist? We worry about our worthiness: could He love me? We remember our sins: is He really willing to "rescue a soul so rebellious and proud as mine"? (*Hymns,* 1985, no. 193.) We want to find Him. We would like to yield to His will. But how do we do that? How do we qualify for the relationship that we so earnestly desire?

We do this through prayer, of course, and through studying the scriptures. I believe we can find Him best by learning to know the Christ, who seems nearer, who was "made flesh and dwelt among us," and of whom Paul wrote that "God was in Christ, reconciling the world unto himself." (2 Corinthians 5:19.) God was making Himself known through His Son. "If," Paul declared to the Romans, "when we were enemies [that is, apart from God], we were reconciled to God by the death of his Son, [how] much more, being reconciled [brought back into unison with Him], we shall be saved by his life." (Romans 5:10.)

Saved by His Life

Being reconciled to God by Christ's death, we can be saved by His life. That means we have to *know* about His life, doesn't it? We are reconciled to God through the life of His Son. When we've seen Him, Christ said, we have seen the Father. He came to do the Father's will, to say what He had heard His Father say, to do what He had seen His Father do. In coming to know Him, we come to know the Father and the Son, and knowing them is peace in this world and life eternal in the world to come.

The scriptures constantly encourage us to —

"Seek this Jesus of whom prophets and apostles have written" (Ether 12:41)

41

"Be faithful in Christ" and remember Him (Moroni 9:25)
"And partake of his goodness" (2 Nephi 26:33)
"And bring forth works of righteousness" (Alma 5:35)
"And lay hold upon every good gift" (Moroni 10:30)
"And partake of his salvation" (Omni 1:26)
"And be perfected in him" (Moroni 10:32).

We are taught to "remember, remember that it is upon the rock of our Redeemer, who is Christ, the Son of God, that [we] must build [our] foundation" (Helaman 5:12); "feast upon the words of Christ; for behold, the words of Christ will tell you all things what ye should do" (2 Nephi 32:3). Christ is "the right way." (2 Nephi 25:29.)

Nephi, at the height of his concluding testimony, said that he had charity for his own people and great faith in Christ; he had charity also for the Jew and for the Gentile. "But," said he, "behold, for none of these can I hope except they shall be reconciled unto Christ, and enter into the narrow gate, and walk in the strait path which leads to life, and continue in the path until the end of the day of probation." (2 Nephi 33:7–9.)

These scriptures are a sure source of discovery. Each of the standard works has remarkable windows of knowledge and understanding and insight to lead us to Him. Nephi said that the writings of prophets "persuadeth them to do good; ... maketh known unto them of their fathers; and ... speaketh of Jesus, and persuadeth them to believe in him, and to endure to the end, which is life eternal." (2 Nephi 33:4.)

Why are we to read the Book of Mormon, along with the other magnificent scriptures? Because the book, like all the other scriptures, has a single central aim; and that is to prepare the world for the coming of Christ, to celebrate His meridian advent, His holy atoning sacrifice, and His death and resurrection, and to prepare the earth for His coming again.

Each of these great volumes that constitute our scriptural heritage testifies in similar fashion. But they respond not to the lazy, or to the indifferent, or to the unconcerned, or to the mind diluted with too much of what one may see in books or television programs or otherwise that is inconsistent, indeed incompatible, with the Spirit of Christ. One does not need to be a scholar to learn from and rejoice in the scriptures, but they do not yield their spiritual treasures to those who do not seek, ask, knock, search.

We are promised personal revelation. As we read, as we listen more carefully than perhaps we have done, as we seek to organize our comprehension of the gospel, as we get the strength of it into our bloodstream and share it with others, personal revelation becomes the key to our understanding, to our use of agency and our accountability. Through the Spirit we may know the truth of all things.

That leads me to the major thing I want to say to you.

The Temple

There is a special place where one may learn more about the Savior than anywhere else I know. If we are praying and seeking and trying to learn, and if we are walking reasonably well on the path He laid out, there is a place to go where He has promised to "manifest himself to his people," where we can come to know Him. That place is the temple.

The temple has been called by someone "the binding point of heaven and earth," but the meaning of that is not immediately comprehensible to many of us. My soul was really comforted when President David O. McKay spoke to me of the "bewildering" experience of going for the first time to the temple. That is why we must know we are involved in a long learning experience, not a single journey "through the temple."

In the temple one may learn many things, chiefly, I believe, by thinking and feeling and learning to comprehend and apply in our own lives the concepts beyond the symbols. There *are* concepts beyond the symbols. Again, one does not have to be a scholar, but a little guidance may help.

What is done in the temple is often thought of as chiefly benefiting the dead. Perhaps the greater blessing comes to the living who serve the dead in the pattern of their Lord and who pray and worship and put themselves in the path to enjoy the Spirit that is constantly accessible in the temple.

In the dedicatory prayer of the first temple of this dispensation, a prayer revealed from God, the Prophet made known the great personal blessings that can come to us from going to the temple in the right spirit and often enough in order to begin to comprehend the experience through repetition, through thought, through prayerful effort.

Listen to these four promises as indicative of what may be experienced through temple service, temple worship. They can be read in the dedicatory prayer of the Kirtland Temple.

> "That they may grow up in thee,
> and receive a fulness of the Holy Ghost,
> and be organized according to thy laws,
> and be prepared to obtain every needful thing."
> (D&C 109:15.)

What a magnificent picture of what can be — to "grow up" in the Lord, to enjoy a fulness of the Spirit, to organize our lives according to His laws, and to be prepared to obtain every needful thing. In the temple we may "grow up," *mature*, in the Lord. *Maturity* is a key word to me. God is perfectly mature in every eternally important quality. There is no immaturity in His response to one who makes a mistake, no quick judgment, no condemnation. There is love and a way provided for us to recover from the consequences of our mistakes. There is no immaturity in Christ, no lack of love.

Peter — who knew Him well, who himself failed Him and denied Him, and who wrote, I have no doubt, through tears and a broken heart — said: "[Jesus], when he was reviled, reviled not again; when he suffered, he threatened not; but committed himself to him that judgeth righteously." (1 Peter 2:23.)

Christ was perfectly mature. We are not. We are learning.

When God made these promises, there was an historical preparation. When He first instructed Moses and his people to build the little tabernacle in the wilderness, their prototype temple, He said, "Make me a sanctuary; that I may dwell among them." He revealed the pattern of that building and all that pertained to it and said, "There I will meet with thee, and I will commune with thee." (Exodus 25:8, 22.)

In that remarkable dedicatory prayer at Kirtland in 1836

are these opening words, after the salutation: "For thou knowest that we have done this work through great tribulation [the people have sacrificed for this temple]; and out of our poverty we have given of our substance to build a house to thy name, *that the Son of Man might have a place to manifest himself to his people.*" (D&C 109:5; italics added.)

A temple is built that the Son of Man might manifest Himself to His people! A few days later in that same temple, the Lord declared: "Let the hearts of your brethren rejoice, and let . . . all my people rejoice, who have, with their might, built this house to my name. For behold, I have accepted this house, and my name shall be here; and *I will manifest myself to my people in mercy in this house.*" (D&C 110:6–7; italics added.)

What does that mean? Does that mean that occasionally God will come to His house and occasionally the pure in heart may see Him? Hear the words of Elder John A. Widtsoe, that pure and saintly man with the great mind and the humble heart. I wish your generation could have known him better, or at all. He said of this promise of God that He will "meet" and "commune" with His people there—does it mean the occasional visit or the occasional personal manifestation or *"does it mean the larger thing, that the pure in heart who go into the temples, may, there, by the Spirit of God, always have a wonderfully rich communion [communication],"* with the Lord?[3]

In the temple we can, as the scriptures attest and as I personally attest, feel the presence of the Lord in the warmth, the love, and the kindness of those who serve there, in the sense of spiritual presence one may feel. This, to me, is the glorious blessing of the temple, that in temples the Son of Man *does* manifest Himself to us through the Spirit in the principles and ordinances and covenants. A temple truly is a place of revelation to those who go with minds freed from ordinary earthly cares and there learn to walk with Him on the path He has walked and prescribes for us.

Has it occurred to you in going to a temple or thinking about it that the principles around which the sacred covenants of the temple are formed, which are often thought to be the heart of the experience, are those principles that were absolutely fundamental in the mortal life of the Lord Jesus Christ? It is His pattern we are following, through His blood we are symbolically cleansed and blessed, through His life, "saved by his life," that we are learning.

We do not discuss in detail or in the exact vernacular what happens in the temple, but we are learning the gospel there, and we are learning it out of the scriptures and revelation and in a way understandable to those who prepare themselves. We learn, for instance, that we make a covenant with reference to the principle of doing the will of God. We have spoken of that. *Christ* came to do the will of the Father. *We* came to do the will of the Father. That is our mission. In the temple that principle is strongly taught. Does it not become manifest to us as we sit and ponder that the highest and holiest exemplar of this great quality, the capacity to do the will of the Father, in all history is the One who in Gethsemane said, "Not my will but thine be done"? Do we not walk in His paths, even though they lead us through our own Gethsemanes, when we seek to do the will of our Father?

In service, in sharing, in giving, are we not representing in its highest and holiest form the path of the Savior? When we make a commitment to give what we have to give, to serve usefully, are we not following in His path and pattern?

What is the basic principle by which God governs and which was central in the life of our Lord? Was it not that love which Christ declared, the love of the individual for God, of person for person, of each of us for our neighbor? Was it not the love of God and love of our fellowmen that He said are those commandments upon which all others depend for meaning and for substance? Was it not that love that caused Him to give everything? "Therefore doth my Father love me, because I lay down my life, that I might take it again. No man taketh it from me, but I lay it down of myself." (John 10:17–18.) *"No man taketh it from me, but I lay it down of myself."* (Italics added.)

And what of our commitment to purity and honor and integrity and self-discipline, of loyalty to holy commitments?

46

In His great encounter with the devil at the beginning of His mission and throughout His ministry, Christ was "in all points tempted like as we are, yet without sin." (Hebrews 4:15.) He met the tests we are meeting right now, and He positively and absolutely rejected the enticements and blandishments of the tempter. Is not this the path we are here to learn to follow?

And finally, what of priorities? We are taught priorities in the temple: "Seek ye first the kingdom of God, and his righteousness" (Matthew 6:33), and then whatever else you need that is important to your joyful life will be added.

But a respected writer has said:

"We are half-hearted creatures, fooling about with drink and sex and ambition when infinite joy is offered us, like an ignorant child who wants to go on making mud pies in a slum because [she] cannot imagine what is meant by the offer of a holiday at the sea."[4]

In the temple we walk for a time with One who bought us with a price. We cannot fully understand the price, but we can seek to understand this: "Know ye not that your body is the temple of the Holy Ghost which is in you, which ye have of God, and ye are not your own? For ye are bought with a price: therefore glorify God in your body, and in your spirit, which are God's." (1 Corinthians 6:19–20.) "Daily in the temple," it is written, "and in every house, they ceased not to teach and preach Jesus Christ." (Acts 5:42.)

You may be interested to consider one last matter. There are some women who come from the temple (thoughtful, very bright women, sensitive, sweet women) uneasily thinking that somehow they have less value than men in the eyes of God. I have the sure conviction that that is not true, not what we are meant to learn. Repeated exposure to the remarkable institution of the temple leaves me believing the opposite to be so.

The scriptures teach us that Adam and Eve are placed in the garden in a beautiful union. Lucifer finds Adam alone and tries to convince him and fails. He then finds Eve alone and holds out the importance of knowing good and evil to her. She with spiritual perception and intuitive wisdom sees, beyond the blandishments of the tempter, the importance of the commandment that they multiply and replenish the earth. Somehow she understands the mighty importance of that instruction. She partakes of the fruit and then finds Adam and tells him about this special commandment, which they cannot in their present condition fulfill. He eats, they become mortal, and, when God calls him to account for that decision, notes that he was led to do so by the woman whom God had given him with the commandment that she should *remain* with him.

Alma explained: "Now we see that Adam did fall by the partaking of the forbidden fruit, according to the word of God; and thus we see, that by his fall . . . [they became] as Gods, knowing good from evil, placing themselves in a state to act, or being placed in a state to act according to their wills and pleasures, whether to do evil or to do good." (Alma 12:22, 31.)

In short, they became free—free to have a family, free to learn to truly love, free to act according to their wills, whether to yield to the plan of God or subject themselves to the devil, free to enjoy the fruits of the plan of redemption, the plan of mercy, the plan of happiness, free to choose and to be accountable.

Eve did the right thing, made the right choice, had the intuitive comprehension to see the end from the beginning. What if they had made a different choice and stayed in the garden? That seemed so plausible; it seemed so good there. Somehow she knew better.

"And in that day Adam blessed God and was filled, and began to prophesy concerning all the families of the earth, saying: Blessed be the name of God, for because of my transgression my eyes are opened, and in this life I shall have joy, and again in the flesh I shall see God.

"And Eve, his wife, heard all these things and was glad, saying: Were it not for our transgression we never should have had seed, and never should have known good and evil, and the joy of our redemption, and the eternal life which God giveth unto all the obedient." (Moses 5:10–11.)

Most of us know Lehi's declaration that concludes "men

are, that they might have joy." Preceding it are these words: "Adam fell that men might be." (2 Nephi 2:25.)

Eve made a choice. We honor her. *We honor her.*

And so we must choose, and sometimes the choices are between options that are or seem good, or may seem against counsel—whether to remain in the garden in unchallenged comfort, or to become vulnerable, subject to death, and candidates for eternal life.

I come from the temple believing that Eve understood, that through a woman's intuitive faith she knew what must be done, that Lucifer intensified the difficulty but illuminated the vital importance of her choice. I have always believed since I began to think at all seriously that that dramatic event is meant to emphasize the absolute importance of the principle of agency and accountability, the magnificent miracle of motherhood—that incredible, dangerous journey into the deep valley to bring forth life; the responsibility of fatherhood—the lifelong love and labor of a priesthood leader in a family.

Hear these words from the scripture: "Ye [who] have . . . received Christ Jesus the Lord . . . walk ye in him: Rooted and built up in him." (Colossians 2:6–7.)

Oh, there is so much we have yet to learn, and I think many of you here are way ahead of the rest of us, you pure and sweet women.

I said there were several writings on the wall in my office. I have already quoted one, and I end with another. A young lady came to my office years ago declaring her confusion because the father whom she loved was not the father she felt she could respect. I talked with her a long time about him. There were things she didn't know, dear things, unselfish, lovely things to balance, or at least to be taken account of in her criticism, in her anguish. I talked to her of the Savior. I wanted to help her know and love her father and her Savior, and I was praying a simple, familiar prayer: Lord, help me now.

She went away, and things changed at home and have remained changed. A year later she came back just before Christmas, with a shadow box for me. She had dried beautiful flowers and hand lettered and put in the box these words:

> Though Christ a thousand times in Bethlehem be born,
> If he is not born in thee, thy soul is still forlorn.

She was and is no longer forlorn.

I think we will not be forlorn if we come unto Christ, if we learn patiently that we cannot accommodate everybody's estimate of what we ought to be or do, if we walk in the way our own conscience will approve, if we seek to measure as God measures, and if we esteem ourselves and others as He esteems us. I testify that He is good and loves us and wants us to "make it," that He is pulling for us, that His anxiety, His whole plan, His great sacrifice in sending His Son and the sacrifice of that Son in giving His life, all were meant to help us meet the dramatic or drastic or difficult test life lays upon us.

I thank the Lord for this sweet opportunity. In the name of Jesus Christ, Amen.

Notes

1. Dr. Joan Hoff-Wilson, *Salt Lake Tribune*, 7 Mar. 1987; italics added.
2. Marion D. Hanks, " 'Magic Aplenty,' " *Woman* (Salt Lake City: Deseret Book Co., 1979), pp. 99–101.
3. John A. Widtsoe, "Temple Worship," *The Utah Genealogical and Historical Magazine* (Apr. 1921), p. 56.
4. C. S. Lewis, *The Weight of Glory and Other Addresses* (Grand Rapids, Mich.: William B. Eerdmans Publishing Co., 1965), p. 2.

No Respecter of Persons: Equality in the Kingdom

A. D. SORENSEN

*T*hose who speak for the women's movement unanimously condemn patriarchal societies. They point out that in such societies the male-dominated hierarchies and structures of control leave women with diminished opportunities for self-fulfillment and self-determination. They argue that patriarchal societies exclude women from the centers of power and creativity, ranging from science and industry to art and communication, and confine them to subordinate positions from which they can only serve the interests of men. They contend that the rule of women by men works ultimately because the driving ethos of patriarchal society embodies masculine perspectives. This means that women receive their very identity from men by virtue of the fact that the prevailing visions and images by which women live are creations of men. Consequently, men see women — and women see themselves — as adjuncts to men, as satellites, as helpmeets, as the "other half." Thus defined, women by nature stay in the background, do the chores that would impede men in their work, cheer men from the sidelines, provide men with sexual satisfaction, and assure men of paternity. The upshot is that in patriarchal society, women cannot reach full personhood. Some who speak for the women's movement even claim that the barriers to full personhood for women, and indeed for all people, cannot be

A. D. Sorensen is professor of political science at Brigham Young University. After receiving his Ph.D. from the University of Illinois, he taught for several years at Indiana University before joining the faculty at BYU, where he has taught courses in political and moral philosophy, law and morality, and the philosophy of science. His Church callings have included bishop and president of a BYU branch. He and his wife, Necia Marie Lee Sorensen, have six children.

overcome until we eliminate from culture the very distinction between male and female.[1]

From the feminist viewpoint, Mormon society is a patriarchy par excellence. The men occupy the positions of power and privilege, while the women, defined from the male perspective as helpmeets to man, have children, do housework, and sustain their husbands. Like women in all patriarchal societies, Mormon women fail to realize themselves fully as persons. The final barrier that blocks their way to full personhood is the male-female distinction that operates in Mormon culture. That distinction, some believe, has its roots in the master myths out of which Mormon patriarchy arises and receives its rationale. The central myth has it that God made woman so that man would have a helpmeet and not be lonely. (Moses 3:18.) Then God tells the woman that her desires should be to her husband, and that he should rule over her. (Moses 4:22.)

Some critics of the Church think that patriarchy in Mormon society creates for LDS people a crisis of faith that has no satisfactory remedy. For, on the one hand, the liberation of women from patriarchal rule is an idea whose day has come. It is an idea that has freedom and justice as its allies and cannot be convincingly resisted by a group that claims to be the people of God. Yet, on the other hand, patriarchy is so deeply rooted in the Mormon society's foundation and system of beliefs that it cannot be removed without a major revision of belief and practice, which would undermine the Church's claim to be the restored Church of God. So some believe that the LDS people face the unwelcome dilemma of either not giving up patriarchy in the face of change that has right and good on its side, or forsaking patriarchy by sacrificing doctrines and practices supposedly received by revelation from God Himself which form the very core of Mormonism.

It must be admitted, as some of our critics claim, that sex discrimination exists among LDS people more or less as it does in the societies surrounding them. But the explanation for this discrimination does not lie at all in the belief system of the restored gospel but in the fact that we live too much in the world and fail to realize the equality between man and woman that living in the kingdom requires. The fact is that the doctrines and principles of the kingdom are the proper remedy for the unequal treatment of the sexes in the Mormon society, not its cause. So as a people we do not, in fact, face the dilemma of either resisting the women's movement for equal freedom and justice or giving up central tenets of the faith; but as always, we must choose whether or not to continue living as the world does. The real crisis of faith will come from postponing the right choice for too long.

In this essay I propose to lay out what I see as the fundamental social structure and ultimate aim of the earthly kingdom and the equality between woman and man within it. If I am successful, the results will be a general framework within which all relations between the sexes should be understood. Anyone who attempts what I do here faces the difficult and sensitive task of untangling the beliefs and practices not of the kingdom — especially those we cling to as a result of living so much in the world, with its deep-rooted traditions of false patriarchy — from those peculiar to the kingdom. This task can best be done simply by strictly confining the analysis to officially recognized revelations on the subject and by laying out each step in the discussion as fully as space permits, beginning with what I take to be elementary but fundamental truths and building from there. Needless to say, in discussions of this kind the author should not make authoritative claims that he has the final truth.

First, I will discuss the fundamental organizing principle of the kingdom — the principle of divine love — and the absolute equality among all persons who participate in it. My task here will be to examine in sufficient depth only those properties of divine love that I will need later in order to justify the distinction between male and female and to illuminate the equality between them that should characterize every operation and goal of the kingdom. Next, I will consider the kingdom's basic social structure and ultimate aim and the equality between persons within it. Finally, I will take up in a general way the distinction between male and female in divine love, review the justification for its existence, and explain the sexual equality that should extend throughout the organization and purposes of the kingdom.

II

We know from scripture that the earthly kingdom must be organized according to "the law of the celestial kingdom." (D&C 105:4.) "Otherwise," the Lord says, "I cannot receive her unto myself." (D&C 105:5.) As we also know, divine love, in the words of Paul, comprehends and fulfills the whole law (Galatians 5:14; Romans 13:8–10), including the law that governs the celestial world and determines the organization and aims of the earthly kingdom. So if we want to grasp the meaning and significance of the equality between persons that distinguishes the organization and purpose of the kingdom, the place to begin is to examine the human equality inherent in divine love as fundamental law.

But before that can be done, we must understand the general meaning and significance of divine love itself. To grasp its general meaning and significance, we need to review divine love's twofold relationship with the scriptural categories of spiritual life and death as humankind's ultimate possibilities. Only by considering this twofold relationship can we grasp the ultimate justification of the very distinction between male and female and fully appreciate the final importance of equality between the sexes in organizing the kingdom. The relations between divine love and humankind's ultimate possibilities — spiritual life and spiritual death — provide the minimum framework for discussing what equality in the kingdom means and what role it plays in the organization of the kingdom. As we will see, unless we can achieve the equality between persons required by divine love, the spiritual life of neither the man nor the woman can be full.

In scripture the term *life* (the Greek term *zoe*) means fulness of life everlasting, not primarily life biologically understood. Life in the sense of *zoe* represents the highest possibility of humankind, its final good, the ultimate point of the human existence. Death, the opposite of life, is explained in terms of life in its fulness. When fully realized, it means the weakest form of human "life," human existence drained or emptied of its distinctive vitality — existence that is spiritless, dark, without meaning. Together, life and death constitute the grand alternatives, the overall possibilities, of human existence. The picture of humankind individually and collectively facing these grand possibilities as the caretakers of their own existence and having a natural desire to realize life and avoid death represents the scriptural view of the universal human situation.

Divine love has the meaning and significance it does — it comprehends and fulfills the whole law of the gospel — because of its twofold relationship to the grand alternatives of life and death. First, divine love has for its ultimate aim that humankind avoid death and realize everlasting fulness of life. The achievement of that aim represents, as we have observed, the highest possibility of humankind, their ultimate good, and the final purpose of God. But second, divine love also makes possible, indeed literally constitutes, fulness of life. Scripture provides us with a powerful metaphor that reveals how this is so, the metaphor of the seed that grows into the tree of life.

In the Book of Mormon the "tree of life" represents at once both "the love of God" (1 Nephi 11:21–23) and "everlasting [fulness of] life" (Alma 32:40–41). Alma describes the "seed" that grows into the tree of life as "the word" (Alma 32:28) that is contained in "the words" (Alma 32:27), both written and spoken, by which Christ offers his gospel to the world. The word in Alma's sense Paul calls "the word of life" (Philippians 2:16) and John "the words of eternal life" (John 6:68). Alma tells us that if we "plant" the word of life in our "hearts" (Alma 32:28) and "nourish" it properly (Alma 32:39), then it "swelleth and sprouteth" (Alma 32:28, 33–34), "enlarge[s the] soul" (Alma 32:28), and expands the mind (Alma 32:34) until the person reaches "everlasting [fulness of] life" (Alma 32:41–42). We can see that the enlargement and expansion of life and its fulness have to do with the degree and quality of our distinctive vitality as living beings.

Now, in its fundamental meaning, the word of life represents the perfect love of God. We know this because Alma tells

55

us that "every seed bringeth forth unto its own likeness" (Alma 32:31) and, as we know, the seed — "the word" — develops into "the tree of life" (Alma 32:28, 40–41), which represents divine love (1 Nephi 11:21–25). So the word as a seed must represent the germ of divine love, just as the tree of life symbolizes divine love perfectly formed. In this John agrees with Alma. John tells us that "whoso keepeth his word, in him verily is the love of God perfected" (1 John 2:5), and everyone in whom God's love is perfected is "born of God" (1 John 4:7) and has "passed from death unto life" (1 John 3:14).

Clearly, the life of divine love and fulness of life are not two things, but one. The seed is both the germ of divine love and the source of life. The development of the seed is both the growth of divine love and the increase in the degree and quality of life. And the tree of life itself represents both divine love perfected and fulness of life. So as we see, divine love constitutes life as well as aims at life — everlasting fulness of life. Indeed, divine love constitutes life by being aimed at life in its distinctive caring-for-life way. Fulness of life actually consists in being a caring-for-life person in the rich and comprehensive sense implied by divine love.

That divine love constitutes life by the way it aims at life explains the law of the harvest (Galatians 5:13–26): if we live lives of sin, we will reap death. Paul writes, "The wages of sin is death." (Romans 6:23.) But if we fulfill the requirements of righteousness, we will harvest everlasting fulness of life. Righteousness produces fulness of life because righteousness consists of satisfying the requirements of divine love that comprehends and fulfills the whole moral law and all righteousness. (Romans 8:1–13; 13:8–10.) And the reason sin produces death is that in sinning we violate the conditions that make life lasting and full — the requirements of divine love. The bottom line is that we must lose our lives to find our lives. We lose our lives by becoming people of divine love and serving its ultimate aim. And we find our lives because the divine love present in us when we live this way constitutes fulness of life. To repeat, divine love is the fundamental law by virtue of its twofold relationship to our ultimate good — it both gives life and governs life.

We now have the minimum scriptural framework in place for introducing the concept of equality. Equality between persons forms an integral part of divine love, and, consequently, it plays a critical role in its power to give fulness of life. Clearly, each person has supreme worth, and his or her everlasting fulness of life has supreme value, in view of divine love. It is easy to see that in divine love there is no respecting of persons: in range it encompasses every person, past, present, and future; its scope embraces each person's total well-being, his or her everlasting fulness of life; and in strength, measured by the suffering Jesus willingly underwent on the cross, it does not vary with regard to persons. We may say that from the perspective of divine love, persons are equally everything. Because divine love reaches out to all persons totally and equally, it embodies the rich and comprehensive caring for life that constitutes fulness of life. If persons were not equally everything as subjects of love, then life could not reach fulness. If inequality infected divine love — if it singled out any person from others by excluding her from all concern or by not caring for her total welfare or by taking a weakened interest in her well-being — then love ceases to be perfect, and life cannot be full. And whenever inequality in caring for life invades human relations in a large way, as it often does, it greatly impoverishes life.

III

The kingdom on earth and in heaven is a society of divine love. It has the same ultimate aim as divine love — bringing about humankind's fulness of life everlasting — and the organization through which its aim can be accomplished consists of relations of divine love. For this reason the earthly kingdom conforms to "the union required by the law of the celestial kingdom." (D&C 105:4.) Since it fulfills the requirements of divine love in its purpose and organization, the kingdom can promise fulness of life to its members. Indeed, by reason of being a community of divine love, the full operation of the kingdom itself constitutes fulness of life for its members. So, as we should expect, the equality inherent in divine love characterizes every operation and objective of the kingdom. It begins with the fact that all persons are everything in view of divine love, and this principle extends throughout the kingdom's organization. If it did not, if inequalities invented by the world because of sin infected the kingdom, then the kingdom would lose its power to give fulness of life.

The law of divine love that determines the basic structure of the kingdom is the law of consecration. That law combines both elements of divine love — serving and being served, giving and receiving, loving and being loved — into one formula. It obligates every person to help realize the purpose of the kingdom, to perform a stewardship of love, to the full extent of his or her ability. And it requires that each person receive and be cared for according to righteous wants and needs. As we will see, the equality inherent in divine love distinguishes both parts of the law of consecration and the operations of the kingdom to which it gives rise. Accordingly, in the kingdom, persons labor together in love as equals and receive in accord with their wants and needs as equals. Both in the doing of and the receiving of things persons are equals in divine love. Let us bear in mind that, as a principle of divine love, the law of consecration itself contains power to help make life full and never-ending. As a precept of divine love, it aims at life and helps constitute life that is full and without end. That power to create life remains untapped unless we abide the law of consecration and achieve in our daily affairs the equality inherent in divine love.

Let me mention a word about how I will now proceed in describing the equality that marks the law of consecration as a principle of divine love. The most detailed scriptures we have on the everyday working of the law of consecration are concerned with its operation in the economic order of the kingdom. So what I will do is identify a general form of equality that characterizes the law of consecration in all its workings, and then illustrate that form with scriptures about the economic operation of that law. I should emphasize that my interest is not so much in the particular economic form of the law of consecration as in its general form and the overall organization of the kingdom as a community of equality to which it gives rise.

I have noted several times that the earthly kingdom must be organized according to the law that governs the celestial kingdom. (D&C 105:4–5.) The law of consecration is one such law. When we inquire into how celestial beings organize themselves, we should not be surprised to find that the equality of divine love obtains among them and that we, like them, must attain this equality. We learn from revelation that in preparation for a "place in the celestial world," the Saints must be "equal in earthly things" and "equal . . . in heavenly things." (D&C 78:5–7, 13.) Continuing our inquiry, we discover that persons in the celestial world carry out their stewardships as required by the law of consecration according to a system of equal power. In the words of revelation, all those "who dwell in his presence" He makes "equal in power, and in might, and in dominion." (D&C 76:94–95.) And, as I intend to show, when we examine the revelations on how the earthly kingdom should operate, paying particular attention to who can make what decisions and carry out what actions, we discover that the earthly kingdom clearly exhibits a system of equal power. Just as we would expect, the earthly kingdom is indeed modeled after its heavenly prototype.

This, then, is one form equality must take in the earthly kingdom when it is modeled after its heavenly prototype and becomes a society of divine love: each person carries out his or her stewardship in obedience to the law of consecration within a structure of equal power. How fitting, not to mention how necessary, it is that in the society of divine love, wherein persons are equally everything, they should share equally in power in accomplishing the ends of divine love.

Since analyzing equal power as set forth in scripture can itself be a lengthy undertaking, I limit myself to several carefully selected examples of how equal power operated, or at least was meant to operate, in the united order of the Prophet Joseph's time. I think I will depart this once from using recognized scripture as a source and begin with instructions the Prophet Joseph once gave concerning one way power should be equal in the kingdom. The passage is worth quoting at length:

"The matter of consecration must be done by the mutual consent of both parties; for to give the Bishop power to say how much every man shall have, and he be obliged to comply with the Bishop's judgment, is giving to the Bishop more power than a king has; and upon the other hand, to let every man say how much he needs, and the Bishop be obliged to comply with his judgment, is to throw Zion into confusion, and make a slave of the Bishop. The fact is, there must be a balance or equilibrium of power, between the Bishop and the people, and thus harmony and good will may be preserved among you."[2]

Note how clearly the notion of equal power figures here in the Prophet's teachings. In acts of consecration the requirements of divine love prevail and, consequently, "there must be a balance or equilibrium of power" among all parties involved.

The second illustration of how power operates in the kingdom concerns the relationship between each steward (or particular group of stewards) and the order acting as a whole. Like the relation of power between the bishop and the individual steward, this relation involves the law of consecration. The text I have chosen is section 104 of the Doctrine and Covenants. There the Lord instructs the Saints that "all moneys that you receive in your stewardships, by improving upon your properties . . . shall be cast into the treasury as fast as you receive moneys." (D&C 104:68.) Here we see the law of consecration in operation, but this time the "moneys" go into the "treasury" controlled by the order acting as a group, rather than being "laid before the bishop" (D&C 42:31–34), as in the first example.

The principle of equal power determines how the moneys of the treasury will be redistributed. From revelation we learn that "there shall not any part of it be used, or taken out of the treasury, only by the voice and common consent of the order."

(D&C 104:71.) The right of counsel and consent is to be exercised according to equal power. Again I will quote at length:

"And this shall be the voice and common consent of the order—that any man among you say to the treasurer: I have need of this to help me in my stewardship—

"... the treasurer shall give unto him the sum which he requires to help him in his stewardship—

"Until he be found a transgressor, and it is manifest before the council of the order plainly that he is an unfaithful and an unwise steward.

"But so long as he is in full fellowship, and is faithful and wise in his stewardship, this shall be his token unto the treasurer that the treasurer shall not withhold." (D&C 104:72–75.)

The words the Prophet Joseph used, which were quoted earlier to describe the relation of power between the bishop and a steward, may be repeated here. Between the order as a whole and the steward "there must be a balance or equilibrium of power." On the one hand, as the quoted passage indicates, if a steward is both wise and faithful, his or her just claims (see D&C 82:17) cannot be turned down. If this were not so, the members as a collective could become the center of initiative and decision in the performance of his or her stewardship; this would give the order "more power than a king has." On the other hand, if a steward is unwise or unfaithful, the membership may instruct the treasurer not to honor that steward's request for funds to run his or her stewardship. If this veto power did not exist, an unwise or unfaithful steward could assume power to direct the order itself or to usurp another steward's power to carry out his or her own stewardship. This would "throw Zion into confusion." There must be a "balance or equilibrium of power."

So as we can see, the relation between the steward and the order, much like the relation between the steward and the bishop, is a relation of equal power.

I offer one last illustration of how equal power was meant to work within the united order. From the first two illustrations we learn that each person within the kingdom enjoys self-direction equal to every other person in carrying out his or her individual stewardship. But stewardship also includes helping determine the overall direction of the order as well as performing individual tasks within it. In the order "all things" are done "according to the counsel . . . and united consent or voice of the order." (D&C 104:21.) Each steward has an equal voice in the membership's power of counsel and an equal say in its power of consent. Thus, persons in the order are equal in being *joint* stewards as well as in being *individual* stewards.

This joint aspect of stewardship is an important aspect indeed: it prepares each steward for life in the heavenly kingdom in ways in which individual tasks alone do not. In eternal life, being "one" with others and the Lord consists of a joint stewardship as well as individual stewardships. As the scriptures read, if we are faithful and wise we shall become "heirs of God, and joint-heirs with Christ." (Romans 8:17.) In the kingdom of darkness there is no joint stewardship, for Satan seeks to "reign over" people (2 Nephi 2:29), not to make them joint heirs. Preparation (D&C 78:6–13) for this sort of kingdom would, of course, be quite different. A different structure of power would be required—one that is hierarchical and authoritarian.

It is important to notice the degree of human freedom that the kingdom's system of equal power makes possible. Every steward in his or her individual work enjoys the highest degree of self-direction compatible with each steward's enjoying the same freedom. And in things that concern the whole group, each shares the power of counsel and consent equally with others. As a result, a person has the greatest opportunity for self-direction that this social order can allow. This is as it should be within a community of divine love.

Consider now the second part of the law of consecration. That law requires that each person receive equally according to righteous wants and needs. Wants and needs can be conveniently divided into two kinds. First, there are the wants and needs the person has in carrying out his or her stewardship. Concerning these, the Lord tells members of his kingdom that "you are to have equal claims on the properties, for the benefit of managing the concerns of your stewardships, every man according to his wants and needs, inasmuch as his wants are just." (D&C 82:17.) Here equality is part of the system of equal power already discussed. But persons have other wants and needs that may not be immediately related to the daily work of the kingdom, yet essential to a full life. These include the desire to learn or know for its own sake, to enjoy things of beauty, to play, to celebrate life itself. In the opportunities to fulfill these wants and needs, persons also must be equal in the kingdom, every person being treated as an "equal according to his family, according to his circumstances and his wants and needs." (D&C 51:3.) When equality in this sense operates among the Saints, there exist no rich nor poor among them. Only then are they truly a Zion people (Moses 7:18; 4 Nephi 1:3) — a people living as one in an earthly kingdom that is organized according to the law of heaven.

So we see that under the law of consecration, because it is a principle of divine love, persons labor together in love as equals in power, and as equals all receive alike. When the Lord's people are not equal, then they, like the world at large, "lie in sin" and "the abundance of the manifestations of the Spirit shall be withheld." (D&C 70:14.) Life for them will not be full, because the total and equal caring for life required by divine love does not exist among them.

IV

We now have before us the framework of beliefs within which we can understand the distinction between male and female in the gospel and the equality that should define all relations between woman and man in the kingdom. Every major point covered so far will now be used in arriving at this understanding. I will begin with the basic task of laying out the justification for the very distinction between male and female implicit in the design of divine love. I do this having in mind the view of some critics that the distinction between woman and man in Mormon belief and practice has its roots in myths of patriarchy that justify man's ruling woman and woman's being an adjunct to men. Then I will consider the equality between man and woman that divine love requires. I will argue that the law of consecration requires that women and men be equal as stewards in doing the work of the kingdom and in receiving its blessings.

Let us consider first, then, the ultimate justification of the distinction between male and female (implicit in scripture). I suppose that God could develop a kingdom wherein the cultural difference between woman and man hardly exists, or even create intelligent nature that is biologically unisexual. So the reason God made persons male and female must finally be a matter of their fulness of life everlasting, which is the defining aim of His work and glory as well as their ultimate good. We may say that without male and female, fulness of life would be less than it is.

This implies that the distinction between male and female must be essential to divine love itself, since divine love makes possible fulness of life. How essential it is can be seen when we consider briefly two things. For one thing, scripture describes the kingdom first and foremost as a family—the family of God. Better than any other term, *family* expresses the essential character of the kingdom as a community of divine love. In the kingdom persons are one in the bonds of love as sons and daughters of God and as brothers and sisters to each other forever. If the everlasting community of divine love were not a family, it would be very different indeed. And without the distinction between male and female, the essential relations of divine love that make the kingdom a family would not even be possible. Divine love itself would be radically altered and would not be what it is.

How essential the distinction between male and female is to divine love can be seen by considering a second closely related principle. We know that the growth of divine love in the heart enlarges the soul and expands the mind until the person reaches fulness of life. (Alma 32:27–41; 1 Nephi 11:23–25.) This process of rebirth and purification involves in an essential way the transformation of persons as male and female. Scripture tells us that those who thus attain fulness of life are "born of [Christ]" and "become his sons and his daughters."

(Mosiah 5:7.) They put off old definitions of man and woman and put on new ones. They become truly woman and man as measured by their fulness of life.

It seems apparent that fulness of life is constituted essentially by kinship relations in all the variety and subtlety that divine love comprehends. Without the distinction between male and female, the kinship relations of divine love that comprise the kingdom as a human family would vanish, and the possibility of fulness of life would be irredeemably diminished. The resulting void in eternal existence could not possibly be filled by the remaining relations between human beings defined simply as persons. We may say that in a comprehensive sense male and female — as well as female and female, male and male — are not without each other in the Lord.

In divine love woman and man are equal — absolutely equal. There can be no doubt that this is so. In light of their equality before God's love, all rankings and gradings of woman and man favored by the world melt away, and they appear as they really are, equals. All illusions of ruling over, being better than, or possessing more than dissolve. Then woman and man can see each other as equally everything: each as a person has supreme worth, and the fulness of life of each has supreme value in the eyes of the other. Their total, and therefore equal, caring for each other helps make possible fulness of life together. If inequality infected the relations between woman and man, divine love would be corrupted and life could not be full for either of them.

Once man and woman fully grasp that they are equals in divine love, they are prepared to labor and benefit as equals in the work and blessings of the kingdom. This means particularly that woman and man work and receive as equals in obedience to the law of consecration. Consider once more what we observed earlier about how the equality inherent in divine love characterizes the law of consecration as a precept of divine love. In doing so we should bear in mind that the earthly kingdom should be modeled after the heavenly kingdom in its operations. (D&C 105:4–5.)

The law of consecration requires that all people labor in

the kingdom according to their talents and to the full extent of their ability. We saw earlier that, in accord with divine love, persons serve together under the law of consecration in a system of equal power. This should be true of women as well as men. We can say this because it is in accord with the order of heaven after which the earthly kingdom models itself. From scripture we learn that if the marriage between man and woman is "sealed" by the "Holy Spirit of promise," then they "shall inherit thrones, kingdoms, principalities, and powers," and "they" shall "be gods," because "they have all power." (D&C 132:19–20.) Furthermore, we know from scripture that *all* those who "dwell in his [God's] presence," *all* members of the highest kingdom, women as well as men, are "equal in power, and in might, and dominion." (D&C 76:94–95.) There, one sex does not rule over the other.

The same equality operates in the earthly kingdom when it is organized, as it should be, in accord with its heavenly prototype. (D&C 105:4–5.) Revelation tells us that to "prepare" ourselves for "a place in the celestial world," we must be "equal in the bonds of heavenly things" and "earthly things also" while in this world. (D&C 78:5–7.) So in the only way befitting beings of divine love, man and woman labor together to accomplish the purposes of the earthly kingdom in a system of equal power. Not only as individual stewards do they do this but as joint stewards as well. Each has an equal voice in counsel and an equal say in consent in those matters in which both participate together as stewards. Thus, each enjoys equal maximum freedom compatible with social order. The man does not reign over the woman in the earthly community of divine love any more than he does in the heavenly community.

There is a principle here that should not be missed. It is a principle designed to guide how all power should be used in the kingdom. It says that power must be exercised "by persuasion, . . . by gentleness and meekness, and by love unfeigned." (D&C 121:41–42.) This principle is not, I think, about one person's being kind and loving in exercising authority over another in a hierarchical system involving unequal power. Rather, it is a principle that springs from divine love itself and reflects the system of equal power based on that love. Divine love demands that men and women in the kingdom perceive and treat each other as equally everything and, therefore, work together as equals in carrying out their respective stewardships within the kingdom. No hierarchy exists between them, only different stewardships, different labors of love, that they perform individually and jointly. So, based on divine love, the kingdom's system of equal power requires that persons exercise it through persuasion, meekness, gentleness, and unfeigned love in serving with others.

Let me summarize the main points just made. In carrying out their stewardships in obedience to the law of consecration, all persons in the kingdom, women as well as men, labor together within the system of equality required by divine love. This means that women as well as men share equally in the power of the kingdom, even though at this time only men are ordained to priesthood offices. Because power is equal, priesthood power must necessarily be handled with persuasion and love unfeigned. It is unrighteous dominion for any man or woman to think he or she is a ruler.

I hardly need to mention that the law of consecration's second requirement of equality also applies to women as well as men. Both should enjoy "alike" — all should receive equally — the opportunities to grow offered by the kingdom according to their "wants" and "needs" so they "may be one." (D&C 82:17; 51:3, 9.) If they do not, then like much of the world at large, they "lie in sin" (D&C 49:20), and God withholds from them "the abundance of the manifestations of the Spirit" (D&C 70:14). The inequalities favored by the world stand as a barrier to the fulness of life that might otherwise be theirs.

V

Let me conclude with a simple observation. The society in which we live, and in which the Restored Church had its origin, is characterized by inequalities of power, status, and wealth. From the viewpoint that sees power, status, and wealth as things of value, these inequalities favor men over women. About this there can be no doubt. But the inequalities of the world around us stand in stark contrast to the equalities between all persons, however they might be categorized, that divine love requires as the fundamental organizing principle of the kingdom. Insofar as we choose to be of the world, we exhibit its inequalities, which our critics misperceive as being inherent in the gospel and the kingdom.

These inequalities cannot be eliminated from among us, or from society at large, simply by removing sex discrimination from the existing order of things as some propose. For even if all discrimination were removed, the inequalities between persons would remain. They are inherent in the worldly system itself. So we and the world would continue to live in sin even if all "sexism" were eliminated. (D&C 49:20.) The only way we can finally escape the sins of inequality is to embrace the order of life required by divine love — to become a Zion society. The kingdom can be built up in no other way. (D&C 105:5.) The reforms offered by many of our critics will not work for us any more than they will work in the world. Those reforms leave intact inequalities that prevent persons from realizing the fulness of life which the gospel alone promises.

Notes

1. See, for example, Simone de Beauvoir, *The Second Sex* (New York: Alfred A. Knopf, 1953); Sheila Ruth, "The Naming of Women," in *Issues in Feminism* (Boston: Houghton Mifflin Co., 1980), pp. 84–97.
2. Joseph Smith, Jr., *The History of The Church of Jesus Christ of Latter-day Saints,* ed. B. H. Roberts, 7 vols. (Salt Lake City: Deseret Book Co., 1971), 1:364.

A Struggle for an Eternal Order

DONNA LEE BOWEN BARNES

*I*n all the accounts of creation, the primeval state of this universe is one of chaos. In the Babylonian story of creation, chaos, the most ancient of gods, is represented by a great dragon, Tiamat, who destroys all before her. A god, Marduk, is sent to slay the dragon and thereby impose order upon the cosmos so that man may flourish, rather than being consumed in the vast yawning abyss of the void.

In our tradition, the need for order is equally apparent. In creating the world, God imposes form upon the void and light upon darkness. (Genesis 1:2–4; Moses 2:2–4.) There is no question of the source of power or of the source of order in the formation of this earth—all reside in God.

The need for order extends throughout God's creations— beyond that of the physical earth, to the regulation of all that falls within its purview. The intelligences and spirits given bodies on this earth also have a critical need for harmony in their relations and a guiding method in their progress through life. Although God's universe is ordered, we can create our own lives and can live them observing God's order or we can create our own chaos.

The earth was ordered to pull itself back from chaos and remove itself from dangers far greater than the fiery breath of the dragon Tiamat. In our mortal existence, we need to find

Donna Lee Bowen Barnes, associate professor of political science at Brigham Young University, received her Ph.D. in Near Eastern languages and civilizations from the University of Chicago. She has conducted extensive research in Morocco as a recipient of Fulbright-Hayes, National Institute of Mental Health, Ford Foundation, and BYU Kennedy Center research grants for work in that country. The author of numerous scholarly publications on the Middle East, she has taught classes in Arabic, comparative politics, the Middle East, Islam, and the Book of Mormon. She has served in all the Church auxiliaries, including most recently as a Sunday School teacher.

an order to give sense and structure to our existence and to thrust the chaos far from us; we need to recognize God's overarching eternal order.

An Eternal Order

Too often the idea of order conjures up the term *orders* and connotes a sense of hierarchy, power, and authority. Once having recognized that an order exists, mortals seem to react by either meekly obeying it or rebelling. In both cases, they may see the rules but not the meaning of an ordered system.

We have our personal peace to make with the universe. If we realize how we are a part of this system, then it is possible to work within it. Otherwise, we try to dominate it, establishing our own demands and procedures, discarding what does not please us, reasoning through our own philosophies or setting up some substitute authority that we choose to obey.

As one of five billion persons on this earth, I recognize that my religious and cultural system is one of many. And, because my world is a pluralistic world where one cannot be condemned for differences in belief, I am often confused. How can I convince my friends of the importance of chastity when their world claims love and its physical expression to be a primary value? How can I assert the truth of the gospel of Jesus Christ to my Catholic, Hindu, or Muslim friends who have their own scriptures and knowledge of the divine and live a more exemplary life than I do? How can I resolve the conflict when Church leaders tell me to marry when I haven't had the opportunity to marry or to raise children when all my efforts result in miscarriage? Often when such friction results, individuals begin to construct their own systems and establish independent personal orders.

Nevertheless, the order established by God cannot be voided by personal inconvenience or appeals to alternate authority, however reasonable. A personal mortal order can never supersede an eternal one.

The order established by God in this world affects us on two levels—an eternal one and an immediate, personal one. The eternal level of order began in the preexistence. It regulates our lives through mortality and into eternity; it gives us the plan of salvation and hope for exaltation.

The plan of salvation is an elegant and simple part of this order—that we may have a method to receive salvation and, beyond that, exaltation. Such is the importance of His system that, having set it up, even God is bound by its precepts if we follow His commandments.

"For behold, this is my work and my glory—to bring to pass the immortality and eternal life of man." (Moses 1:39.)

This order is predicated upon the sustaining force in this world and the next—that of the power of God, also known as the Spirit of the Lord. The Spirit of Christ, the agency by which God governs and controls in all things, fills the immensity of space. (Bruce R. McConkie, *Mormon Doctrine,* 2d ed. [Salt Lake City: Bookcraft, 1979], p. 752.) This spirit of light strives with the righteous to guide and induce them to seek the truth of the gospel and prepare them to receive it and ready themselves for eternal life. God's power is the means by which He creates, governs, and controls all things that are, were, and will be. This is the power by which the plan of creation, redemption, and exaltation operates throughout eternity, binding on earth and in heaven. (McConkie, p. 594.) The terms *order* and *command* have meanings that are very close, both based on the concept of authority. Since all authority is God's, He alone possesses the power to establish order and to command.

On a personal mortal level, the order of the gospel leads us to structure our lives to realize both our own needs and our place in the larger plan. As a literal spirit child of God, each person has a unique place in His divine plan. Separated from God by a veil, we stumble to find our place in the system unsure of how we fit in the overall schema and what our actions should be. If, rather than stumbling, we hold sight of our goal (reunion with our Father in Heaven), our everyday progress can be more surefooted and serene.

The gospel of Jesus Christ makes no pretense of being an unstructured system. Rather, there are numerous steps in a progression through which we are led if we act in righteousness in accord with the Spirit of God. In this life, it is illogical to

71

perform ordinance work out of order — to ordain to the priesthood before baptism, to receive temple endowments without proving one's worthiness. This order makes sense to us because we have been taught a certain logical progression and have practiced it, but it makes eternal sense as well as we are guided from one step to another. This progression ranges from ordinances such as baptism through those of the temple, through the priesthood hierarchy, each with its respective keys, to individual lessons that we each experience, each capable of building faith and strength in the gospel of Christ. We must realize that the priesthood is a means to funnel the power of God to us on this earth. It is the means by which order is imposed, by which the steps are established that we must follow to return to the Lord. The Spirit of God empowers us through the priesthood and gives us earthly ordinances that help us make sense of life through the eternities.

Imagine trying to discern God's wishes for us without prophets, without scripture, without guidance from the tribulations and triumphs of the Israelites, the Nephites, the Lamanites. How could we know of a Messiah if we had to construct His existence from rational proofs and without the reports of His disciples? Even with the scriptures, most of the world's population doubts the historical veracity of Christ, although most postulate the existence of God.

Although we don't deal with cosmic questions every day, the same principles apply. Our lives are made up of the ordinary: alarm clocks, three square meals, bus schedules or consistent automobile maintenance, work, some exercise, and a little entertainment to restore our good humor. If one area of our life slips out of synchronization and moves into the space allotted other areas, we notice — fall out of sorts, suffer from gastric distress, inordinate weight gain, car troubles, or loss of our jobs. Chaos, or the lack of order, throws us off and can have at first annoying but often ultimately distressing symptoms.

More seriously, disobedience to God's laws can pull us into real chaos. Disregard for chastity results in a living hell of deception, the agony of a family unit being ripped into separate concerns. If we turn aside from ethics or moral considerations and condone killing, theft, or lying, we reduce society to a jungle where the strongest rules.

Late in her long life, my dear grandmother suffered from constricted blood flow to her brain. The result was loss of memory and increasing disorientation. Nights I would find her wandering from room to room in her home trying vainly to remember where she was and what she was doing there. I would calm her panic for a moment, but when I left, I knew the disorder of thoughts returned. The loss of her sense of place and time had panicked her, and she could not bear the emptiness. My grandmother's confusion was physiological, but the spiritual chaos that we flee is a deep and lasting hell. We can create this hell ourselves through actions that scorn God's order.

If we, however, are aware of the natural world and our place within it, we notice the system of order whereby the elements were molded to God's purpose. Each enzyme, each chromosome, each spiral of DNA has its separate function, which combined with that of others takes on purpose and meaning. Likewise, we have talents that enable us to perform certain functions. Each is given certain abilities. (D&C 46:11–26, 29, 33.) And each has certain roles. The logical extension of each of our receiving certain gifts is that none can supply all the abilities needed to run the world.

All of God's children share certain tasks. The first is to make ourselves worthy to return to His presence. We must work hard, study, and acquire knowledge of God's plan revealed through His prophets in order to learn how to return to Him, as well as develop the most important component—the will and the desire to regain His presence. Inherent in this mortal slice of the divine order is the idea that we are given roles, duties, and the agency to decide how we will respond.

The second task we are given is to replenish the earth and instill in our children, as well as in all others, the desire to live forever in His presence and to learn the means to achieve that goal.

In order to keep the first task in mind—that of our returning to our Father in Heaven, it is vital that the second — bearing and raising children and teaching others — be correctly understood. We are responsible for ourselves and can guarantee no one else's exaltation. Even our spouse, whom we need for exaltation, cannot be forced to the celestial kingdom. We can only help and guide; we cannot determine another's eternity. We can bear and raise children, but while their births are *one* purpose for which we were created and placed on earth, they are a means to our goal, not the goal itself. Our goal is eternal life, which comes to us only through obedience and righteousness and reliance on Christ's atonement.

Our major role in this life that leads to the life beyond is parenthood. Thus, much is commanded regarding it. In addition to bringing life into the world, we have the responsibility to guide it; however, if we see being a father or a mother as our end goal in this life, we further misconceptions. If we see it as a necessary part of an eternal goal, then all the pieces fit well together.

Maturity within God's Order

An example of one who found his place within God's order and gained in maturity and strength is Nephi, probably my favorite person in the Book of Mormon. I am fascinated by his growth from a single-minded, tactless young man, dedicated to his parents and his God, but incapable of enforcing his convictions and obeying God's commandments without raising the hackles of his older brothers, Laman and Lemuel. As he matured, his qualities of courage, his faith in the Lord and strength in obeying His commands, however difficult or foreign, triumphed. His care for and his belief in his father, Lehi, was absolute. When asked by the Spirit of the Lord what he desired (1 Nephi 10:2), a question reminiscent of that asked of Solomon, he disdained any personal gain and answered that he wanted to see what his father had seen. He was then shown a revelation foreshadowing the rest of the Book of Mormon, depicting the future history of the world, and outlining the plan of salvation. He saw great things, things "even too great for man." (2 Nephi 4:25.)

Although he was blessed by God's attention, Nephi often offended his brothers. They accused him of seeking power and authority over them. Before his death Lehi reproved them:

"Ye have accused him that he sought power and authority over you; but I know that he hath not sought for power nor authority over you, but he hath sought the glory of God, and your own eternal welfare.

"And it must needs be that the power of God must be with him, even unto his commanding you that ye must obey. But behold, it was not he, but it was the Spirit of the Lord which was in him, which opened his mouth to utterance that he could not shut it." (2 Nephi 1:25, 27.)

At Lehi's death, the prophecies that had so grieved Lehi began to play themselves out as the two older sons separated from Nephi, Sam, Jacob, and Joseph. Feeling his weakness and mortality, Nephi, in writing upon the plates of brass, berated his own limitations and left a record of his innermost thoughts for our learning and profit. (1 Nephi 4:15.)

What follows is for me one of the most inspiring parts of scripture, the psalm of Nephi, as Nephi expresses both his delight in the gospel of our Lord and the recognition of his own imperfections.

"Nevertheless, notwithstanding the great goodness of the Lord, in showing me his great and marvelous works, my heart exclaimeth: O wretched man that I am! Yea, my heart sorroweth because of my flesh; my soul grieveth because of mine iniquities.

"I am encompassed about, because of the temptations and the sins which do so easily beset me.

"And when I desire to rejoice, my heart groaneth because of my sins; nevertheless, I know in whom I have trusted.

"My God hath been my support; he hath led me through mine afflictions in the wilderness; and he hath preserved me upon the waters of the great deep.

"He hath filled me with his love, even unto the consuming of my flesh.

"He hath confounded mine enemies, unto the causing of them to quake before me.

"Behold, he hath heard my cry by day, and he hath given me knowledge by visions in the nighttime." (2 Nephi 4:17–23.)

Then Nephi, who is worthy of revelation from God, goes on to lament his own weakness—his propensity to yield to sin, to allow a place for the evil one in his life.

As quickly as he has realized his weakness, he acknowledges the source of his strength and delivers a strong testimony of the power of the Lord, echoing the earlier verses, calling on the Lord to grant him strength and to guide him.

"O Lord, wilt thou encircle me around in the robe of thy righteousness! . . . Wilt thou make my path straight before me! Wilt thou not place a stumbling block in my way—but that thou wouldst clear my way before me, and hedge not up my way, but the ways of mine enemy.

"O Lord, I have trusted in thee, and I will trust in thee forever. I will not put my trust in the arm of flesh; for I know that cursed is he that putteth his trust in the arm of flesh. Yea, cursed is he that putteth his trust in man or maketh flesh his arm.

"Yea, I know that God will give liberally to him that asketh. Yea, my God will give me, if I ask not amiss; therefore I will lift up my voice unto thee; yea, I will cry unto thee, my God, the rock of my righteousness. Behold, my voice shall forever ascend up unto thee, my rock and mine everlasting God. Amen." (2 Nephi 4:33–35.)

The plan of God for this life was revealed to Nephi, as well as matters too great for him to speak of. Yet being human, he doubted his own strength but knew that of the Lord. The paradox here is that Nephi was both weak and strong. As he recognized, he himself was weak, but with the Spirit of God, he gained strength as he accepted and relied upon the place of God's power in his life and deeds.

Without a revelation as overpowering as Nephi's and without a faith as strong and purposeful as his, we confuse mortal goals with eternal goals, mortal order with eternal order, mortal concerns with eternal concerns in trying to make sense of life on the earth. We fail to realize how all-encompassing the strength of the Lord can be and how much comfort and serenity His Spirit can impart, if only we are willing to request strength, comfort, or serenity.

My Search for an Eternal Order

Unfortunately for my parents, or perhaps because of them, I was born with a restless, rebellious, and willful spirit. My basic redeeming quality was my willingness to see reason and the other side of any question. All of the faith and meekness in our family went to my siblings — especially my younger brother Cacey and my youngest sister, Kristey. I have always had a difficult time taking things on faith or obeying because it was commanded. I always needed to know why and how. The order upon which I based my life was centered in the gospel, but it was a difficult centering — more responsive to reason than to faith.

A few years ago I came up against something that reason and logic could not crack. My husband, a good man whom I loved dearly, ran into a personal crisis and reacted by gradually and then rapidly pulling away from the Church, from me, and finally from his own self. As I struggled to sort out and then put back together the scraps my marriage had been reduced to, I attempted to make sense of what was happening and to understand my place in all of this. I quickly found that reason was insufficient for my needs (it further confined me), but that prayer sustained me.

My patriarchal blessing tells me to pray at all times, in all places, and regarding all things. Those words suddenly had new meaning, and I prayed constantly for the strength and serenity to get through each night, each morning, each afternoon, and often each hour. Although I have always relied strongly upon my Father in Heaven, never had I needed Him so much. And as my need increased, so did His sustenance.

Never have I been better behaved. I clung to the Lord's commandments, used the scriptures as a marriage counseling handbook, and followed all they suggested. In return, I found that I could command serenity, peace of mind and of heart during the greatest period of turbulence in my life. If I prayed for calm, I received it. If I prayed for guidance, inspiration followed. If I needed patience and understanding, new depths of meekness were made available. Family and friends sensed my needs and supplied them. I was truly blessed, and I learned so much.

One night, as I was reading the scriptures I was struck by a recapitulation of the Beatitudes in chapter 3 of Colossians. Paul instructs us how to be risen with Christ:

"But now ye also put off all these; anger, wrath, malice, blasphemy. . . .

"Lie not one to another . . . ;

" . . . put on the new man, which is renewed in knowledge after the image of him that created him: . . .

"Put on therefore, as the elect of God, holy and beloved, bowels of mercies, kindness, humbleness of mind, meekness, longsuffering;

"Forbearing one another, and forgiving one another, if any man have a quarrel against any: even as Christ forgave you, so also do ye.

"And above all these things put on charity, which is the bond of perfectness." (Colossians 3:8–10, 12–14.)

I realized as I read that I had learned some lessons in the past months: that anger would not get me anywhere, that meekness and forbearance were far better suited to my needs than arrogantly asserting my rights, that longsuffering, forgiveness, and, finally, charity—or love—were essential if there were to be a solution to our problems. And, finally, I realized they were necessary even if there were no solution—as there was not. I stopped needing to have all the answers immediately—to fit them together in a tight mosaic, any one piece which would not fit immediately invalidating all the rest. I learned to live with space and with ambiguity, and I learned that I could wait for some answers, that in time all would be comprehensible. I did not learn all this in pleasant ways. I learned it by having it pounded into me by experience. And the lesson is more valuable for the cost.

Close to the beginning of this experience, I took a deep breath and looked around at the new world I had discovered as others, learning of my difficulties, began to confide their problems in me. I saw a world of turmoil, not calm, a world of tears rather than joy, a world of endurance rather than triumph. I was overwhelmed at the trials men, as well as women, suffered at each other's hands.

I realized that many of them, as they dealt prayerfully with their situations, after being struck blows of adversity, were learning lessons that better equipped them to enter the celestial kingdom than others who had more agreeable lives. In recognizing their weakness, they were not misled by ideas of their own strength or by goals of fame, status, position, or material goods.

Meekness and forbearance and forgiveness are qualities not easily acquired. In addition, these traits are not valued in today's world, which teaches assertiveness and how to stick up for ourselves. None of these former qualities, of course, imply not realizing our self-worth and defending it. Rather, to my mind, they demand our knowing our place in God's system and holding firmly to it.

Through our absolute need for free agency, we are left to make our own choices, including if and to what extent we wish to involve God in our lives.

Once I turned to God to give me strength, recognizing my own inability to affect another's behavior and realizing my total ability to determine my own behavior and my own course of action, I began to feel a sense of liberation, freedom born of working within a discipline and an order. I established order in my life and, by placing myself under God's care, avoided the dark chasm which threatened to engulf me.

The knowledge of one's relation to oneself and to others and to God, and the dependence on His Spirit and adherence to the ordinances are the best means to develop the qualities to regain God's presence. I had to realize that the spirit and the power of God are there to be tapped and brought into our lives. We are denied nothing if we ask in righteousness.

"He that asketh in the Spirit asketh according to the will of God; wherefore it is done even as he asketh.

"And again, I say unto you, all things must be done in the

name of Christ, whatsoever you do in the Spirit." (D&C 46:30–31.)

Unfortunately, although the scriptures systematically teach us of the availability of spiritual help, we usually coast along relying upon our own abilities and following our own will until we reach a problem we cannot overcome. So we turn to the Lord and request His Spirit in times of frustration and great need, times when we have found that we cannot trust in the "arm of flesh" that Nephi spoke of in his psalm:

"O Lord, I have trusted in thee, and I will trust in thee forever. I will not put my trust in the arm of flesh; for I know that cursed is he that putteth his trust in the arm of flesh. Yea, cursed is he that putteth his trust in man or maketh flesh his arm." (2 Nephi 4:34.)

Maturity for me came when I recognized the paradox of my existence. If I held to my strength and my own system of organizing and understanding my life, I was weak — more than weak, for I was brittle and I could break.

Conversely, by recognizing my weakness and inability to manage by myself, and by asking for help, I was given, so generously, the Spirit of God — a power that enabled me to deal with problems and to understand and see beyond myself. But holding this power is not a constant or permanent process. It ebbs and flows with my receptiveness to the Spirit of Christ. It must be worked at.

Clumsy Mortal Attempts to Live Immortal Principles

Although through the Spirit of Christ we can be given all the help, strength, and comfort necessary, to gain this spiritual help for ourselves certain things are expected: that we are righteous, that we obey the precepts and commands of the gospel, and that we seek help from the Lord on our knees in prayer. Access to the Spirit is not granted by office held in the Church, or by wealth, by status, by gender or color. It is available to those who truly desire it and are willing to humbly do as they are commanded.

Thus, all the power of God is at our disposal to be used in our behalf when we need it, dependent only upon our righteousness, our spirituality, our desire to bow to God's command.

Unfortunately, the harmony that results from adherence to these divine injunctions is sometimes shattered by selfish human concerns. If the divine order is upset, the result is a kind of chaos with individuals' imposing their own means of ordering their lives rather than living in accordance with the divine plan.

"For although a man may have many revelations, and have power to do many mighty works, yet if he boasts in his own strength, and sets at naught the counsels of God, and follows after the dictates of his own will and carnal desires, he must fall and incur the vengeance of a just God upon him." (D&C 3:4.) Too often when this happens, order becomes command, and force is introduced into human affairs. Often materialism, recourse to wealth, status, fame, and influence, become overriding goals.

At this point the whole order of the gospel is upset. Our order is one of service, of stewardship. Whatever function we perform in the Church, we work within parameters established to guide that work. Positions in the Church, to my mind, are very far from reflecting power. Rather they force us to be sensitive to the Spirit of Christ, to seek, to listen, and to obey. Our stewardships are to induce us to serve, not to command. They give us responsibility, not glory. The more responsibility an office entails, the more tightly a person is tied to obedience to the Lord's commands and to attention to the Spirit. As Nephi gained in knowledge, maturity, and spirituality, he became more, rather than less, dependent upon the Spirit of God. Thus, in reproving Laman and Lemuel for wrongly accusing Nephi of seeking power and authority over them, Lehi contrasted the two senses of power: first, the mortal sense of power and authority as command with its implicit sense of force and repression; second, the immortal sense of power as Lehi described it, the "power of God within him," the "truth according to that which is in God which he could not restrain." (2 Nephi 1:25–26.)

Our major purpose on this earth—besides sustaining life,

81

which necessitates food, shelter, and a modicum of other needs — is to help teach and influence others to enable them to achieve celestial life. In my opinion, that which furthers this goal is worthwhile, that which detracts from it, misplaced energy. We have life-styles and professions that help. First of all are the nurturing roles of mother and father. Second, there are professions, work, and callings which, pursued correctly, can help steer others to God: the positions of teacher, doctor, nurse, neighbor, visiting teacher, bishop, Relief Society president, and so many other roles that can add to our understanding of our place in this life and make it richer, healthier, better. Nevertheless, these same jobs, if not pursued correctly, can be more damaging than any other. I have friends who trace problems of members of their family to uncaring or malicious teachers or inattentive health professionals. These possibilities provide a yardstick to help us determine how we wish to spend our professional lives — as Anne Sullivans or as Ivan Boeskys.

If we fall victim to what is known in the Church as "unrighteous dominion," we are in a sense helpless. The Church organization is being used against us, and for purposes opposed to the divine order. Often reasons for command rather than service tie in with misunderstandings of the role of men and women in the gospel, sometimes with personality problems being played out in interpersonal relations. Too often those commanded are women. And women — or more personally, I — get very tired of being told what to do, how to do it, how I should feel, how I should react, and how I should interpret the scriptures. The Spirit of Christ is there to guide me if I make use of it. If not, then I am the loser.

The concept of priesthood is often misused by both men and women. Rather than seeing it as the structure that makes the universe intelligible to us, which permits us to follow the order — baptism, confirmation, ordination — that God has set down, we confuse it with the Spirit of Christ or the power of God. Priesthood funnels God's power to man; it does not replace it. Any righteous person can partake of God's Spirit; indeed, that is how prayer and repentance function. Therefore, we can never place responsibility for our actions on anyone else, for each of us has access to the Spirit of the Lord. Conversely, we can never take responsibility for another by virtue of priesthood office and thwart the working of free agency. Women are not saved by their husband's priesthood (although they can be greatly aided by him—just as the husband is aided by the wife); they are saved by their faith, works, and the atonement of Christ. This principle is the same for all of us.

Every reference to power in the scriptures speaks of it as residing only in God (if it is used righteously), although it can be delegated to those having authority and acting in righteousness. The missionaries in my father's mission years ago always impressed and touched me when they insisted that *they* did not convert investigators to the Church—"the Spirit of the Lord did." The Spirit of Christ or the power of the Lord is intended for our assistance. It is offered for the benefit of mankind. We know from the scriptures and from statements by President Spencer W. Kimball that the Spirit of Christ exists for all, not just for Mormons or those living in Salt Lake City, Utah County, or the Wasatch Front. In some degree, all, regardless of religious background, can call upon the Spirit of Christ and be given help. I have seen this in experiences in other cultures, and there is no other explanation than that the Spirit extends Itself to all.

In 1978 President Kimball said in "A Statement of the First Presidency Regarding God's Love for All Mankind": "We believe that God has given and will give to all peoples sufficient knowledge to help them on their way to eternal salvation, either in this life or in the life to come."

The major qualification to this statement is that *all* power cannot be extended to *all* inhabitants of the earth without all following the gospel. In other words, there is one eternal order and one eternal truth that all must follow. Authority—and the power of God that fuels it—comes from Christ and is vested in the priesthood and ordinances of the Lord. This priesthood is only available under the direction of one who has the keys of prophecy and the stewardship of the community of the saints to direct the Church of Jesus Christ.

The Mortal Clash of Temporal Orders and Divine Order

In my medium-long lifetime I have been exposed to various temporal orders ranging from peer pressure in Bountiful, Utah, to attempts to convert me to Islam in the desert oases of Morocco. In graduate school my life was bound by formal rules and orders. Two years of one language, four years of another. Expertise in fourteen centuries of Middle Eastern history, command of a system of doctrinaire philosophy, understanding of the theological arguments that underline that philosophy. Four years of tuition paid into the university (or the approved equivalent thereof). Annual applications for fellowship funding. Reports and financial accounting to the Fulbright Commission. Signatures of advisers for the finished Ph.D. dissertation. Fees paid to the graduation office. The lists run on and on.

In addition I had others' systems influencing my life: friends from Chicago's North Side, New York City, Pakistan, Sweden, Tunisia, Iran, Sioux Falls, and Alpine, Utah, with varying needs and their own methods to resolve those needs. In some ways, these temporal orders were the most trying of all. Close friends and peers seemed to have inordinate influence when I was far from my family. We all had so many problems at that time and needed each other's support to keep going through romantic attachments, academic disasters, family problems, and the trials of daily life in southside Chicago. Determining a basis upon which to resolve problems was a major conflict in itself. Religious teachings did not seem viable bases when arguing my position with friends who were fiercely agnostic rationalists or were simply of a different religious tradition. I did not feel free to impose my values upon them. At times I even felt reluctant to bring up religion in our discussions and tried to develop reason-based arguments to support my position.

The most puzzling of the collisions is related to my work and continues still. As I work professionally in the Middle East and North Africa with non-Mormons and non-Christians, my adherence to a principle of one eternal truth makes my treatment of their religions and their traditions inherently difficult.

If I declare my religion to be the only truth, I thereby declare their religion to be false. If I take an easy out and weasel around this dogmatic position, I trivialize both religions. Dealing with foreign cultures, traditions, and customs is tricky. When religion comes into the picture, it becomes triply complex.

Trying to work within all of these orders, each of which has had a strong impact on my life, is enough to make my head spin. Resolving the dissonance so all systems can operate in tandem, given their mutual irreconcilability, requires adroit juggling. There is no single answer for resolving conflicting temporal orders as many of them cannot be reconciled. But knowledge that they cannot be reconciled and that they are mortal orders, not eternal ones, and that they do not have to be reconciled provides an answer in itself.

A scholar of Native American culture, Gary Witherspoon, once stated that the similarities on this earth come from the pre-existence. The differences come from this earth. When we were divided at the Tower of Babel and given different languages, we also developed different customs and habits separating us from each other. As a scholar, I relish and learn much about others and myself from the differences of our cultures, but my soul yearns for unity. This unity I find in the gospel of Christ, a truth that transcends diversity. In the gospel, all begins to come together, and I find truth from the diversity, not in spite of it.

Recognition of the divine order, which stretches for eternity, removes the uncertainty and ambiguity in dealing with our varieties of temporal orders. For many, giving in, surrendering oneself to a heavenly order is not easy for it necessitates great faith and humility. But once accomplished—when the leap is made—one finds that no control over life is lost, no freedom is surrendered. Instead, far more control is gained, and the freedom of the eternal order is far sweeter than anything this earth can offer.

Once I achieved this level of maturity and delighted in the freedom I had found in following the rules of the gospel, I wanted more than anything to share this feeling with my former husband. He could not comprehend what I was talking about.

This was the most bitter part of those years: knowing that what Nephi said was true—that we had to depend upon our Father in Heaven and follow His strictures—and yet being unable to persuade my husband that this was the answer, or the beginning of the answer, to our problems.

Free agency is a double-edged sword that is often used in a most painful manner. It is part of our Father in Heaven's order that we are responsible for our own destiny and none other. We can help, support, guide, but we do not have the power—even God does not have the power—to influence anyone unless he or she wishes that influence. So many times I prayed for my husband to turn to the Lord to calm his personal demons. I could not understand for many years why such a righteous prayer was not answered. Finally, I realized that I could govern only my own spiritual relationship; others were in charge of theirs. Although my prayers might open doors, my husband had to walk through them himself. If our positions had been reversed, he would not have been able to do any more for me, despite his priesthood. This plan reflects great eternal wisdom, but it is sometimes difficult for mortals to accept and live when we want instant answers and relief for our pain. Now, a few years later, my former husband has worked things through himself in his own time and is returning to the gospel.

A few years ago I taught an honors Book of Mormon class. At the end of the year I gathered the class together at my house to share insights about the Book of Mormon. One freshman related an experience I have never forgotten.

She told how her father had died early in the year and what a hard time she had had accepting his death, an occurrence made more difficult by being at BYU and absent from her family. She said she could not understand how God could have done such a thing to her and she was inconsolable. Then one day in class we discussed the psalm of Nephi and the importance of asking our Father in Heaven for help. She said she was very skeptical at that, believing that her grief was unique, that no one could understand, care, or relieve it, but she decided she had nothing to lose. The next night she prayed for help. At that point her voice broke. When you ask, she admonished us, you had better be ready, because the Spirit of the Lord will come pouring out faster and stronger than you can ever imagine.

Then she opened the Book of Mormon to 2 Nephi 4:35:

"Yea, I know that God will give liberally to him that asketh. Yea, my God will give me, if I ask not amiss; therefore I will lift up my voice unto thee; yea, I will cry unto thee, my God, the rock of my righteousness. Behold, my voice shall forever ascend up unto thee, my rock and mine everlasting God. Amen."

The Repentance of Eve

SUZANNE EVERTSEN LUNDQUIST

dam, Eve. . . . Where art thou?" and "Who told thee that thou wast naked?" stand as two of the most significant questions posed by God to our original parents in the Garden of Eden. (Genesis 3:9, 11.) And if God asks such questions to first man and first woman, by implication, we too are asked. Perhaps at no other time in the history of humankind has "discovering our nakedness" been so necessary. Where, indeed, are we in understanding what it means to be man — male and female? Wounded and wounding we go, still ignorant of beginnings, divine intentions, creation — standing, as it were, between the "tree of the knowledge of good *and* evil" and "the tree of life."

Essentially, life is a journey from "the tree of life . . . in the midst of the garden" (Genesis 2:9) to "the tree of life, which is in the midst of the paradise of God." (Revelation 2:7.) The "fruit" of the tree in Eden, in Lehi's dream, in the midst of God's eternal landscape, can be eaten by those who have ears, eyes, and a will to discover how to overcome ignorance — to know, to become. The temple ceremony provides the clearest indications of what is required of each initiate — how, through voluntarily accepting and living covenant laws, one can move from Eden, through mortality, into the presence of God. In order to take full advantage of the atonement of Jesus Christ, we must individually and collectively answer the questions

Suzanne Evertsen Lundquist received her doctorate in English with an emphasis on Native American literature at the University of Michigan. She is assistant professor of English at Brigham Young University, where she has taught classes on the Old Testament, Native American sacred texts, and novels from the Third World. She has written extensively on her specialties. Her Church callings have included Gospel Doctrine teacher, chorister, Relief Society teacher, and membership on the activities committee of her Orem, Utah, ward. Sister Lundquist is a single parent with six children.

posed to Adam and Eve, and, like Adam and Eve, eat the fruit of these trees. By so doing, we can become "sons and daughters of the Gods."

Traditional interpretations of Genesis 1–3 have had a powerful impact on the lives of men and women, and, for the most part, these interpretations come from negative misreadings. Any review of the criticism available on the Adam and Eve story would require a seminar. Indeed, universities such as Princeton offer a semester's study of Adam and Eve literature. Biblical scholars everywhere are revising, literally giving a new vision to, the meaning of the text. Those looking for the correct version will be at a loss to find it. Even within the Latter-day Saint faith, there are four (Genesis, Abraham, Moses, and the endowment text); each, however, illuminates the others in very meaningful ways. Perhaps this is what the Savior did when He expounded "all the scriptures in one." (3 Nephi 23:14.) Through proof-texting, comparing the available sacred literature written by Saints from the beginning, Christ was able to help the Nephites come to more correct notions about the nature of mortality. The familiar rabbinic formula for such exegesis would be: "you have heard it said, . . . but I say unto you. . . ." (See Matthew 5.) During Christ's ministry on earth, He was constantly turning His audience to correct interpretations of familiar, standard works.[1]

I believe this same spirit of correction is moving many twentieth-century men and women to reevaluate the Adam and Eve story. This reappraisal is a result of the fact that, among other things, the notions of patriarchy, the origins of evil, and the nature of male-female relationships stem from this narrative. As both men and women move towards new understandings of what it means to be whole (a creation partaking in Gods' image), the idea that the Gods created woman to be ruled over by man, that she is a secondary creation, is no longer acceptable. Nor is the notion that Eve's seduction (with all the attending sexual overtones) was an experience exposing womankind's weakness for the flesh. What, really, did Eve do? What transgression did she make that requires repentance? Why is what happened to Eve in the Garden an event we ritually repeat in order to move towards salvation? As Carl G. Vaught so rightly suggests, "the quest for wholeness moves in two directions": "forward toward a larger, more inclusive unity [and] back to the origins of our individual existence."[2]

What Vaught suggests, then, is that before we, as women, can experience renewal, wholeness, the Second Coming, we must understand the origins of our being—which, by definition, includes the creation of woman "in the beginning." In essence, then, this paper is two directional: it first explores traditional, more negative approaches to Genesis 1–3 and then moves towards overcoming those interpretations through a revision of the text and, by implication, a new vision of what it means to be a whole woman in relationship to a whole man. We must be willing to know *the good* and *the evil* interpretations.

Two attitudes towards the Genesis story prevent women from arriving at a more correct understanding of their origins. The first attitude involves innocence and ignorance. Many women accept the traditional interpretation of the tale. Such women are more literalist in their approach to reading sacred texts; that is, they read *only* on the literal level, ignoring symbolic dimensions, word studies, and alternate readings. Imagine discovering, for example, that the words *help meet* (*'ezer* in the Hebrew) have multiple meanings in the context of this story, the most important being a beneficial "helper equal to man."[3] Or consider the delight at discovering that Moses, the presumed author of the text, was punning with words when he describes Eve's being made from Adam's rib. Ancient Sumerian texts describe the Goddess Nin-ti, a goddess created to heal Enki's rib, "the lady of the rib" or "the lady who makes live."[4] Certainly Moses, the writer, was aware of the literary milieu. What better way to symbolize the creation of the "mother of all living" than by drawing on local "rib" imagery? Adam's wife is "the lady who makes live"—a powerful role and purpose for Eve and her daughters.

The second attitude towards the creation story that prevents women from arriving at a more correct understanding of their origins involves arrogance. Many women insist that Eve has nothing of which to repent, no matter what multiple texts suggest to the contrary (i.e., Moses, Abraham, temple texts, and apocryphal and pseudepigraphal works). Eve is seen as a pawn in the plan of salvation—a character acting out key elements of a plot or script written by the Gods. Often, however, this arrogance comes from a failure to understand fully the nature of agency, accountability, and repentance.

For example, of the four versions standard to Mormon theology (Genesis 1–3, Moses 3–4, Abraham 5, and the endowment text), one pattern emerges: (1) God creates man (male and female) in the image of the Gods—indicating equality; (2) through Eve's choice to eat of the Tree, she becomes subject to Adam—indicating the beginning of patriarchy and inequality; and (3) through Eve's disobedience, mortal existence comes into being—separating Adam and Eve from the presence of God, the source of wholeness. According to Phyllis Trible, the "subordination of female to male signifies their shared sin. This sin vitiates [makes faulty or defective] all relationships: between animals and human beings ([Genesis] 3:15); mothers and children (3:16); husbands and wives (3:16); people and the soil (3:17); humanity and its work (3:19)."[5]

What all the texts I have read seem to indicate, finally, is that this story calls females and males to repent.[6] Through their actions, Adam and Eve pervert (turn away from the original order) creation and must suffer the consequences—mortality. In other words, they *really* do have agency and are accountable for their state of being. And they must change that state through repentance. One real theme in the Adam and Eve story, then, is exile and return—salvation through repentance. Repentance, then, "exists to repair a breach in relations between the Gods and an individual."[7] Repentance, meaning, literally, "to rethink," is the process that Adam, Eve, and we must go through to continually overcome ignorance as accountable humans.

The title of this address, "The Repentance of Eve," is taken from a book called *The Life of Adam and Eve*[8] by an unknown author. This text, originally written in Hebrew, dates back to one hundred years before Christ and essentially deals with the events recorded in Genesis 1–5. There are hundreds of texts claiming authorship by familiar biblical characters. Joseph Smith encouraged the Saints to consult these texts because they contain many truths. According to the Prophet, those who read with the Spirit can be enlightened by these works. (D&C 91.) This has certainly been the case with my reading. One verse from *The Life of Adam and Eve* particularly arrested my attention. In it, Adam and Eve have already been thrust from Paradise and are finishing a seven-day fast. They are both hungry, so Adam walks another seven days looking for food but can find none like the food eaten in the Garden. Full realization of the difficulty of mortality begins to burden Eve. In anguish for her part in Adam's suffering, she cries out to him: "Would you kill me? O that I would die! Then perhaps the Lord God will bring you again into Paradise, for it is because of me that the Lord God is angry with you." (2:1–3.)

Adam explains to her that he cannot harm his own flesh. Adam does admit, however, that they should lament before the Lord "with a great penitence." (4:3.) Because of their penitence (their sad and humble regret for not keeping God's commands), Adam believes the Lord might pity them and provide a way of life: a pattern for acting and existing in a mortal world.

For me, this outburst of Eve's is representative of the attitude both men and women have historically propagated about Eve and the nature of women. In this episode, Eve accepts the blame for their situation. I believe women, to this day, are made to feel responsible for what goes wrong in families and societies. We are often reminded, for example, that if women will do what they are supposed to, the evils in society will be reversed. Blame, in this context, implies guilt, shame, even crime. Certainly, in the above episode, Eve has become conscious of the difficult nature of mortality, and she is also aware that her choice brought her and, because of her, Adam into an environment full of trials. To be responsible, accountable, to feel the effects or consequences of choice, is agency. If "blame" means this (to be responsible, accountable, to feel the effects or consequences of choice), then Eve is to blame.

Perhaps a verse from The First Book of Adam and Eve in

The Forgotten Books of Eden will further illuminate this notion of blame as accountability. In chapter 13, the Lord explains why He warned, even commanded, Adam and Eve not to partake of the fruit of the tree. The Lord says:

"Had I not been and spoken to thee, O Adam, concerning the tree, and had I left thee without a commandment, and thou hadst sinned — it would have been an offence on My part, for not having given thee any order; thou wouldst turn round and blame Me for it."[9]

In effect, in this passage the Lord is saying, "I gave you knowledge and you chose based on that knowledge." Certainly, this has not been the most common interpretation given to the events described in Genesis 3.

Indeed, traditional interpretations of Eve's part in the fall of man portray her as being selfish, easily tempted to do evil, and governed by the desires of the flesh. Eve, contrary to God's counsel, partakes of the fruit of the tree "in the midst of the garden," because the serpent convinces her she may become as the "gods, knowing good and evil." (Genesis 3:3–5.) Eve's desire for the fruit increases because it will satisfy her hunger, is "pleasant" to her eyes, and will also make her wise. Once she has eaten of the fruit, she gives some to her husband. This woman, then, that God gave to Adam (because it is not good for man to be alone), makes a decision, the most important decision affecting mortality, without consulting Adam. (Of all the allegations against Eve, this one seems most insightful.) Lucifer has successfully separated Eve from her husband. Typical interpretations of this event also point out that Eve satisfies her hunger, her desire for pretty things, and her yearning for status and adventure while being seduced by the serpent — the symbol of evil and sexuality (the phallus). To top it all off, she is so blind in her desires, she does not consider what effect her actions will have on her companion. No matter, though. She will simply seduce him too. He can become fallen like her. Then when she must suffer the consequences for her actions, she cries.[10]

When the Lord calls out to Adam and Eve and asks: "Where art thou?" a rather charming exchange follows. Traditional readers seldom see the humor (the humanness) in this dialogue. Adam has discovered his nakedness and explains to God that he ate of the fruit. Nevertheless, Adam does not accept the responsibility for his own choice and blames Eve: "The woman . . . thou gavest to be with me, she gave me of the tree, and I did eat." Eve also blames another: "The serpent beguiled me, and I did eat." (Genesis 3:12–13.) The Lord, however, insists that both be held accountable for the part they played in this drama. Because Adam listened to his wife, he must labor all the days of his life in a world subject to corruption. Eve's desires are to be unto her husband; she will bring forth children in much pain, and, because she was the first to sin, her husband will rule over her. The real problem with this punishment, however, is that Adam and Eve represent every man and woman. Eve is the prototype. She defines womanhood.

John A. Phillips's remarkable book *Eve* discusses the varied negative interpretations of Eve's behavior and what they have meant to the role of women in the various cultures that accept the story. "The introduction of Woman into the world," Phillips claims, is seen as having caused this earth to change "from a paradise into a problematic place where hard labor, birth, and death are facts of life." Eve is a trickster figure who introduces paradox, ambiguity, sin, and a preoccupation with sex into the life of Adam, who would prefer to keep all of God's commandments.[11] Because language, the power of naming, is seen as the key to having dominion and power over creation, Adam is asked to name the woman and thereby define her role; he calls her Eve: "the mother of all living."[12] Eve's expansive motherhood is limited and controlled. She, and, by implication, all women, must raise up seed to their husbands and to God.

The religious communities which trace their view of the world back to the Adam and Eve story have shaped their views of women from this text. Ecclesiasticus, an apocryphal book, claims that "from woman was the beginning of sin, and because of her we all die." (25:23–24.) The Essenes, pious men from the Dead Sea community, would not take a wife for fear of being corrupted. The Aramaic and Arabic words for snake are similar to the Hebrew name for Eve. One Jewish mystic de-

94

scribed Eve as the last of the animal creations and "the source of all lechery." Eve was the Devil's gateway into the world.[13] Because womankind has from the days of Eve been considered susceptible to evil, of course it was through them that witchcraft came into the world, or so the Puritans thought.

Despite the Savior's redemption of mankind from the Fall, and from the notions that men and women are punished for the sins of Adam and Eve, the New Testament epistles reflect typically negative attitudes towards women. In the second letter to the Corinthians, Paul warns the early-day Saints: "But I fear, lest by any means, as the serpent beguiled Eve through his subtilty, so your minds should be corrupted from the simplicity that is in Christ." (2 Corinthians 11:3.) Paul also appears to uphold the implications of the Genesis narrative by claiming that "the man is not of the woman; but the woman of the man. Neither was the man created for the woman; but the woman for the man." (1 Corinthians 11:8–9.) Timothy claims: "I suffer not a woman to teach, nor to usurp authority over the man, but to be in silence. For Adam was first formed, then Eve. And Adam was not deceived, but the woman being deceived was in the transgression. Notwithstanding she shall be saved in childbearing, if they continue in faith and charity and holiness with sobriety." (1 Timothy 2:12–15.) This is an offensive image of women; these scriptures even cause anger, frustration, and loss of self-esteem among righteous women.

In his book, *The Image,* Kenneth Bolding warns modern man that "behavior depends on the image."[14] If cultures and societies have become inured to the negative image of Eve and of women, what behavior can be expected from women? How can each woman continue to strive when she is seen as an appendage to man? What woman wants to be expendable, used, controlled, defined by men who seem unable to discern her spirit, men who are essentially, biologically, emotionally, and spiritually different from her?

In one of *The Forgotten Books of Eden,* Adam and Eve are outside Eden in a dark cave. There is some humor in the work. Adam assumes that earth life will be lived in blackness. He is overwhelmed by the thought and cries out to the Lord. The

Lord, however, gently explains to Adam that he is merely enduring what is called night; in twelve hours, day will come. In this same passage, however, a very telling exchange occurs between the Lord and Adam. Adam explains:

"For, so long as we were in the garden, we neither saw nor even knew what darkness is. I was not hidden from Eve, neither was she hidden from me, until now that she cannot see me; and no darkness came upon us, to separate us from each other. . . . [N]ow since we came into this cave, darkness has come upon us, and parted us asunder, so that I do not see her, and she does not see me."[15]

Is this what the Fall, in part, is really about? Is this the pain of mortality: that men and women cannot see each other? Are we failing to understand the very essence of the male and female relations the Lord intended?

Richard R. Niebuhr believes that the women's movement is basically an expression of a "deep woundedness," a "verbal and public sign of immeasurable pain." This pain, claims Niebuhr, is registering on the "seismograph of the spirit" and is representative of "dislocations in the deepest recesses of our being."[16] No revolution in the history of human affairs is equal to the one now taking place to heal the separations felt between men and women.

Bert Wilson, a noted folklorist at Brigham Young University, has collected many folk tales representative of the ways contemporary Mormon women perceive certain institutions. One typical tale concerns a woman with twelve children. One evening, her husband brings home a new wife without telling her. The first wife is instructed to fix a wedding supper and to make the bedroom ready for the evening. When these chores are completed, she is then sent to the attic to sleep with her twelve children. While in the attic, she has her children relieve themselves into a chamber pot. She then pours the contents between the planks of the ceiling of the bedroom downstairs. Following this act, she leaves home with her children, never to return again.[17] What is important here is the attitude of the husband towards his wife, the implication of the attitude of men towards women in the kingdom. There is often a disturbing and sometimes inhuman disregard for women on the part of men — a lack of vision.

I believe that, in part, women gather at conferences directed toward both faith and issues for two reasons. One reason is to share what it means to be a woman with women who understand — to bear one another's burdens. Perhaps this need to share with women comes because we are not seen or well regarded by the Adams who share our lives. I believe that, for the most part, women will always choose to love and be loved as the Lord would have us do. The second reason we come together is to re-create the image of male-female relations so that those who follow after us may re-create the world in a more healing setting. May I now share with you the image I feel we are trying to establish and how we must proceed?

One of the most profound postulates of the restored gospel is this: Men and women are punished for their own sins and not for Adam or Eve's transgression.[18] In Joseph Smith's revision of Genesis (Moses), Adam asks the Lord, "Why is it that men [and women] must repent and be baptized in water? And the Lord said unto Adam [and Eve]: Behold I have forgiven thee thy transgression in the Garden of Eden." (Moses 6:53.) What is even more important to this discussion are the implications of this forgiveness to the children of Adam and Eve:

"Hence came the saying abroad among the people, That the Son of God hath atoned for original guilt, wherein the sins of the parents cannot be answered upon heads of the children, for they are whole from the foundation of the world." (Moses 6:54.)

Latter-day Saint theology clearly rejects the notion of original sin. Yet, we tend to take the punishments given in the garden as our own. As part of a creation text, these punishments merely describe the origin of the toil that is man's and the labor of childbirth. The notion of patriarchy, the subjection of Eve to Adam because of their transgression need not be answered on the heads of all men and women.

There is, however, clearly a division of labor. When the division of labor is misunderstood, some men turn their faces away from home, believing that their work and glory come through positions in the Church or in the world. Being president of a corporation, author, artist, Church leader—toiling by the "sweat of his brow"—often becomes a man's measure of his place in creation. Some women also measure their worth by the work their companions do. Do we somehow value husbands more if they are elders quorum presidents, bishops, or better still, stake or mission presidents?

In his national best seller, *Habits of the Heart,* Robert N. Bellah analyzes how Americans view marriage today. Of particular significance to my thesis is Bellah's description of Christian marriages. Often, because partners in a Christian marriage love Christ, their marriage is held together by sacrifice, obligation, and duty.[19] What is missing in all of this, however, is love. It occurred to me, while reading this text, that the ability to truly love one's partner is a way of loving Christ. Real love does not require denial of one's essential self. Incorrect notions of sacrifice (a term meaning "to be made sacred" and not surrendering personal integrity or identity) have caused women to act inappropriately in love relationships. The fullness of love is given and received freely out of a sense of full identity.

According to Bellah, the tendency to view relationships as fulfillments of individual needs is one of the by-products of individualism. How often do we hear phrases like: "He doesn't make me happy" or, "She gives me what I need"? In this line of reasoning, loving another is a way of loving self. And somehow, the notion of romantic love is all mixed up with self-love.

M. Scott Peck, a popular psychologist, explains that the feeling of "falling in love" is "not an act of will"; there is no "conscious choice" involved. So often, falling in love isolates a couple; it excludes others. Real love, on the other hand, enlarges the capacity to love others. It is inclusive. Says Peck: "Real love is a permanently self-enlarging experience. Falling in love is not."[20]

"Falling in love" also suggests the notion that the most significant human relationships are determined by desire—sexual passion. It is here that men and women get very confused. Current research shows that when one is driven by passion, pushed by emotions beyond one's control, long-lasting relationships become difficult. Multiple sex partners deplete an individual. When the Lord commanded Adam and Eve to keep their desires focused on the other, He was indicating that profound passion occurs within the bounds that He has established. Chastity increases the power to connect with another in deeply emotional, sexual, and spiritual ways. Bridled passions, paradoxically, generate more excitement, fun, joy, giggles, because they are acts of will exchanged with another in an everlasting context.

Closely connected with romantic love and sexual passion is the issue of personal validation. Does a woman validate her existence by means of the man she marries or the children she has? What happens in this situation when the husband leaves his family or children sin? Most often, the woman loses her sense of identity and worth. And if a woman does not marry, what then? The other possibility in this area of dependency is the notion of self-sacrifice. Often, in a false sacrificial role, many women literally lose themselves. Through too much giving, through adopting the role of caretaker or rescuer, they never find a true and unique identity. This is not what was meant by "help meet." This is bondage. In such a situation it is time for an exodus towards the sacred mountain, time to stand on holy ground and become complete. Perhaps it is time to repent.

I would like to share with you a definition of sin. D. M. Dooling explains that "creation myths from everywhere show how man was produced from the wholeness of God in an incomplete form: 'Male and female created He them'. . . . Christians call this human incompleteness 'sin,' a word that comes from the same root as the word to be (Indo-European *es*, participial *sont*)."[21] The notion of imperfection literally means to be "incomplete" or "unfinished." Ira Progoff, a depth psychologist, believes the genius of the Talmudic creation text comes from the fact that God did not complete his task when creating man:

"He refrained from making man perfect, but left that as a task remaining to be done. He left it for man himself to do, specifically for man to achieve in his existence as an individual.

The human being is therefore neither perfect nor complete according to his nature, as other, more limited species are. His life is open-ended in its possibilities, and this is precisely why man is the species that holds the possibility of carrying the evolution of life to further levels."[22]

The most profound realization of this truth came when the Savior stated: "I Am." (Exodus 3:11–14.) He has a complete identity. The qualities of love, humility, endurance, and power do not float somewhere out in space waiting to be discovered; they are characteristics housed within a personality. That is why we can say that Christ is the law (3 Nephi 15:9), that Christ is love (1 John 4). Jeremiah explains that Christ's real children have His law in their inward parts. (Jeremiah 31:33.) Because Christ's attributes are constant, complete, He was able to atone for our sins. He did not feel guilt for them; He felt sorrow. A complete person can endure this life and its trials, can truly help another, because her identity is constant, sure. Identity becomes sure, however, only when a woman clearly understands the laws of the gospel, the law of sacrifice, the law of chastity, and the law of consecration, because she has studied and applied these laws to her own life. A sure identity comes by continually overcoming ignorance, by moving towards a condition of being complete through repentance.

Karl Barth, a Protestant apologist, extends the notion of completeness to marriage. He believes that creation can never be "completed" if man exists without woman. Explains Barth: "the completion of man by creation of woman, is not only one secret but *the* secret, the heart of all the secrets of God the Creator. The whole inner basis of creation, God's whole covenant with man, which will later be established, realised and fulfilled historically, is prefigured in this event, in the completing of man's emergence by the coming of woman to man."[23] The metaphor of "one flesh," the fact that this union is the primary relationship established by God in the beginning, demonstrates the first order of existence. In the eternal marriage covenant, a man and woman are commanded to "receive" the other — bone to bone and flesh to flesh.

The heart of the everlasting covenant can be found in these

notions of completeness. The message of the Sermon on the Mount, then, is clear. This clarity can, perhaps, best be seen in some translations other than the King James Version. The Savior invites humankind to "Be ye therefore true [or 'complete'] as your Father which is in Heaven is true [or 'complete'] (Anchor Bible, Matthew 4:48.) The Greek word *teleioi,* from which the King James translators derived the word *perfect,* has various synonyms. Besides bearing the notion of being complete, the word also carries the meaning of being mature. This maturity comes to the initiate who becomes "pure in heart" (Matthew 5:8) through participation in the rites of passage ordained by the Lord.

The plan of salvation, the progression towards completion through successive initiatory experiences, is the message of the restoration. Repentance becomes the action we take to overcome those things which fragment our lives and prevent our connections with self, others, nature, and God. Marriage is the union of two complete individuals. This is why the Lord so frequently uses marriage as the symbol of His love for us. He is the Bridegroom; His Saints are the bride. The wedding feast is a metaphor for God's joy in our righteous covenant with Him.

Throughout the Old Testament, the Lord uses family relationships to help us understand His function in our existence. God prefers the title Father. His work and His glory are to "bring to pass the immortality and eternal life" of His children. (Moses 1:39.) Christ consecrates all of His talents as Maker, Redeemer, Savior, Advocate—all His light and truth—for the benefit of His bride and His children (metaphorically, Christ is both husband and father). I believe that the scriptures give us insight into what is meant by provider. A provider offers those experiences necessary for his wife and children to develop, to become all they can be.

Just prior to my divorce, I was driving to work on a brittle winter day. My children were suffering; my soul could not be comforted. I cried unto the Lord. "I don't want to be tried; I don't want to be a God. All I want is a complete, righteous family." The Lord quickly responded saying: "That is all I want."

That tender message has given me a vision of my own work. All that I am and ever hope to be I willingly give to my children and extended family. While teaching the book of Isaiah in my Old Testament class last winter, I realized something else about the Christ. In Isaiah, Christ describes His love for us at His second coming with these words:

"Be glad with [Jerusalem], all ye that love her: rejoice for joy with her, all ye that mourn for her:

"That ye may suck, and be satisfied with the breast of her consolations; that ye may milk out, and be delighted with the abundance of her glory.

"For thus saith the Lord, Behold, I will extend to her like a river, and the glory of the Gentiles like a flowing stream: then shall ye suck, ye shall be borne upon her sides, and be dandled upon her knees.

"As one whom his mother comforteth, so will I comfort you." (Isaiah 66:10–13.)

Christ's love is like a mother's love. My personal experiences with the Savior also let me know that He not only loves me as a unique woman, but He is interested in my particular life. I have also had blessings from my father, my oldest brother, my counselor and my bishop which provided detail about what Christ wants me to know about my life—blessings I am only starting to comprehend. I am loved and known. I also am coming to see that as I keep the laws intended for all mankind, my life, paradoxically, develops in unique ways. I discover my place in the Body of Christ. He has need of my witness, my talents. I can be a vehicle in the transformation of others. I can see this especially in my role as a professor.

Jeremiah also saw something about our day. He explains that at the time when the law of God will be in our inward parts, at the time of the new covenant, the Lord will create "a new thing in the earth, A woman shall compass a man." (Jeremiah 31:22.) One Hebrew scholar explained to me that what is meant here is the notion of circumambulation. It is the ritual circle, the moving around towards completion. Works by Joseph Campbell and others validate this notion. We are moving towards a time of renewal, a time when a new vision of our connections with other peoples, with God, with family, with our own capacities is being born.[24] Traditional readings of sacred texts have caused and are still causing wars: Protestant against Catholic, Muslim against Jew, Hindu against Muslim — even man against woman. A new heaven and a new earth are needed, are coming. And in this reality, women will play a major role, a healing role: not as despots, corporate bosses, honorary men, but as women who understand that those who stand at the foot of the cross and watch their daughters, husbands, and sons struggle to claim "I Am" can do so because we know who they are, who we are, and because we know that God is.

There are metaphors all around us for how this is done. Eve can tell us. Joseph F. Smith saw her on the third of October, 1918. Eve was someone before this life. Like Adam, who was Michael (one of the creators of this earth), Eve had a great premortal identity. She also exists now, carrying redemption to the dead. President Smith related this: "Among the great and mighty ones who were assembled in this vast congregation of the righteous were Father Adam, the Ancient of Days, and father of all, and our glorious Mother Eve, with many of her faithful daughters who had lived through the ages and worshiped the true and living God." (D&C 138:38–39.) She is with God, there with Adam and her children. Each time any of us present a woman who is dead at the veil during an endowment ceremony, we do so in the name of Eve. She takes us all, as the mother of all living, into the presence of Father, if we are also true and faithful.

The story of the Garden of Eden, as far as the man and woman are concerned, is a metaphor of great significance. There we are instructed how to become one flesh. Hugh Nibley explains the tale as a metaphor for a condition of checks and balances that must exist in male-female covenant relationships. Adam is to obey Christ as Eve is to obey Adam, through covenant. The discrimination being made here is not as evident as interpreters have indicated. Adam seems to be given a superior, legislative position in relationship to Eve with the words "rule over." The phrase, however, is modified by a qualifier:

"in righteousness." Dr. Nibley explains that Adam and Eve are to "supervise each other. Adam is given no arbitrary power; Eve is to heed him only insofar as he obeys their Father—and who decides that? She must keep check on him as much as he does on her."[25] The law of opposition, so necessary to creation and completion, finds powerful definition in this episode. Knowledge, wisdom, Godhood become possible only through relationship, through the resolution of contraries.

In conclusion, I can say that in my experience with creation stories, one character must adhere to the given pattern—all of the commandments—while the other character challenges the pattern. This is part of the law of opposition. And Adam and Eve are symbols for this essential order in the universe. Throughout Genesis, this reality is made manifest. Abraham, in his desire to keep the law of the firstborn, chooses Ishmael to inherit the covenant blessings; Sarah challenges that rule because she understands the spirit of the law and Isaac's ability to fulfill the covenant. The same holds true in the case of Esau and Jacob. The Pharisees are perfect examples of men's using God's laws without understanding their intent. Man is not saved by law, especially when it is used to burden, abuse, and suppress.

When God commanded that Adam and Eve not partake of the fruit of the Tree of Knowledge of Good and Evil, He allowed first man and first woman to become accountable for their choices, He established agency and the opportunity for us to create our own natures in God's complete image. In love, we can journey to the Tree of Life, hand in hand, with divine connections, in relationship.

Certainly, living as "one flesh" requires another kind of labor, an enduring, striving, working throughout life so that this kind of love can be born. The scriptures are rather sparse in examples of couples who have loved well within the covenant. Aside from Genesis and 1 Nephi, the scriptures are silent. Surely Alma had a wife, even daughters. And what of Moroni, Mormon, Jacob and the rest? Where are the examples to follow? Spencer W. Kimball, in his lovely poem, "When I Look Back," written to his wife, Camilla, describes an exemplary marriage. Through great trials, they "mingled" their years together to form "one pattern," a "finished tapestry" whose threads were spun with sorrow, disappointment, failure as well as joy.

> When I look back across our mingled years,
> I know it is not just the joys we shared
> That made our lives one pattern, but the tears
> We shed together, and the rough, wild seas we fared.
> Through all the disappointments we have faced,
> Through this world's faults and failures, we have come
> To heights of understanding that are based
> More on the sorrows than the joys of home.
> Young love is beautiful to contemplate
> But old love is the finished tapestry
> Stretched out from oaken floors to heaven's gate.
> We wove on earth for all eternity
> With threads made stronger by the steady beat
> Of hearts that suffered but knew no defeat.[26]

I hope, as our lives grow to old age, that we may "mingle" years with another—that we too can say that we "knew no defeat" as we worked out our salvation with husbands, children, and our fellow beings.

Notes

1. W. F. Albright and C. S. Mann, "Jesus and the Law," in *The Anchor Bible* (Garden City, N.Y.: Doubleday, 1971), vol. 26, *Matthew*, cvii–cx.
2. Carl G. Vaught, *The Quest for Wholeness* (Albany: State University of New York Press, 1982), p. 4.
3. Phyllis Trible, "Eve and Adam: Genesis 2–3 Reread," in *Womanspirit Rising: A Feminist Reader in Religion*, ed. Carol P. Christ and Judith Plaskow (San Francisco: Harper and Row, 1979), pp. 74–83.
4. Samuel Noah Kramer, "Mythology of Sumer and Akkad," in *Mythologies of the Ancient World*, ed. Samuel Noah Kramer (Garden City, N.J.: Anchor Books, 1961), pp. 102–3.
5. Trible, p. 80.
6. Ibid., pp. 76–80.
7. Mircea Eliade, ed., *Encyclopedia of Religion* (New York: Macmillan, 1987), s.v. "Repentance," by David E. Aune.

8. James H. Charlesworth, ed., *The Old Testament Pseudepigrapha* (Garden City, N.Y.: Doubleday and Co., 1985), vol. 1, *The Life of Adam and Eve*, p. 258.

9. The First Book of Adam and Eve 13:18, in *The Forgotten Books of Eden* (Cleveland: The World Publishing Co., 1927), bound with *The Lost Books of the Bible*.

10. See John A. Phillips, *Eve* (San Francisco: Harper & Row, 1984), for a history of this interpretation.

11. Ibid., pp. 19 and 16–37, respectively.

12. See Mircea Eliade, *Myth and Reality* (New York: Harper and Row, 1963), pp. 5–19; and Phillips, p. 32.

13. Phillips, p. 51; p. 181, note 20; pp. 55–77, respectively.

14. Kenneth Boulding, *The Image* (Ann Arbor: University of Michigan Press, 1973), p. 6.

15. The First Book of Adam and Eve 12:9–10.

16. Richard R. Niebuhr, "The Strife of Interpretation: The Moral Burden of Imagination," *Parabola* 10 (Summer 1985): 36–37.

17. William A. Wilson, "Folklore and History: Fact Amid the Legends," *Utah Historical Quarterly* 4 (1973): 55.

18. Joseph Smith, "Articles of Faith," *Pearl of Great Price* (Salt Lake City: The Church of Jesus Christ of Latter-day Saints, 1981), p. 60.

19. Robert N. Bellah et. al., *Habits of the Heart* (New York: Harper & Row, 1986), pp. 108–9.

20. M. Scott Peck, *The Road Less Traveled* (New York: Simon and Schuster, 1978), p. 89.

21. D. M. Dooling, "The Way Back," *Parabola* 10 (Summer 1985): 49.

22. Ira Progoff, "Form, Time and Opus: The Dialectic of the Creative Psyche," in *Form als Aufgabe des Geistes,* ed. Adolf Portmann, *Eranos Jahr Buch 1965* (Zurich: Rhein Verlag, 1966), p. 265.

23. Karl Barth, *Church Dogmatics,* vol. 3, part 1 (Edinburgh: T. and T. Clark, 1955), p. 295.

24. Joseph Campbell, *The Inner Reaches of Outer Space* (Toronto: St. James Press, Ltd., 1986), pp. 11–51.

25. Hugh W. Nibley, "Patriarchy and Matriarchy," in *Blueprints for Living,* ed. Maren M. Mouritsen (Provo: Brigham Young University Press, 1980), p. 48.

26. Spencer W. Kimball, "When I Look Back," *Brigham Young University Studies* 25 (Fall 1985): 162; used by permission.

Becoming Bone of Bone and Flesh of Flesh

EUGENE ENGLAND

A good friend said to Charlotte and me, during our courtship, "Happiness in marriage consists not so much in finding the right person as in *being* the right person." I was certainly trying to become that right person. I was feeling some of the happiness and pain that comes from any real growth, but many of my mistakes—and much of the pain I caused Charlotte, then and later—were because of some dangerous notions I had about men and women. I want to discuss some of those dangerous notions and what can be done about them to improve our marriages, present and future.

In the Book of Mormon, Nephi claims that the Lord "doeth nothing save it be plain unto the children of men" and that "he inviteth them all to come unto him and partake of his goodness" and "denieth none that come unto him." (2 Nephi 26:33.) Nephi gives us some specific examples of the "all" who are thus invited—and who are, he says, "alike unto God": They include "black and white" and "male and female." What evidence do we have that male and female are indeed equal in this fundamental sense? How do we know they are alike to God and invited equally to come to Him and to be blessed equally when they do? In our time, there seems to me no more important matter for men and women to understand and agree

Eugene England is professor of English literature at Brigham Young University where he has taught courses in Shakespeare and American and LDS literature. He received a Ph.D. from Stanford University. He has written three books, Brother Brigham, Dialogues with Myself, *and* Why the Church Is as True as the Gospel, *and is preparing two others:* Shakespeare's Avengers and Healers *and a collection of personal essays,* The Quality of Mercy. *He has served as bishop, branch president, and high councilman, and is currently a counselor in a Provo bishopric. He is married to Charlotte Hawkins England, and they are the parents of six children.*

about if we are to have effective courtships and build eternal marriages.

We have an immediate problem. In this passage Nephi assures us God is "plain" in all He does for us — which would have to mean that the record we have of God's doings must be plain, at least when the "plain and precious things" Nephi earlier tells us were lost from the Bible are restored through modern revelation. But we have clearly not always *seen* this plainness, even in modern scripture like the Book of Mormon. For instance, shortly after the revelation giving blacks the priesthood was announced, Elder Bruce R. McConkie asked a group of Church educators to disregard what he had previously said on the subject. He stated that because of the recent revelation there was now available new understanding of that scripture from Nephi about all being alike to God: "Many of us never imagined or supposed," he said, "that these passages had the extensive and broad meaning that they do have."[1] He implied that we must use greater vigilance against such misunderstanding in the future. That warning, it seems to me, might suggest that if we didn't understand for such a long time what it means that "black and white" are alike, perhaps we *still* don't understand what it means that "male and female" are alike to God.

What could possibly cause such misunderstanding? Many times the Lord warned Joseph Smith that the plain gospel of light and truth had been lost to God's children because of "the tradition of their fathers." (D&C 74:4; 93:39.) Joseph understood specifically that "our wives and children" have been made "to bow down with grief, sorrow, and care" because of "that spirit which hath so strongly riveted the creeds of the fathers, who have inherited lies, upon the hearts of the children, and filled the world with confusion." (D&C 123:7.) All around us we can see examples of how the traditions of human culture, passed down through the fathers' false patriarchal creeds, have destroyed the plainness of God's equal dealing with male and female and have caused women and children sorrow and care and all of us confusion.[2]

The process that produced this continuing tragedy is now becoming plain: in the apostate creeds of Christianity, which

God told Joseph were an abomination but which have been the main tradition of Western civilization, Eve was blamed for the fall and thus women for all evil on the earth. In fact they were blamed for *subverting* God's plan for his children on the earth. They were assigned a place inferior in every way, defined and treated as property, and it was seriously debated by theologians whether they had souls. Even when women were exalted, as in the cult of the Virgin Mary or in the chivalric code of "courtly love," the female image was being made to serve "male" purposes: the image of a few women raised on a pedestal was used to debase most other women and to undermine such "female" purposes as a healthy, equally shared sexuality and equal fidelity *within* marriage — as well as to excuse male neglect of the values of peace and mercy. One of the main purposes served was what Robert Heilbrun has called the "man-honor-fight" dogma.[3] It is a dogma that Shakespeare opposes in much of his greatest work, both in his early festive comedies like *The Taming of the Shrew* and *As You Like It*, which are centered on strong, witty, merciful women who lead men eventually to salvation in a marriage of equals, but also in his powerful anti-revenge tragedies like *Troilus and Cressida* and *Hamlet*, where women and "feminine" values of mercy and forgiveness are destroyed by male allegiance to war and vengeance.

That "man-honor-fight" dogma, along with the apostate Judeo-Christian notions about women's inferiority, survived even into the Victorian period, where men fostered the perverse image of woman as either a madonna to be worshipped and thus "protected" from the demands of real living and relationship — or a prostitute to be exploited (often by men who were bored by a madonna-like wife they had created themselves). I believe it was at least partially in response to this perversity in American culture that the Lord endorsed the practice of polygamy for a time in His Restored Church. He thus attempted to provide for nearly all women the challenge of child-bearing and home-building in a sanctified but down-to-earth relationship.

There seems to have been little chance for madonna-like

posturing or for degradation in successful polygamous homes. Mormon women formed remarkable bonds of sisterhood and developed unusual skills and confidence while running farms and businesses with their husband absent on missions or at his other homes. They developed a great tradition of equal and often superior accomplishment in ranching, economics, politics, writing and publishing, Church leadership, and (perhaps most important but least remembered) in receiving spiritual gifts, such as healing others and speaking in tongues and prophesying.[4] At the same time they passed the Abrahamic test of polygamy and successfully used that great and painful trial to teach the spirit of covenant sacrifice to their children in ways that produced much of the strength of the Church to this day.

I honor those, including some of my own ancestors, who were willing to pay the cost of polygamy, in response to commandments that I believe came from God. They were thus worthy of blessings that outweighed the costs for a time, as well as countering some of the difficulties caused in nineteenth-century America by the false traditions of the fathers about the value and needs of women. But the nineteenth century is past, and I do not believe the costs or blessings of polygamy are a good basis for imagining what eternal marriage will be like.[5] They are certainly a *bad* basis for imagining what marriage *now* should be, when we are clearly commanded and encouraged to practice perfect, one-to-one fidelity.

What *is* a good basis for imagining eternal marriage, then? The plain scriptures, I believe. In the first place, modern scriptures and revelations suggest quite plainly that we would more accurately and profitably read the scriptural references to "God" as meaning God the eternal *partnership* of Heavenly Father *and* Heavenly Mother. They have a more perfect unity even than that of God and Christ and the Holy Ghost, and so the word *God* implies *both* of them, at least as much as it denotes the three beings in the classical Christian trinity called "God."

Such a more correct identification of "God" might help us better comprehend the direct role our Heavenly Mother played in our creation and salvation. When we read in Genesis that God said, "Let us create man in our image," it makes most sense to read it as God the Father and God the Mother speaking as One. When we read in John that God sent His only begotten Son to save us, it would be better to understand, as it certainly makes more sense, that our Heavenly Parents sent *Their* only begotten Son. This process is truer to the evidence—and to our real needs as men and women—than looking for a *female* God between the lines in the scriptures or in apocryphal works or mythologies, as many feminist theologians are doing. It might help us better imagine our futures as husbands and wives, equally yoked in what Shakespeare called "the marriage of true minds"—and to work toward that future now.

Second, modern revelation tells us that when God put "man" on the earth, "in the image of mine Only Begotten created I him; male and female created I them." (Moses 2:27.) Clearly men and women were *both* created in the "image" of Christ. That would seem to mean we are created in the image of the Heavenly Parents who *together* make up the "God" whom Christ came to reveal, that is, the perfect eternal partnership He came to teach us how to achieve and to show us in His life and character what we would be like when we achieved it.

One of the false traditions about women that survives into the twentieth century is expressed in statements, meant to be compliments, such as "She thinks like a man" and "She fought like a man," or those, meant *not* to be compliments, like "He wept just like a woman" and "He gave in like a woman." We still imagine and approvingly describe men as rational, objective, even tough-minded and revengeful. Women, on the other hand, are supposedly all intuitive, gentle, even immaturely emotional and merciful. Isn't it strange that these qualities we belittle in women are the very ones that best identify Christ? We should remind ourselves constantly that the Pearl of Great Price tells us God made *both* male and female in the image of Jesus. Mormons believe that when Christ came to earth He said plainly, "What manner of men [clearly meaning 'humans,' male *and* female] ought ye to be? Verily I say unto you, even as I am." (3 Nephi 27:27.) We believe He both showed us what He is like, in His infinite patience and mercy, and also *taught* us: "Take my yoke upon you, and learn of me; for I am meek and lowly in heart" (Matthew 11:29) — or literally, in the Greek, "gentle and humble." Male and female, we all are made in the same image and have the same ideal. It is a terrible stumbling block to us all that, in the false traditions of the fathers, that image and ideal of Christ is the one that has been assigned to women and thus thought of as inferior and avoided by many men.

Clearly, we are combinations of qualities, some merely individual, some associated with our great gift of being male or female. Our culture, not the gospel, names certain of these qualities feminine and certain masculine. But our task is to transcend culture, to value all the Christ-like qualities — both in ourselves and in our eternal companions — and to learn how to discover our full selves, *all* of our individual qualities, through mature relationships, especially in marriage.

Modern scriptures help us understand how men and women are alike unto God in a third way by making it clear not only that the references in Genesis and elsewhere to God actually mean our Heavenly Parents but also that those passages referring to Adam often actually mean Adam and Eve together in *their* eternal partnership. This corrects what is perhaps the most damaging false tradition of the fathers, one which underlies most degradation of women in Western civilization and is amazingly still subscribed to by many Mormons: I mean, of course, the idea that Eve was the only one deceived by Satan and partook of the forbidden fruit first, that she was thus responsible for Adam's fall and most of our troubles, and that she was rightly punished accordingly with child-bearing and subservience to her husband. Such a notion is terribly, destructively false doctrine. In the first place, if Eve really did act first, since Mormons supposedly believe that action was *intended* by God and the *right* one to make the plan of salvation work, we should *honor* her as being brighter and more courageous than Adam — who in the scriptural account seems, like modern husbands, mainly able to blame his wife for what is happening that he doesn't understand.

112

Honoring Eve *over* Adam is simply reverse sexism, how-ever, and, in fact, modern scriptures say plainly that *Adam* was responsible for the fall. God teaches Joseph Smith that "the devil tempted *Adam,* and *he* partook of the forbidden fruit and transgressed the commandment. . . . Wherefore, I . . . caused that he should be cast out from the Garden." (D&C 29:40–41; italics added.) Clearly, the Lord is not reversing the Genesis story and blaming Adam alone. He is using "Adam" to mean *Adam and Eve* in perfect partnership. Just as we might have assumed, our first parents, our model for eternal marriage, made that most crucial decision *together* — and both had the same understanding and courage and love for us.

I realize that many Mormon men who blame Eve and, thus, to some extent denigrate all women — and Mormon women who degrade or trouble themselves over Eve's "mistake" — take their notions from the temple endowment ceremony as well as from Genesis and the writing of Paul (for example, 1 Timothy 2:14–15). But if they do so, they act in error: they fail to heed the clear warning given at the beginning of the en-dowment that what they see and hear concerning Adam and Eve is "only figurative." The endowment drama teaches a great truth about God's involvement in the creation of man and woman and in the process by which they entered into a world of moral choice and growth together, but it does not presume to depict with cinematic accuracy the literal events through which that happened. If we assume such literal accuracy, de-spite the warning, we reinforce destructive stereotypes about both men and women.

Now what does this all have to do with becoming "bone of bone and flesh of flesh"? Those are the words used by Adam to create a symbol for both the reality and the ideal of that first earthly eternal marriage created with Eve in the Garden. They imply a unity that is unique in the universe, not possible even for the gods, except with *their* eternal partners in mar-riage, because it directly suggests not only spiritual and intel-lectual and emotional unity but also physical unity. Only eternal marriage partners can enjoy a "continuation of the seeds for-ever." (D&C 132:19.) Only they can participate in sexual relationship in the largest and most profound sense: the unity of equal opposites, male and female, expressed fundamentally in the literal sexual act but in many other ways as well. Sex in that largest sense makes mortal life possible. But according to Lehi's law, sex also, as one of the complementary oppositions which undergird all reality, makes possible all life in the universe, all meaning, godhood, even existence of any kind. (2 Nephi 2:11–15.)

The Mormon view of sex, therefore, is not merely positive; it is, in every sense, grand. Like the priesthood, however, sexual relationships can operate only on the principles of righteousness, that is, "without compulsory means" but rather "by long-suffering, by gentleness and meekness, and by love unfeigned." (D&C 121:36–46.) Mormons believe God is neither a lonely male nor a lonely female—but an eternal partnership of equal opposites, one male and one female who have become "bone of bone and flesh of flesh" in the perfect creative unity that we begin to build in our painful, struggling, exasperating real marriages in this life.

Becoming bone of bone and flesh of flesh is itself, of course, a very sexual image. The Lord makes this even more explicit when He continues, after Adam's recognition that he is now "flesh of flesh" with Eve, "Therefore shall a man leave his father and his mother, and shall cleave unto his wife; and they shall be one flesh." (Moses 3:24.) We who are married know that sexual intimacy can be the fundamental expression of our deepest unity and purposes as eternal partners capable of eternal increase. We are able through intercourse to literally create something new in the universe that is partly each of us but potentially greater than our sum. We thus symbolically image forth the eternal increase of godhood, creation not only of spiritual children but also of universes. Such intimacy can also be a delightful, uniquely intimate counterpoint to the repetitive, public cares of career and homebuilding—a relief even from the cares of the parenthood it makes possible. After literal childbearing (or in cases where the couple cannot have children), it can continue to be a reminder and pledge of the partnership that produced those children and of the unity that continues to nurture them (or will do so for spirit children). It can be none of these things, however, if it is entered into without fidelity, without perfect trust that the partner is unwilling to violate that deepest unity and perfect vulnerability, or if it is entered into with shame or lust, or only as an act of self-sacrifice or self-gratification.

Paul said some things about sex that are not plain, that in fact seem to me quite strange. Fortunately, he said most of them, as he admitted, on his own. But he did say one thing that captures well the perfect equality and modest but affirmative attitude about sex that the gospel implies generally (and here I use the Phillips translation for better plainness): "The husband should give his wife what is due to her as his wife, and the wife should be as fair to her husband. The wife has no longer full rights over her own person, but shares them with her husband. In the same way the husband shares his personal rights with his wife. Do not cheat each other of normal sexual intercourse, unless of course you both decide to abstain temporarily." (1 Corinthians 7:3–5.) Because of both the repressions and obsessions about sex in our culture, as well as our individual trials and tragedies as we form our sexual identities in such a culture, that ideal of Paul is not easy to attain. And the very effort to make certain both husband and wife are equally "willing" can itself become obsessive rather than liberating; however, such an ideal is far superior to destructive actions of male dominance and aggression and female passivity and resentment rampant in our traditional culture – or their reversal in much feminist and playboy fantasizing.

The ideal sexual relationship can best be achieved by applying another ideal articulated by Paul. He borrowed Adam's image of becoming "bone of bone and flesh of flesh" as a metaphor for the perfect unity possible both within the Church and between the Church and Christ. He also wrote, "So ought men to love their wives as their own bodies. He that loveth his wife loveth himself. For no man ever yet hated his own flesh; but nourisheth and cherisheth it, even as the Lord the church: For we are members of his body, of his flesh, and of his bones." (Ephesians 5:28–30.) Using marriage as a symbol he taught, in 1 Corinthians 12 and 13, how the members of that body of Christ, the Church, should relate to each other — and by reverse implication, of course, how the members of the eternal one flesh of marriage should relate to each other in order to become bone of bone and flesh of flesh with Christ. Let me make some additions to make this parallel plain:

"Now there are diversities of gifts [between husband and wife], but the same Spirit.

"And there are differences of administrati[ve responsibilities], but the same Lord.

"And there are diversities of operations [in the family], but it is the same God which worketh all in all.

"But the manifestation of the Spirit is given to every [person] to profit withal. . . .

"But now are they [two] members [in marriage], yet but one body.

"And the eye cannot say unto the hand, I have no need of thee: nor again the head to the feet, I have no need of you.

"Nay, much more [either] member of the body, which seem[s] to be more feeble, [is] necessary:

"And [whatever partner] of the [marriage] which we think to be less honourable, upon [that partner] we [should] bestow more abundant honour; and our uncomely parts [then] have more abundant comeliness.

"For our comely parts have no need: but God hath tempered the body together, having given more abundant honour to that part which lacked:

"That there should be no schism in the body; but that [both] members should have the same care one for another.

"And whether one member suffer, [both] the members suffer with it; or one member be honoured, [both] the members rejoice with it. . . .

"Have [both] the gifts of healing? do [both] speak with tongues? do [both] interpret?

"But [both of you should] covet earnestly the best gifts: and yet shew I unto you [both] a more excellent way. . . .

"Though [either of you] have the gift of prophecy, and understand all mysteries, and all knowledge; and though [you] have all faith, so that [you] could remove mountains, and have not charity, [you are] nothing. . . .

"Charity suffereth long, and is kind; charity envieth not; charity . . . is not puffed up,

" . . . is not easily provoked . . . ;

"Beareth all things, . . . endureth all things."

Martin Luther once said that marriage is "the school of love," and of course he was talking about charity, the pure love of Christ. Marriage is not the result or even the home of love so much as it is the *school* of love—and it is a school of hard knocks. I am still in school, and it is not easy. I am constantly challenged, threatened, embarrassed, even wounded at the very core by my struggles and my failures to respond to the challenges Charlotte's love and our covenanted partnership pose to me—not because she wants to wound me but because of what she is, an honest, complex Other, meek and lowly in heart, to whom I am eternally bound and whom I want to be like. I am painfully becoming, in increasing unity with her, what I want and need to become, though it is what, without her, I might not have chosen to become.

Becoming bone of bone and flesh of flesh, together, does not mean that I am trying to be more "womanly" and Charlotte more "manly"—nor that I am neglecting my own gifts and responsibilities, some of which are given, though only temporarily I think, because I am a man. I believe that the Melchizedek Priesthood and bearing the bodies of mortal children are simply assignments made for mortality. This does not mean the two are equivalent: certainly priesthood should not replace the nurturing duties of fatherhood nor does bearing children replace the spiritual gifts, including healing, nor the administrative gifts and duties given to women. But I believe priesthood and child-bearing are alike in providing, if we let them, similar opportunities to learn charity, to love and serve unconditionally. If we learn those lessons, we will pass beyond Melchizedek Priesthood and physical motherhood to a higher state of more perfect equality. That higher state, promised in the eternal marriage covenant, is called *becoming kings and queens, priests and priestesses unto the most high God.* Fatherhood and motherhood *are* equivalent right now in their in- trinsic responsibilities. (President Lee said to *both* men and women that the most important work we will ever do is within the walls of our own home — and President McKay said to us *both* that no success could compensate for failure there.) The roles of man and woman are absolutely equivalent in their intrinsic joys and opportunities to learn the greatest joy — and the ground of our salvation — which is that pure love of Christ.

The lesson to be taken from all this is not that women need more devotion to their careers in order to be equal with men, but that men need *less* devotion to their careers. For the first ten years of our marriage I simply assumed that where we lived, what graduate school I accepted, what job and how much time and attention must be paid to keep and advance in that job, were simply *my* decisions, to be made from the perspective of myself as breadwinner. That was simply wrong — and destructive. A kind of charity that could have seen how wrong that was is what I think both men and women, equally, must learn in order to make eternal marriage work — and to found a good courtship upon. The core curriculum of the school of marriage is unconditional love, mercy, long-suffering, forgiveness.

I know of a successful marriage that began in the forgive- ness of a man for a woman's abortions in her teenage years that left her unable to have children. I know of another marriage that was able to continue because of a woman's forgiveness of a man's long-continued promiscuity after marriage. Elder Mar- ion D. Hanks, at a BYU devotional, told us of a marriage that had recently ended with the death of the husband, who had left his wife and children to "be himself," had contracted AIDS, and finally came home to die, in the words of Mother Teresa, "in sight of a loving face." He found that blessing in his family, particularly a wife who "read Walt Whitman to him and played Beethoven to him" for those last days.[6] I know of many mar- riages that endure, despite male chauvinism or female passive aggression, despite a man's or a woman's habits, conditioned by our sexist American culture or spiritually handicapped par- ents or personal tragic experience. I know many that fail because one or both partners, with smaller problems than those I have mentioned, cannot forgive, or think they can trifle with the covenant bonds of fidelity without wounding others — and themselves — deeply. They leave the school of love, the god-producing arena where we only can know the pain and joy of becoming bone of bone and flesh of flesh.

Bruce Jorgensen, of the BYU faculty, has written a fine short story called "A Song for One Still Voice," which tells of an ordinary man with an extraordinarily firm and reflective sense of husbandry over his crops and his family. He wakes in the night to take his irrigation turn; then he changes a daughter's diaper and kisses his wife on the temple but resists his passion, his desire to awaken her, because he feels her need for sleep — and reflects: "There is no loneliness like the body, nor any delight."[7] The pain and joy of being bone and flesh go together, but the joy is certainly worth the pain.

Modern revelation (as well as our own intuition) teaches us that we have existed eternally as unique individuals — and always will. A modern Mormon thinker, B. F. Cummings, has put the case this way: "The self is insubordinate, wandering, imperially aloof, solitary, lonely, withdrawn, unvisited, impenetrable. . . . This aloneness is a fact for men and Gods to live with, for it is inherent in existence."[8] Such cosmic loneliness is a source of pain that can only be assuaged by finding our deepest selves, our fullest being, in relationships — ultimately · in eternal partnership and continuation of the seeds, becoming bone of bone. That yearning for relationship is painful, too; it often seems a threat to that eternal uniqueness that is our original joy as individuals.

Becoming one flesh, especially in the central act of that becoming, which is making love, contains within its joy the full implications and responsibilities of having children. For a woman it means literally risking her life in bearing them. For both women and men, it means caring for our children, even when because of genetic defects or social problems the care of them devastates us emotionally and financially, and it means nurturing them, even when they turn on us in misunderstanding and hatred. Would we have children if we could see them first as teenagers? Yet we *do* have them, partly because there is no greater joy than coming to know those we have nurtured when they become mature individuals in their own right—our children as dearly loved friends. When we make love we are already expressing incredible courage—the courage to enter the valley of the shadow of death and of failure and of rejection. I believe our Heavenly Parents have the same kind of courage when, in whatever is Their equivalent of making love, They begin a universe. That courage makes possible existence, and the greatest joy, that of being bone of bone and flesh of flesh.

Notes

1. Bruce R. McConkie, "All Are Alike unto God," in *Charge to Religious Educators,* 2d ed. (Salt Lake City: The Church of Jesus Christ of Latter-day Saints, 1982), p. 152.
2. For a thorough review of this destructive process in Judeo-Christian history—and a sobering analysis of its continuation, to some degree, in Mormon history, despite our corrective modern revelations—see Jolene Edmunds Rockwood, "The Redemption of Eve," one of many fine essays on Mormon women in *Sisters in Spirit: Mormon Women in Historical and Cultural Perspective,* ed. Maureen Ursenbach Beecher and Lavina Fielding Anderson (Urbana and Chicago: University of Illinois Press, 1987), pp. 3–36. See also Suzanne E. Lundquist, "The Repentance of Eve," pp. 88–106 in this volume.
3. Quoted in Linda Bamber, *Comic Women, Tragic Men* (Stanford, Cal.: Stanford University Press, 1982), p. 17.
4. See the many examples related in Eliza R. Snow's "Trail Diary," in *Eliza R. Snow, an Immortal: Selected Writings* (Salt Lake City: Nicholas G. Morgan Foundation, 1957), pp. 316ff. See also Carol Lynn Pearson, comp., *Daughters of Light* (Provo: Trilogy Arts, 1973), and Linda King Newell, "Gifts of the Spirit: Women's Share," in *Sisters in Spirit,* pp. 111-50. Newell documents the amazing outpouring of spiritual gifts on Mormon women in the nineteenth century and the gradual restriction on practice of those gifts in the twentieth.
5. For evidence and argument that polygamy, though a divinely inspired earthly practice, will not be part of the celestial order, see my essay, "On Fidelity, Polygamy, and Celestial Marriage," *Dialogue: A Journal of Mormon Thought* 20, 4 (Winter 1987): 138-54.
6. Marion D. Hanks, "Follow the King," in *Brigham Young University 1985-*

86 Devotional and Fireside Speeches, ed. Karen Seely (Provo, Utah: University Publications, 1986), pp. 106-107.

7. Bruce W. Jorgensen, "Three in the Morning—A Song for One Still Voice," *Ensign* (Mar. 1979), pp. 57-58; revised as "A Song For One Still Voice," published in *Greening Wheat: Fifteen Mormon Short Stories,* ed. Levi S. Peterson (Midvale, Utah: Orion, 1983), pp. 1-5.

8. B. F. Cummings, *The Eternal Individual Self* (Salt Lake City: Utah Printing Co., 1968), pp. 7, 69.

Resolving Differences/Achieving Unity: Lessons from the History of Relief Society

JANATH R. CANNON AND JILL MULVAY DERR

*I*n the early spring of 1842 a small group of Nauvoo women organized themselves. Stirred by the hope that their collective efforts would further work on the Nauvoo Temple, they formed a ladies' society, a "mini-democracy," complete with constitution and officers. Almost certainly they were following the example of their contemporary American sisters who had been organizing such societies, usually for benevolent purposes, since 1800.[1] Invited to examine their proposed constitution, the Prophet Joseph Smith told the sisters he felt the Lord desired something different for them. So he organized them "under the priesthood after a pattern of the priesthood," indicating that the Church was "never perfectly organized until

Jill Mulvay Derr received a masters of arts in teaching degree from the Harvard Graduate School of Education, joining the LDS Church Historical Division soon thereafter. She is presently a research fellow with the Joseph Fielding Smith Institute for Church History at Brigham Young University. A co-author of Women's Voices: An Untold History of the Latter-day Saints, 1830–1900, *she has published numerous articles on early Mormon women and is co-authoring a book on the history of the Relief Society with Janath R. Cannon. She resides in Alpine, Utah, where she has taught the Gospel Doctrine class and edited the Alpine Country Paper for several years.*

Janath R. Cannon, currently serving with her husband as directors of the Visitors' Center in Nauvoo, Illinois, also served with him in the Ghana-Nigeria and Switzerland missions, where he presided, and filled a mission to France and Canada. Prior to her first mission, she was graduated Phi Beta Kappa from Wellesley College. A former member of the Tabernacle Choir, she was also a member of the Relief Society General Board and first counselor in the general presidency of the Relief Society for four years. She is co-authoring a history of the Relief Society with Jill Mulvay Derr.

the women were thus organized."[2] For women of The Church of Jesus Christ of Latter-day Saints the fact that the Relief Society was organized under "a holy form of government" and after a pure and protective priesthood pattern distinguished their organization from similar ladies' societies and determined the sacred principles by which it would operate.[3]

Unity was a key principle for Latter-day Saints who received as commandment the Lord's admonition that "if ye are not one ye are not mine." (D&C 38:27.) Joseph Smith reiterated this ideal for Relief Society women, telling them: "All must act in concert or nothing can be done."[4] Acting in concert required sisters to work in harmony not only with each other but with the brethren who advised them. In Nauvoo, in the Mountain West, wherever branches of the Relief Society were organized, sisters came to understand that unity was critical to their achievements — charitable, social, economic, political, educational, and spiritual. In 1869, Salt Lake City's Fifteenth Ward Relief Society president Sarah M. Kimball was asked how that society had been able to accomplish so much, and she replied, "It was because we had acted in unison." Eight years later, the society still going strong under her direction, she observed there "had not been the least jar" between Bishop Robert Burton and herself.[5]

By contrast, in some wards and branches diverse opinions and interests prevented sisters from meeting the challenge to act in concert, and progress was halted. In May 1917 a member of the Relief Society general board reported "that on her recent visit to Rigby [Idaho] stake, she found one ward delinquent in all its work because of difference between the bishop of the ward and the Relief Society president — the difference occurring over the manner of procedure in a charity case."[6]

How do women work "under the priesthood after a pattern of the priesthood," achieving unity so that their collective endeavors can bless themselves and others? The history of Relief Society offers interesting answers to that question: real-life examples of diversity, difference, resolution, and reconciliation. We have chosen to confine this discussion to twentieth-century examples because many readers are already familiar with events and personalities of the nineteenth century, but—more importantly—because twentieth-century examples include related issues with which Latter-day Saint women are still grappling. One is the gradual merging of the once separate spheres of men and women which has required that women's former organizational autonomy make way for more complex interdependence with men. Another is the growth of the Church, which has provoked increased centralization, standardization, and correlation.

A significant twentieth-century change in Relief Society work was the introduction of prepared lesson outlines for Society meetings. Relief Society was the last Church organization to follow the trend toward centralization and adopt a standardized curriculum. Originally sisters gathered to sew for the needy and share their testimonies. In the 1870s meetings were used for reporting progress of cooperative ventures such as Relief Society halls and stores, silk raising, and grain storage. Some wards studied topics such as physiology—a very popular one—or used the scriptures, Church books, or national periodicals as a way of enriching their testimony and sewing meetings. During the 1890s it became clear that adopting a course of study such as the Doctrine and Covenants could indeed increase attendance and stimulate interest.[7]

By the turn of the century Relief Society had a strong core group of allegiant and aging members, but its program appeared outdated to younger women, most of whom chose not to participate. "We don't have enough young mothers in our society," Alpine Ward president Sarah Marsh told the Alpine, Utah, Stake Relief Society conference in April 1901.[8] The concern was widespread, and a year later the general board decided that mothers' classes should be introduced as a regular part of the Relief Society program. Each stake would prepare outlines for lessons to be given in that stake and submit them to the general board for approval. Approved mothers' class outlines would be published in the *Woman's Exponent*. The classes seemed to meet the need, and many stakes reported new support from young mothers in their areas.

By the time Emmeline B. Wells became Relief Society general president in 1910, stakes had been preparing their own outlines for eight years. Some had expanded their course work beyond mothering and homemaking. In 1912, for example, the indefatigable Utah Stake Relief Society published a comprehensive five-year outline, including theological and political topics among others. Less energetic stakes were tired, bored, and anxiously looking to the general board for direction. Indeed, for several years the general board had considered publishing a standardized course of Relief Society lessons, but Emmeline B. Wells and some older board members objected. At Relief Society general conference in April 1910, Emmeline "explained why the Relief Society did not have a general outline of Mother's work for the entire society, and stated that it was to help educate and develop the sisters in their own locality by doing the thinking and studying of the subject required, which is helpful to the mind and heart."[9]

The proposal continued to be agitated during 1912 and 1913, but eighty-five-year-old Emmeline stalled decision on the matter, tabling the motion time after time or promising she would bring it up for a vote of stake Relief Society presidents. Finally, on 4 September 1913, her second counselor, Julina Smith, asked the privilege of appointing a committee on outlines. This was granted, and one month later the seven-member committee, composed primarily of younger women, reported that the outlines would be ready for publication in January. The 1914 *Guide* featured lessons in genealogy, home ethics, home gardening, literature, art and architecture, and health. Beginning in 1915 lessons were carried in the successor to the *Woman's Exponent,* the *Relief Society Magazine,* edited by Susa Young Gates, a key proponent of standardized lesson outlines.[10]

The response to the new material was overwhelmingly positive. Emmeline never attempted to thwart or sabotage the new endeavor, but she did continue to articulate her uneasiness, expressing her "fear that in these outlines we are getting too far away from the spiritual side of our great work, and from the thought that inspired the first organization of the Relief Society. The Society stands first for spirituality, and then for charity and mercy." Seeking to accommodate this concern, the board voted to give President Emmeline Wells space in each month's magazine to emphasize these aspects of Relief Society work.[11]

While this anecdote is not particularly dramatic, it offers some insight into the process of working in concert. The board wrestled with the question of general outlines from 1910 to 1913. Even after tension started to mount, resolution was not easily obtained. One is struck by the respect the board showed for the aged and experienced Emmeline. Indeed, their respect was charity which "suffereth long, and is kind; . . . is not easily provoked, . . . [and] endureth all things." (1 Corinthians 13:4–7.) Changing the course of the institution was a slow and laborious process. In this case, however, once the board had made the decision to change they moved forward quickly with implementation. The dissenting voice of Emmeline, once the obstacle to change, became a useful warning, a wise balancing voice as sisters pursued a new direction. Anyone who has listened to a Relief Society teacher read a thirty-minute lesson straight from the manual knows standardized lesson plans can, in fact, get us "far away from the spiritual side of our great work."

Working in concert means bringing into effective balance differing demands, talents, or perspectives. This process is ongoing in any marriage, family, friendship, presidency, bishopric, board, or council. Relief Society sisters, at both the general and local level, repeatedly have sought a comfortable balance between continuity and change, enduring considerable discomfort in the process. As we have seen, Susa Young Gates supported modernization of Relief Society lessons, but she opposed changes in the Society's traditional charity or welfare work. She strongly disagreed with the chief proponent for change, her friend Amy Brown Lyman, a woman sixteen years her junior with whom she had worked closely in preparing and publishing the new lessons. The mutual affection and respect of these strong, bright women survived their diverse approaches to charity work.

At the Society's April conference in 1916, Aunt Susa reached out to comfort Amy, sensing that the job of general secretary (some responsibilities of which Susa herself had assumed for a short time) was exhausting her. "God bless you," Susa scratched a note on Amy's conference program. "Be comforted — You will feel better and stronger after this Conference than you have felt for many days. . . . Go on, there is a great work awaiting you."[12] Ironically, this great work would be one of which Susa disapproved.

Three weeks following the conference Amy was contacted by the head of Salt Lake City's Charity Organization Society (COS) and asked if she would be willing to represent the Relief Society in a proposed monthly meeting of those in Salt Lake City "dealing with current social problems."[13] The COS, committed to new methods of "scientific charity" or social work, wanted to coordinate the charity work of the Church with that of other relief agencies in the community in order to avoid duplication of effort. Amy had a personal interest in the new methods, piqued in 1902 when she took a pioneer course in social work at the University of Chicago. In December 1916 she represented the Relief Society in a meeting with other representatives from priesthood quorums and Church auxiliaries to discuss social and welfare issues, including the possibility of training Church volunteers to use the new methodology in connection with Church charity work.[14]

An opportunity for training Relief Society women to perform social casework came in the wake of the United States' entry into World War I. The War Department and the American Red Cross urged governors to appoint delegates to the June 1917 meeting in Pittsburgh of the National Conference of Charities and Correction, forerunner of the National Conference of Social Work. Delegates, including Amy Brown Lyman who was one of two representatives sent by the Relief Society, heard experts discuss "all phases of charity and relief work" and considered how to meet social problems arising from the war. The Red Cross explained its plans for involving volunteers in military relief (preparation of surgical dressings, etc.), as well as civilian relief (distribution of governmental allowances to the families of servicemen).[15]

Eager to participate in both military and civilian relief, the

Relief Society sent Clarissa S. Williams, a counselor in the Relief Society general presidency, and Amy Lyman to an October 1917 Red Cross convention in Denver. Both women were impressed by the need for care and accuracy in family reports submitted to the government and agreed that Relief Society representatives should attend an upcoming Red Cross institute in civilian relief work and become authorized to work with the families of LDS servicemen. Amy and three other delegates from stake Relief Society organizations in Ogden, Logan, and Provo were sent to the six-week Denver Home Service Institute at the expense of the Relief Society general board. After completing this course, each delegate was assigned to Red Cross civilian relief work in her county. Amy Lyman worked with the Salt Lake County Red Cross as chairman of the Family Consultation Committee for the Civilian Relief Department and supervisor of work for LDS families.[16]

Church President Joseph F. Smith "was intensely interested" in Amy's report of the Denver institute. He expressed to her his concern for the Church's own charity work where "there is duplication of effort in which money is wasted, and in many instances, relief funds are not adequate." After having "spent some time examining the sample of [Red Cross] records, case histories, [and] registration sheets," he encouraged her "to devote herself to the study of family welfare work with a view of improving the LDS charity work."[17] The next fall she returned to Denver for more course work. John Wells of the Presiding Bishopric wrote to her there in December 1918, expressing his interest in the new social work: "I hope you will be in a position to educate me to some new ideas and methods of handling the poor of the church."[18] Soon after her return to Salt Lake City in January 1919, Amy set up the Relief Society Social Service Department at Relief Society headquarters. It was to serve as a liaison with other community agencies and use new methodologies to help bishops and Relief Society presidents.

At the same time Annie Palmer, who had attended the first Red Cross training institute with Amy in Denver in 1917, was working with Utah Stake Relief Society leaders in implementing the new social work methods in the charity work of the wards of Utah Stake, an experiment supported and encouraged by the Relief Society general board. Stake priesthood leaders had given them a special blessing in the undertaking and provided them office space in the stake's administration building. The sisters sponsored their own training institute for local Relief Society leaders and then offered bishops their help in investigating families and helping design constructive family relief plans. By October 1919 one bishop had turned over all of his charity work to the Relief Society while others were cooperating with the new stake agency, even bishops who had originally opposed the change. The stake replaced monthly Relief Society donations with an annual stake-wide drive for charity funds.

Susa Young Gates opposed this experiment in the Utah Stake and, much to the dismay of some board members, publicly revealed the board's division of opinion. In an effort to clear up questions regarding the work, Utah Stake Relief Society president Inez Allen was invited to present a progress report on the experiment at the general board's 23 October 1919 meeting. Following her visit Susa Gates, in a letter to the Relief Society general presidency and board, explained that her own views were not "exactly in accordance" with those expressed by Sister Allen.

"We may need to change and modify in this Society," she wrote, "but let us not make fundamental changes nor alter the perfect and wise adjustment of our religious organization to match the world's spectacular methods lest we fall into their mistakes and partake of their errors." Susa objected to exclusive use of trained social workers, feeling that home investigations were after all similar to the work of visiting teachers, many of whom were older women who would not be able to become professionals. Likewise, Susa hated to see responsibility and money shifted to a central office or figure. Proud that "we have always administered our charity without cost," she resented the use of funds for salaries and overhead. She emphasized that "to give money is the cheapest kind of service — to give love and personal services is the most difficult of all impersonal tasks." While the old methods might be less efficient, even if the Church were "imposed upon occasionally that was less harmful and less expensive" than "commercialized charity." Believing help should come from relatives, friends, or neighbors, Susa predicted that individuals receiving "regular financial help" from institutions would find their self-respect stifled and suffer other "demoralizing effects." She also argued that records of those helped should not be kept on permanent file, as it might be a bad reflection upon them once their situation changed. Finally, Susa did not like the approach taken in Utah Stake where an annual drive had been implemented in place of regular contributions, a drive that included members and nonmembers alike and might require a paid staff.[19]

During the winter months of 1919–1920 Susa wrote to several national figures seeking opinions and statistics regarding "the failures which come from administering charity through institutional and paid financial agents." She confided the progress of her campaign to her friend since girlhood, Elizabeth Claridge McCune, furnishing her with a copy of the letter she had sent to the Relief Society general presidency. After receiving a reply from Elizabeth, who indicated that she too felt the Relief Society should lead, not follow in matters of charity, Susa wrote as follows: "Others agree with your opinion . . . but I am advised to keep quiet for a while, and indeed Sister Williams has not permitted me yet to read this letter before the Board. There is a strong sentiment on the other side and the popular trend is in the other direction. Sister Lyman is invited to speak in Denver next Wednesday on this subject. The title of her paper is 'Permeating an Established Relief Agency with Case Work' " — a definite sign of conspiracy from Susa's point of view.[20]

After the Christmas holidays the battle resumed, each woman garnering support for her position from members of the general board, as well as general authorities. On 21 January 1920 a committee from the board called on President Heber J. Grant to discuss the "charity matter." "We asked what was the relationship between the Bishops and the Relief Society President in gathering and distributing charity," Susa reported to her friend Elizabeth, continuing: "Amy said a great deal and so did I. . . . Brother Nibley, who had been invited by President Grant to be present, sized up the situation better than I could have expected, but Amy and I showed such a difference of opinion, that we were referred back to the Board."[21]

Several things happened as a result of this full airing of differing points of view. First, the awareness that duplication of effort wasted resources and could potentially harm those in need led to a stronger working relationship between the Relief Society general presidency and the Presiding Bishopric, the two triumvirates responsible for Church policies on charity. They subsequently surveyed the local Relief Society presidents and bishops who actually administered relief to determine whether they were meeting together regularly to coordinate their efforts. Few were, but new official instructions appeared in 1921 strongly urging regular meetings to plan and coordinate ward charity work.

Second, a firm commitment was made not to rely on outside agencies to administer charity to Latter-day Saints. Bishops were to be responsible for the welfare of their ward members, and Relief Society sisters were to labor under their direction. Nevertheless, charity was not to be disbursed without careful investigations as had too often been the case in the past. Starting in the summer of 1920 with a special course taught by Amy Brown Lyman at BYU, Relief Society women were to learn new scientific methods for investigating families, evaluating their needs, and working with the bishop to determine the plan that would best encourage the family toward self-sufficiency. The new social services department run by Sister Lyman under the direction of the general board would serve as a liaison with community agencies, and as a training center for special social service aids and Relief Society presidents. The Relief Society members at large would become acquainted with principles of social work and sociology through a series of social service lessons.

Certainly, Susa Gates got part of what she had campaigned for. The new charity program was to be run by Church volunteers under the direction of the bishop, not by paid professional social workers, though a handful of them would continue to deal with specialized cases through the Relief Society Social Service Department. Amy Lyman, on the other hand, got a professional department which served as a liaison with the greater community and at the same time trained large numbers of women to utilize the principles of social work in carrying forth their Relief Society charity work. Each achieved part of what she had worked so hard for. "My dear Sister Lyman has been just as single-hearted, as devout, and as dutiful as I could possibly be," commented Susa in 1919. "Then, which may be right and which wrong? Perhaps both in some measure."[22]

We all know of compromises that represent the worst of both worlds. In this case, however, the new program represented some of the best of each. This was possible because neither woman was obsessed with being right or being best. Each wanted to do what was right and implement a decision that was best for those who needed help. Each was committed to something larger than herself. "The sweet influence of the Relief Society work, has been to hundreds of our sisters a consolation in passing through trying ordeals," wrote Emmeline B. Wells to Amy Brown Lyman in 1909. It "is the spirit of love and magnanimous charity that unites us in a fellowship grander and holier than the highest educational organizations among the cultured and learned women of the world."[23]

After resolving productive dissonance into harmony, the Relief Society launched its most productive decade of charity work—combining its traditional program with the new scientific charity. The differences between Amy and Susa actually enriched a program, infused it with new energy, and allowed continuity in the midst of tremendous change.

The Relief Society was for all practical purposes the welfare arm of the Church until the advent of the Church Security Plan in 1936. Under the bishop's direction, the local Relief Society president drew on the resources of the ward and community to give direct help to the poor and needy. She also had the Society's own charity fund, collected monthly by the visiting teachers and managed by the sisters.

Proper use of this fund was a particular concern to General

President Louise Y. Robison during her 1928 to 1940 tenure. To her it symbolized the original charge given by Joseph Smith to the Society. In the April 1935 Relief Society conference she took to task those wards and stakes who were neglecting their responsibility to use the charity fund wisely—one ward had even added the money to its general fund and used it to buy furniture. "But," asked Sister Robison with characteristic candor, "can you be comfortable with the choicest furniture, if little children and aged people are cold for want of quilts, or hungry for things you could give them?" She told of visiting a stake where the Relief Society president was "in despair" because one ward had asked for such a large sum of money for other expenses that "the needy had been entirely neglected." The "other expenses" often included contributions to the missionary fund or ward meetinghouse. In the Ontario, California, Branch, for example, the Relief Society had bought draperies for the stage and foyer, as well as helping with the painting, window-washing, and cleaning of the new chapel. "I do not want to say anything against help you can render," said President Robison, "but your first responsibility is to those who are in distress in your communities."[24]

Assured of the Presiding Bishopric's support in this matter, she concluded confidently, "I do not know of any of the Authorities who have given us the mission of building meeting houses, or sending missionaries. These activities belong to the Priesthood." On another occasion, she asked pointedly, "Do the men in your wards make contributions to the Society?" She reminded her audience of the Prophet Joseph's illustrious example and reasoned that since stake presidents and bishops gave generously to the Community Chest, they should also donate to the Relief Society.[25]

But history was headed in another direction. The institution of the Church Security or Welfare Plan in 1936 required some far-reaching changes in Relief Society's approach to charitable service. Under the new Welfare Program, the priesthood structure—quorums, committees, and presidencies—was given the responsibility for building and managing a vast new system of farms and factories and distribution centers. Relief Society sisters would do much of the work and Relief Society officers would have representation on the governing committees, but the Society's own relief work would gradually be encompassed in a growing priesthood-directed system.

One significant change was the demise of the charity fund. But it was not abruptly terminated. Small changes preceded the Relief Society's decision to discontinue its charity fund. In a departure from President Robison's policies, the general board of her successor, President Amy Brown Lyman, recommended in October of 1942 that ward charity funds be made available for maternal and child health care, emergency relief, and service-oriented Welfare Program projects, but not production. In 1943, however, the use of charity funds was extended to the production of quilts and, in 1944, to the production of clothing for welfare assignments. Gradually President Lyman and the general board reached the inevitable conclusion. "We seriously question whether the Relief Society should continue to collect donations from ward members through the medium of visiting teachers, particularly in view of the apparent lack of need for these funds," stated an April 1944 memorandum from the general board to the Presiding Bishopric.[26]

The collection of charity funds by visiting teachers was discontinued in October of 1944. As of 1 January 1945, the headquarters' charity fund balance of $150,748.14 was combined with the Society's general fund. Relief Society was no longer to provide commodities or funds directly to needy families.

Ward, stake, and general units of the Society continued to raise, spend, and manage their own general funds until 1970, when all the organizations of the Church were put under priesthood-directed budgets. This fiscal unity was not achieved without pain — few changes in the traditional Relief Society structure could have been less welcome to President Belle S. Spafford than the loss of financial autonomy. But she accepted it in the spirit of the Relief Society president of a Mexican branch, a Sister Torres, who had said of the request for every sister to contribute $5 to the Relief Society building, "The First Presidency have permitted [it] and therefore it must be right, and if it is right we can do it."[27]

These examples of Relief Society sisters working in concert to advance their educational programs and charity work are indicative of sisters' commitment to one another and to the mission of Relief Society. Equally challenging for Latter-day Saint women, and in many instances more challenging, has been the necessity of working harmoniously with Latter-day Saint men. Like partners in any strong marriage, priesthood brethren and Relief Society sisters have achieved unity only through the resolution of numerous differences. This is evident at every level of Church organization, but it is revealed with particular clarity and poignancy through ward records.

Ward Relief Society organizations typically managed not only their own charity funds, but other funds and property well into the twentieth century. Some of the separate Relief Society halls, constructed by ward and stake Relief Societies through the 1870s and 1880s, needed to be repaired or replaced as the century drew to a close. New wards also required new halls. When the Provo Fourth Ward was divided, the new Fifth Ward found itself with no public buildings of any kind. The Relief Society borrowed the Fourth Ward's hall for a while, but members became anxious to construct their own. Counselor Amanda Knight was tearing down one of her old brick buildings and offered brick for the hall. The matter was proposed to the priesthood and, while some objected to the hall's going forward at the same time the ward house was being constructed, one brother spoke plainly in favor of the sisters' enterprise. He said he had once lived in a ward where the men objected to the Relief Society building a hall because they feared it "would delay completion of the meeting house." But, he warned, "That house has never been finished and neither was the Relief Society hall. He thought it a good plan to let the sisters have their way in some things, and he predicted that the building of our ward house would be hastened rather than delayed by so doing." Following his remarks "the tide of sentiment turned in our favor," wrote one sister.[28]

Likewise, after the Vernal Second Ward was divided in

January 1910, the sisters had permission to build a Relief Society hall with the understanding that, if necessary, it would be sold when the time came to build a ward chapel. The ward's brethren and members, and even nonmembers, supported the sisters in constructing their hall. "The house was at last finished so we could use it and with thankful hearts moved our belongings," one sister recalled. "It was home. Home for we had built it with hard work. Patience, love, courage, self-denial were in the walls, roof, floor in fact all parts of the structure." Three years later the time came to sell the hall to help build a new ward house in which the Relief Society would have a room. The same sister explained, "Now we are established in our apartments in the ward. It is light and airy the sunny part of the house, we do not have to worry about the coal bill, or the light statements and we can work early or late but we feel like a girl living with her Motherinlaw [sic]."[29]

Thus did priesthood leaders in Provo and Vernal support Relief Society sisters who, in turn, sustained them. These wards had proceeded according to the Lord's command that "all things shall be done by common consent in the church, by much prayer and faith." (D&C 26:2.) Support and common consent, like love itself, must be unfeigned, genuine, and without pretense. At the turn of the century Relief Society sisters in Huntington, Utah, learned a hard lesson about common consent. They passively supported a decision with which many of them secretly disagreed and subsequently struggled not only with the decision, but with their pretense at supporting it. A diligent and insightful secretary, Amy Hunter, kept careful minutes of this desert saga of the Huntington Relief Society Hall.[30]

The Relief Society of the Huntington Ward in Emery Stake was organized in 1882. At that time Bishop Cox gave sisters the opportunity to nominate their own officers, but they deferred to him, asking him to nominate. Despite their initial reluctance, as they participated in the new organization they achieved a sense of ownership and commitment, seeking to visit and bring into their ranks nonmember and inactive sisters. On 17 May 1900 during their meeting in a borrowed brick school house, they discussed the desirability of beginning a home for their society, a hall like those erected by Relief Society sisters in dozens of other Latter-day Saint communities. That fall they began to evaluate the cost of lumber for the enterprise and, during the early months of 1901, they began the work of raising money. They had hoped the project would unite them and, indeed, one sister commented in March upon the "awakening among the sisters." "The building of our house is a burden," another sister said, "but we will be able to accomplish it if we persever [sic] and it will be a blessing to us."[31]

When the Emery Stake Relief Society president Anna Larsen returned from the Society's general conference in May, she reported plans for an additional building. Each Relief Society sister was being asked to donate $1 to the Woman's Building to be erected in Salt Lake City. In doing so, she assured the sisters, they would be blessed and "they would complete their own house sooner." A brother in the ward helped them adjust their bookkeeping records to accommodate various donations and in June a sister in the ward bore witness, "If we are united and faithful the Lord will bless us with mean[s] to pay donations & build our house."[32] The sisters were hopeful of hauling lumber for the hall that winter, but by December it was clear they would have to delay again, presumably because they had not raised enough money. So they held a party, decided to "get up a theater," collected and sold Sunday eggs, and sold a lot owned by the society in order to raise necessary funds. They planned to use donated labor as far as possible and found a carpenter who would "take what produce he could use at store prices" as pay for drawing up a plan for the building and supervising the work. In August 1902 when the stake officers visited they expressed their pleasure at the size of the building. It was not finished, however, and funds were running low.

Later that fall, in October 1902, the ward's new bishop called together the Relief Society presidency and the building committee, indicating at the outset of the meeting that he "wished all to be comfortable and prepared to stay until we arrive at a conclusion [and that he] desired the Spirit of the United Order should prevail." The sisters presented a financial report on the hall, with the president, Esther Grange, indicating she thought construction would have to stop for a while. Two other sisters agreed with her. One favored selling the building. Five felt encouraged to go on. Sister Grange expressed some frustration with the brethren present, who weeks earlier had persuaded the sisters to build a larger hall than they had originally planned for. She even asked the sisters to vote and indicate "who would have favored a smaller house in the first place"—a close-the-barn-door-after-the-horse-is-gone vote.[33]

The new bishop had clearly come to the meeting with his own ideas about the best solution. He "asked if the House could be finished for the ward and the Relief Society paid for all they had done and furnished." The ward finance committee would control amusements held in the hall, appropriating funds to the Relief Society for their charity work as necessary. Ten of those present voted to accept this offer. Only one rejected it. Four days later at a general meeting of the Relief Society, the bishop explained that it would cost the sisters $2000 to enclose their hall, and they voted unanimously to sell, confirming the decision of the earlier meeting. In parting, the bishop told the sisters they "must not have feelings."[34]

Oh, but they did have feelings, feelings which surfaced within hours after the general meeting. The next day when the Relief Society presidency and building committee met with the bishop and his finance committee to effect the transfer, one brother said he had been hearing "slurs and insinuations" that hurt him deeply. A second brother said he would rather go on a two-year mission or pay $200 than do this. A third brother burst into tears, and a fourth said he was "grieved but willing" if they had the "faith and good will of [the] society." The bishop insisted that selling "was the only way in this question," and President Grange tried to be encouraging, hoping that "the people would always thank the society for starting the building." Like others present she did not feel it right to "stand against the priesthood" and wanted to "try to be united."[35]

Ill-will over the decision to sell the hall—a unanimous decision—continued for months. In February the bishopric called a special meeting with the Relief Society sisters in order "to listen direct to complaints." Members of the finance committee were hurt since they had supposed the sisters were in harmony and then found out it wasn't so. The bishopric "asked the sisters not to deceive them and smother their feelings." Sister Grange explained that a member of the finance committee had hurt her feelings with his statements about the inability of the Relief Society to pay its debts. The member stepped forward and "said he did not know he had caused feelings and made an explanation in regard to the time [and] asked her forgiveness." A sister said she had not felt it right at first "but had reconsidered and felt better now." Another sister "was not converted . . . but was willing to be corrected," and another said she remained "hurt in her feelings." One of the men present acknowledged that women surpassed men in some things, but their problem was they couldn't bridle their tongues. The bishop, still trying to learn the ropes of his new position, felt overwhelmed by the ward's thousand dollar debt. He apparently was willing for the society to finish the hall, but not until the ward was out of debt and the society "had some means of their own to go on with." He was sick of the fault-finding and said it must stop, threatening that "those who indulge in it would be humiliated forcibly."[36]

Sister Grange found this meeting particularly painful, acknowledging that she "had not felt as she ought to for some time [and] was hurt in her feelings but would like to keep it private[. She] knew she had talked to[o] much, but was willing to turn over a new leaf or resign her position if requested to." During the next four weeks the sisters poured out love for Sister Grange. Several sisters expressed their willingness to sustain her, one affirming that "she was the right one in the right place." In March the sisters sponsored a surprise picnic for her at the end of their meeting.[37]

The process of healing and reconciliation lasted through the spring. In April the stake Relief Society president came to meet with the presidency and visiting teachers and asked them to speak about their feelings. One sister acknowledged she had "voted against her feelings at first," but since had felt better, though she still did not understand "what [the ward] debt was for." Several made similar comments, and some sisters were "still not converted," though they did not blame the Relief Society presidency. The stake Relief Society president "thanked the sisters for their confidences." A month later in May, when Annie Taylor Hyde visited the ward on behalf of the general board, the Huntington sisters confided their frustration to her. She commended their exertions but sorrowed with them that they had to give up the hall and would not be remunerated until some future time.[38]

At the Huntington Relief Society's first meeting in June a counselor in the presidency, Mary Westover, indicated that she "felt better by coming to meeting than by giving way to her feelings and not coming."[39] The sisters sang a singularly appropriate hymn to close the meeting: Eliza R. Snow's "The Trials of the Present Day."

> The trials of the present day
> Require the Saints to watch and pray,
> That they may keep the narrow way
> To the celestial glory.
> What though by some who seem devout
> Our names as evil are cast out,
> If honor clothe us round about
> In the celestial glory.
> With patience cultivate within
> Those principles averse to sin
> And be prepared to enter in
> To the celestial glory.
> Oh, let your hearts and hands be pure,
> And faithful to the end endure,
> That you the blessing may secure
> Of the celestial glories.[40]

The sisters of the Huntington Ward used the summer months to look inward, examining their motives and seeking to cultivate patience and purity of heart. In coming together they prayed for peace and union. They expressed a willingness to sustain both priesthood and Relief Society officers. One sister, drawing her words from the apostle Paul, indicated she "did not want to give up the good fight." (See 2 Timothy 4:7.)

In July when one sister confessed that she still harbored bad feelings, though not toward anyone in particular, Sister Grange expressed her willingness to try to right all wrongs.[41] And indeed, on 6 August 1903 she testified "the Lord had blessed her and been with her since our last meeting." Additionally, she announced the stake's decision that all visiting teachers should be set apart for their callings "and that the teachers must be in harmony with each other and the board, and the presiding officers of the ward before they can be set apart." A long testimony meeting followed, with many sisters expressing changes in their feelings over the past few months. One "felt like blessing and sustaining every organization." Another "had had her prayers answered and felt to sustain the Authorities and the sisters in the society."

The next week the visiting teachers met with the bishop and his counselors. "We cannot teach love and peace unless we are in harmony with our neighbors," he reminded them. Twenty-six women felt at peace with themselves, their sisters, and their priesthood leaders and were set apart, one sister expressing how good it felt "to see the unity that was with the sisters."[42]

There are sequels to this story to be sure. The bishop ultimately resigned because of continued conflict with members of his ward. The building was completed and was always known as Huntington's Relief Society Hall, used for Relief Society meetings, amusements, and other ward activities and public gatherings. It was destroyed in 1952. The controversy over the hall does not seem to have survived in the town's collective memory, but it serves to prick our memories, reminding us of Emma Smith's original instructions to Relief Society members in Nauvoo "that each member should be ambitious to do good [and] that the members should deal frankly with each other."[43]

At the April 1924 Relief Society conference, General President Clarissa Williams made the following announcement:

"The Presiding Bishop's office has advised that separate Relief Society halls be not built. Where new chapels are being erected, quarters should be provided therein for the Relief

Society. It is felt that it is a waste of money to build a hall which would be unoccupied except one afternoon a week, and that it is far more preferable that all auxiliary organizations be housed in the ward chapel." Then she added a telling comment of her own: "When Relief Societies are assigned a room in a ward chapel, however, they should not be contented with the darkest room in the basement."[44]

No doubt her comment reflects the reluctance of many sisters to give up their own buildings for a room in a ward chapel. They preferred being in control of their own decor. The same year the new policy was announced, the Washington, Utah, Ward Relief Society renovated its hall, adding electric lights, an organ, "sixteen chairs, a rocker, six hymn books, and a white stand for use in laying out the dead."[45] Some halls continued to be used for many years, as the advice from the Presiding Bishop's Office was politely ignored. In 1941 the Santa Clara, Utah, Ward reported, "The Relief Society house is being renovated. So far it has been reshingled, painted, and a cupboard built in the northwest corner. . . . We have bought new curtains and when all is complete we will have a nice home-like place in which to meet." They also gave the bishop $45 toward remodeling the chapel, although they did not choose to meet there. Finally, in 1949, the sisters moved into the ward meetinghouse to which they had contributed for eight years. They moved when they were ready.[46]

As for achieving unity, the sisters' move into the meetinghouses was a symbolic step toward unity with priesthood leaders. That it *could* be taken slowly, without undue pressure, when the sisters were ready, is a lesson in leadership, a model for resolving differences.

What do these incidents from the past mean to us today? There are several applicable principles that emerge. First, we have learned that resolving differences does not necessarily mean *dis*solving them. It is possible to "act in concert" and move forward without full agreement and perfect harmony — if we steer by what we have in common rather than by our differences. There is truth in the metaphor Joseph Smith used in his letter to the Saints from Liberty Jail: "You know . . . that a very large ship is benefited very much by a very small helm in the time of a storm, by being kept workways with the wind and the waves." (D&C 123:16.)

A balance can be achieved between the wind and the waves, and the ship with its helm kept workways, so that the ship moves forward in a kind of dynamic purposeful tension. Much of the Lord's work in our stormy world manages to get done in this manner by His imperfect but persistent servants. After all, Relief Society sisters who have disagreed about lesson content and presentation have continued to give and receive lessons regularly for three-quarters of a century. Despite changing programs and methodologies, sisters still care for the poor, the sick, and the sorrowful through Relief Society charity work and compassionate service. And differences of opinion and orientation have not prevented Latter-day Saint men and women from working toward unity as brothers and sisters.

A second concept that emerges from the past is that the process of achieving unity can be a valuable learning and growth experience, as the example of the Huntington Ward illustrates. The process should be a journey with good companions instead of a race to the finish line where only one wins and the others lose. True unity can be achieved only through patience and understanding.

The power of the priesthood—that ultimate unity with God—must be exercised "by persuasion, by long-suffering, by gentleness and meekness, and by love unfeigned; by kindness and pure knowledge." (D&C 121:41,42.) If the Relief Society is to act, as Joseph Smith said, "after a pattern of the Priesthood," then this should surely be our pattern. Eliza R. Snow said, prophetically, "Let [the sisters] seek for wisdom instead of power and they will have all the power they have wisdom to exercise."[47]

May we, like Solomon of old, seek "wisdom and understanding exceeding much, and largeness of heart, even as the sand that is on the sea shore." (1 Kings 4:29.) B. H. Roberts said it well at the October general conference of 1912, "In essentials let there be unity, in non-essentials liberty, and in all things charity."[48] Perhaps, echoing Paul, he should have added, "but the greatest of these is charity." (1 Corinthians 13:13.) To which we say, in the name of the One who showed us the way, Amen.

Notes

1. Anne Firor Scott, "On Seeing and Not Seeing: A Case of Historical Invisibility," *Journal of American History* 71 (June 1984): 7–21, discusses such societies, noting an observer's remark that "it was as if in the year 1800 a bell rang and all over the country women began coalescing into groups" (p. 12). See also Keith E. Melder, *Beginnings of Sisterhood: The American Woman's Rights Movement, 1800–1850* (New York: Schocken Books, 1977), pp. 42–53.
2. Sarah M. Kimball, "Autobiography," *Woman's Exponent* 12 (1884):51.
3. Brigham Young explained that priesthood "forms, fashions, makes, creates, produces, protects and holds in existence the inhabitants of the earth in a pure and holy form of government preparatory to their entering the kingdom of Heaven." Sermon of 30 Oct. 1870, in *Journal of Discourses,* 26 vols. (Liverpool: Latter-day Saints' Book Depot, 1853–86), 13:281.
4. "A Record of the Organization and Proceedings of the Female Relief Society of Nauvoo," 30 Mar. 1842, microfilm of holograph, Archives of The Church of Jesus Christ of Latter-day Saints, Salt Lake City, Utah, hereafter cited as LDS Church Archives.
5. Fifteenth Ward, Riverside Stake, Relief Society Minutes, manuscript, vol. 1, 1868–1873, 25 Feb. 1869; vol. 4, 1873–83, 6 January 1876, in LDS Church Archives.
6. Minutes of the Relief Society General Board, 31 May 1917, microfilm of typescript, LDS Church Archives.
7. Stakes reported their success with the early course of study at semi-annual conferences of the Relief Society. See, for example, Emmeline B. Wells, "National Woman's Relief Society Record," 10 Oct. 1892 to 8 Apr. 1901, holograph, 3 Oct. 1895, in LDS Church Archives. An excellent discussion of the development of Relief Society curriculum is Carol Lois Clark, "The Effect of Secular Education upon Mormon Relief Society Curriculum, 1914–1940" (Ph.D. diss., University of Utah, 1979).
8. Alpine Ward, Alpine Stake, Relief Society Minutes, 26 Apr. 1901, microfilm of manuscript, LDS Church Archives.
9. "General Relief Society Conference," *Woman's Exponent* 39 (June 1910): 6.
10. An April 1915 editorial by Gates celebrated the new courses of study: "There are no limitations to our possible growth and development. We find admirable truth germs in the literary studies carried on in some clubs; we discover elements of rare joy in the art lessons given by some

other club; while the patriotic societies, both at home and abroad, certainly are doing a good work in fostering a love for history and genealogy among their members. Then why not open up in the Relief Society all of these avenues of culture and education, by establishing departments for the study of all these truths and beauties of life and nature?" "The Scope of the Relief Society," *Relief Society Magazine* 2 (Apr. 1915): 199.

11. Minutes of the Relief Society General Board, 10 Dec. 1913.

12. Aunt Susa to Amy, handwritten note on the back of *Program, Annual Meeting of the Woman's Relief Society . . . April 4th and 5th, 1916,* Amy Brown Lyman Papers, Special Collections, Harold B. Lee Library, Brigham Young University, Provo, Utah, hereafter cited as BYU Special Collections.

13. William J. Deeney to Mrs. Richard R. Lyman, 27 Apr. 1876, holograph, Amy Brown Lyman Papers, BYU Special Collections.

14. For a careful assessment of the work of this committee, see Thomas G. Alexander, "Between Revivalism and the Social Gospel: The Latter-day Saint Social Advisory Committee, 1916–1922," *Brigham Young University Studies* 23 (Winter 1983): 19–39.

15. Minutes of the Relief Society General Board, 28 June 1917. Amy Brown Lyman emphasized the importance of the conference in her "Social Service Work in the Relief Society, 1917–1928, Including a Brief History of the Relief Society Social Service Department," typescript, LDS Church Archives, pp. 3–4. Lyman's history was also inclued in Minutes of the Relief Society General Board, January-October 1928, pp. 117–48.

16. Cora Kasius served as assistant secretary in the Weber County Red Cross Civilian Relief Department, and Mary Hendricksen had the same position in the Logan Red Cross, Annie Palmer was executive secretary of the Utah County Red Cross Chapter. Lyman, "Social Service Work in the Relief Society," p. 4.

17. Minutes of the Relief Society General Board, 31 Jan. 1918; Lyman, "History of Social Service Work in the Relief Society," p. 4.

18. John Wells to Sister Lyman, 11 Dec. 1918, Amy Brown Lyman Papers, BYU Special Collections.

19. Susa Young Gates to the Presidency and Board of the Relief Society, 4 Nov. 1919, typescript, Susa Young Gates Papers, LDS Church Archives.

20. Susa Young Gates to Elizabeth Claridge McCune, 17 Nov. 1919, Susa Young Gates Papers, LDS Church Archives.

21. Susa Young Gates to Elizabeth Claridge McCune, 21 Jan. 1920, Susa Young Gates Papers, LDS Church Archives.

22. Gates to the Presidency and Board of the Relief Society, 4 Nov. 1919.

23. Emmeline B. Wells to Mrs. Amy Brown Lyman, 6 Oct. 1909, Amy Brown Lyman Papers, BYU Special Collections.

24. "Relief Society Conference," *Relief Society Magazine* 22 (May 1935): 272; "Relief Society Conference," *Relief Society Magazine* 18 (Nov. 1931): 633.

25. Ibid.

26. Minutes of the Relief Society General Board, 19 Apr. 1944.

27. *Builders for Eternity* (USA: General Board of Relief Society, 1948), pamphlet, pp. 12, 13. See also Belle S. Spafford Oral History, interviews by Jill Mulvay Derr, 1975–76, typescript, p. 116, James Moyle Oral History Program, LDS Church Archives. Such loyalty to leaders is a necessary step along the path to unity.

28. "A Sketch of the Life of President Martha A. F. Keller" and History of Provo Fifth Ward Relief Society by Olive S. Bean, typescript in Utah Stake Reports, Susa Young Gates Papers, LDS Church Archives.

29. "Vernal Second Ward Relief Society," manuscript, LDS Church Archives.

30. Huntington Ward, Emery Stake, Relief Society Minutes, 1883–1903, manuscript, LDS Church Archives. All information and quotations regarding the Huntington Ward Relief Society have been taken from this source.

31. Huntington Relief Society Minutes, 7 Mar. 1901.

32. Ibid., 9 and 15 May 1901.

33. Ibid., 23 Oct. 1902.

34. Ibid., 23 and 27 Oct. 1902.

35. Ibid., 28 Oct. 1902.

36. Ibid., 10 Feb. 1903.

37. Ibid., 10 Feb. and 6 Mar. 1903.

38. Ibid., 18 Apr. and 25 May 1903.

39. Ibid., 4 June 1903.

40. *Latter-day Saint Hymns* (Liverpool: Latter-day Saints Book Depot, 1851), pp. 138–39. The hymn was included in Latter-day Saint hymnals until 1948.

41. Huntington Relief Society Minutes, 2 and 16 July 1903.

42. Ibid., 13 Aug. and 3 Sept. 1903.

43. "A Record of the Organization and Proceedings of the Female Relief Society of Nauvoo," 17 Mar. 1842.

44. "Relief Society Conference Minutes," *Relief Society Magazine* 11 (June 1924): 321.

45. *Relief Society Memories of St. George Stake, 1867–1956* (St. George Relief Society [printed by Art City Publishing Co.], Springville, Utah, 1956), pp. 77–78.

46. Ibid., pp. 99–101. Today Relief Society halls in good condition can still be seen, some with their original titles intact, like the Salt Lake 19th Ward Relief Society hall — a little jewel that resembles a miniature church. As of March 1987, it was obviously cherished by its occupants — appropriately, a firm of architects. When a Relief Society General Board member visited the Alamosa Colorado Stake in 1984, the sisters showed her a former Relief Society hall that looked like a sturdy red-brick family home. The sisters affirmed that it was indeed a home — their bishop's. It was the kind of "home" the Church is concerned with today, rather than the 1941 "home-like place" of the Santa Clara Relief Society sisters. Relief

Society has contributed more than bricks and mortar to the stability of such homes.

47. Eliza R. Snow to Mary Elizabeth Rollins Lightner, 25 May 1869, photocopy of holograph, LDS Church Archives.

48. In Conference Report, Oct. 1912, p. 30. Roberts acknowledged he was quoting from an unknown source.

"A Voice Demands That We Ascend"—Dare the Encounter: Building a Relationship with God

ANN N. MADSEN

A little over three thousand years ago the children of Israel camped before Mount Sinai. (Exodus 19:2.) The Lord invited the people to become a "kingdom of priests, and a holy nation" (Exodus 19:6) and commanded Moses to prepare the people for a personal encounter with their God.

"Sanctify them to day and to morrow, and let them wash their clothes,

"And be ready against the third day: for the third day the Lord will come down in the sight of all the people upon mount Sinai." (Exodus 19:10–11.)

But the people were not ready. Moses alone climbed to the peak of that mountain.

"And all the people saw the thunderings, and the lightnings, and the noise of the trumpet, and the mountain smoking: and when the people saw it, they removed, and stood afar off.

And they said unto Moses, Speak thou with us, and we will hear: but let not God speak with us, lest we die." (Exodus 20:18–19.)

So they would not go up.

The ideas I share with you here are about "going up," about daring the encounter which our forefathers feared. In Abraham Joshua Heschel's words:

Ann Nicholls Madsen received her master's degree in ancient studies at Brigham Young University where she has taught the Old Testament. More recently she has taught at the Brigham Young University Center in Jerusalem. She served a mission with her husband in the New England States, where he presided, and has lectured with him in Scandinavia, the United States, and Austria. She has contributed articles to the Ensign *and the* New Era *and to two volumes of* Studies in Scripture, *edited by Robert L. Millet and Kent P. Jackson, and* Apocryphal Writings, *edited by C. Wilfred Griggs.*

"Daily a voice demands that we ascend.... There are no easy roads, there is no simple advice.... The way of [man] is a way of rising to the peak of the mountain.... The vision of reaching the peak gives meaning to our touching its border."[1]

How I love the people who have helped me catch a vision of the peak and a glimpse of the Lord there.

Our relationship with the Lord is the prototype for all our other relationships. We had a closeness with the Lord before we came here. We are not establishing, but reestablishing, that relationship. He is no stranger to us. Over and over again, He invites us to come to Him: "Draw nigh to God, and he will draw nigh to you." (James 4:8; also D&C 88.) "Return unto me, and I will return unto you." (Malachi 3:7.) In Jeremiah, the Lord explains, "For I know the thoughts that I think toward you ... thoughts of peace, and not of evil, to give you a future of peace."[2]

"Then shall ye call upon me [probably in that future], and ye shall pray unto me, and I will hear you.

"And ye shall seek me, and find me, when ye shall seek me with all your heart.

"And *I will be found of you,* saith the Lord." (Jeremiah 29:11–14; italics added.)

This is no idle pursuit. How do we find Him? Where do we find Him? I will focus on six areas that have proven fruitful to me in my search.

The companionship of the Spirit is our goal. He it is who bears witness of our Father and His Son and carries their messages to our hearts and minds. Where can we hope to find that companionship, to feel that spirit? In the temple? At sacrament meeting? Is this enough? No, surely not. We all can prepare a home or an apartment where He will feel welcome.

Furnish the home with virtue so that the Lord will feel at home there

Bruce Hafen, the dean of the BYU Law School, speaks of the world today as a polluted river. We are like fish swimming in the pollution, often carried by a current of which we are only vaguely aware, until someone swims against the current, and we see the contrast. The Lord has commanded us to stand in holy places. But how do we do that in such a world? Where are the holy places? I suggest that we should make our homes holy places. And I have five suggestions under that heading:

Furnish the home with great books. I'm the kind of person who finds it very difficult, after I have purchased a volume or have checked it out from the library, not to finish the book. I am a book finisher, or I *was* a book finisher, but I have discovered that is not always the wisest course. Someone has said, "Don't reach your white-gloved hand into mud and expect the mud to come out 'glovey.'" I read reviews of the movie I want to see so I know what to expect. But if I discover, after I arrive at the theatre, that it's not what I had been led to believe, then even though I hate to waste the money, I leave.

Art that lifts can furnish a home. We should fill our homes with precious objects for remembering, things that bring back memories of uplifting moments in our lives—a delicate, painted Japanese fan stands open on my bedside table. There are all kinds of objects that may be beautiful because of what they mean to us and because of what we identify with them. There are all kinds of art reproductions that can be purchased relatively inexpensively. Simple, beautiful art changes the whole character of a room.

Orderliness, another chance at design. Orderliness in the home really is a chance at design. Occasionally I try to see my home with new eyes. I get so accustomed to the stack of papers that gets higher and higher on my desk; then my mother comes to visit, and I think, "That really looks terrible there." When we had the BYU religion faculty in our home for a social some time ago, I saw cobwebs and dirt I didn't realize had been there. We need to look with new eyes once in a while. We would invite the Lord into a clean and orderly place. I've used the word orderly for a purpose. Clean is for Saturday nights. Orderly can be for most of the time.

TV sparingly, so sparingly. It is the polluted water in which we swim. I think the remote control is an essential part of television today. There are things that we can't turn off fast enough to avoid leaving an indelible image in our minds. We need to be able to "click" it away immediately.

The problem with us is, unlike computers, we can't dump trash. My computer has a sign that appears periodically with the message, "The memory is nearly full; store to disk." And then if I want to save what I have, I need to store it someplace else. It also has the commands: "erase" or "erase whole disk." My Macintosh has an outline on the screen of a garbage can labeled "trash." One command I can give is "empty trash." I can put whatever I want to dispose of into the trash file. Then I press the button marked "empty trash," and it's gone forever. But, unfortunately, our minds are not like that. We see an image, and it's recorded indelibly.

I read once about doctors who did a study of patients under full anesthetic who could later remember, under hypnosis, the conversation in the operating room while they were undergoing surgery. That frightens me. The things we see, the things we experience, the things we allow into our minds are there. To remove them requires conscientious effort.

Furnish the home with glorious music. Our spirits respond to certain chords, melodies, and modulations in spite of ourselves. We are lifted or beaten down by music. In 1878 Joseph Young said:

"Man of himself is an instrument of music; and when the chords of which he is composed are touched, and salute the ear, the sounds appeal to his spirit and the sentiment to his understanding. If the strains are harmonious, he endorses and enjoys them with supreme delight; whether the tones are from a human voice or from an instrument, they arrest his attention and absorb his whole being."[3]

We've all seen young people with their whole being absorbed by music. Lex de Azevedo, an LDS musician, gave a talk some time ago called "Put 'No Trespassing' Signs on Your Mind," in which he said:

"Music can also affect your emotions. Music speaks in a language more powerful than words, for it is the language of emotion. Words communicate ideas. Music communicates feelings. While words get stuck in the thinking part of our brain, music sails through to reach the innermost corners of our emotional being. It is our emotions and feelings that really govern our lives and actions. This is precisely why music is such a wonderful, dangerous, exciting power. . . .

"Music is an instant recall mechanism to past memories. We can relive spiritually uplifting moments as well as times we would best forget. Images — good and evil — parade before our minds when we hear the music associated with them. Music is an effective means of indoctrination for good or evil, for we will not soon forget that which we learn with music."[4]

Ads on television teach us that so quickly. How many times have all of us driven in our cars and started humming a tune, the last tune we heard? Often, the music was an accompaniment to an advertisement, whose words were designed to induce us to buy a product. We carry many musical memories with us.

De Azevedo ends by saying our minds are sacred: "Let us put up 'No Trespassing' signs on our minds. Do not allow anyone to pollute your mind. Each thought is important. Do you realize that with each thought we inch our way toward heaven or hell? The key to overcoming the world is in controlling our minds. . . . If we program our minds properly[,] our bodies will follow.

"I submit to you the unclean things of our society are largely the culture that is produced by a telestial world. Let us not ask what evil we can tolerate, but let us find ways of filling our minds with celestial stimuli.

"For only to the extent that we feed our minds celestial food will we have the strength, spirituality, [and] motivation to reach our divine potential."[5]

There are songs that I sometimes find myself singing. I realize that when I'm the most uplifted, when I've felt the Spirit, there are certain songs from "The Messiah," and from other beautiful compositions that give words and music to the feelings of my heart. Good music has the power to put us in tune with Heaven.

Constructing a positive environment that incorporates all

these elements helps us furnish a virtuous home, in which we can practice godliness. We can learn eventually to respond in a godly manner. We can learn godly attributes and incorporate them into our lives. In the Old Testament, the high priest wore on his head a hammered gold crown on which was engraved, "Holiness to the Lord." On each of our temples there also is a sign proclaiming, "Holiness to the Lord." It is a promise to put that on a building. I wonder if we could, at least in our minds, have that kind of promise on our homes. "Holiness to the Lord"—in this place there will be only those things conducive to the presence of the Lord's Spirit. While this is a lofty ideal, we can work to make our homes holy places.

We can be aided in this process by becoming close to people who are close to the Lord. We should invite them into our homes. A beautiful woman in Hawaii shared a line from her patriarchal blessing with me, "Seek women companions who live beautiful and clean lives, lives that our Heavenly Father meant for women to live." After I heard that, I realized I'd done that all my life. I've been drawn like a moth to a flame to women who were spiritual and uplifting. I have looked for and found every year of my life a new friend, full of righteousness, someone who I knew was better than I was, and I knew if I spent time with her, I could become better as well. My friends are such queenly women. As I look back on the thirty or forty years I have known some of them, I wonder how I had the ability as a young woman, wife, and mother to choose such friends, who contribute a continuing righteousness to me. Every day I feel as if I'm bathed in righteousness. Our circle of encouraging, faithful friends will help us to make wise choices. They will be there in our times of struggle, pain, and grief to lift and bless us. Find friends; look for friends. Don't try to go it alone.

We also benefit from those men and women whose full-time preoccupation is to listen to and serve the Lord. In our wards, we must listen to the bishop and our home teachers, who have been called to serve and bless our lives. They are not paid for that service; they do it voluntarily. Sometimes they do it well, sometimes not so well, but they do it. Our home teachers' coming shows they love us. We may not need any message they might bring; their message is inherent in their coming. What we need is to know they care about us.

There is a right way to influence others. It is called righteousness. And righteousness does influence others. As we are righteous, people are drawn to that, as I am drawn to women of righteousness as friends. It is my personal feeling that there is a spirit that accumulates in a home as righteous people come and go there. I had the privilege of living in the New England mission home for three years. I can remember sitting in that living room, sometimes all alone, being so tired. I've never been so tired in my life as I was on my mission. Sitting there very tired and just absorbing the surrounding spirit, I thought, "President McKay was here. Levi Edgar Young was here. Spencer W. Kimball was here. Just a few weeks ago, Hugh B. Brown was here." All the things they said, the prayers they offered, the feelings they experienced in that room seemed to be reflected. We could feel it; it was there; it is still there.

I feel the same way about my own home. When we first moved into our home three years ago, it had been empty for quite a while and had been left by two older people who had passed away. But, I had the feeling that they still lived there. I didn't feel as if it were my house. I kept thinking, "Have I made a terrible mistake? What am I doing in this house?" The house I had lived in for fifteen years had been crowded with the pronouncements of blessings and the settings apart for missions. I remember where the chair sat, facing the fireplace, when our children were set apart for their missions. Now I was in this home where no children of mine had lived. Was it ever going to be the kind of home I wanted it to be? Then I realized, after the first Thanksgiving dinner with our children and grandchildren, it was different. Things were broken; there was dirt on the walls, and the carpet was dirty. But in addition, there was a different feeling. We have family prayer there daily. Now the place in the kitchen where we kneel to have our family prayers in the morning with the sun streaming in the window is a sacred spot. There have been a few blessings given in that home. The members of the BYU Religion Department came a few weeks ago. When I look around, I see them there. I see other people whom I love and admire. That's how I feel about homes. There is a spirit in the home. People used to walk into the New England mission home and say, "What is it about this house?" I wanted to say, "Well, there's Levi Edgar Young, and there's S. Dilworth Young, and there's Hugh B. Brown, and Spencer W. Kimball; that's what's about this house."

You will find the Lord in the scriptures

The scriptures are His books; He is there. "Immerse yourself in the scriptures, and the distance narrows between yourself and Deity." I think it was President Kimball who said that. When I lived in the mission field, we used to study for two hours in the morning with the missionaries. We couldn't send them down to study and then not study ourselves, so for three years, I studied for two hours almost daily. When we returned to Provo from our mission, however, I was really tired and started sleeping in each morning. I did that day after day and, finally, after six months, I felt rested. But I didn't read the scriptures. I didn't have study class with myself for two hours every morning. After six months had passed, I felt as if I were never going to adjust as a returned missionary. I thought, "There's something wrong with me. All the spirituality I've ever known in my life has now leaked out; I used it all on that mission, and I'm never going to have those good feelings again." One day, I thought, "Maybe I should study the scriptures again; that might help me." So I got up every morning, and from then until now, I have studied the scriptures daily. My husband chides me and thinks I'm a "scriptureholic." I teach the scriptures at BYU, so I'm required to study to teach. I'm so glad I need to. It's such a privilege.

Now I study on the telephone with a friend every morning but Saturday and Sunday. I'm so appreciative that we have this appointment, that we call each other every day and read. We don't discuss theology. We have long conversations sometimes, but we just *read* the scriptures. We psychoanalyze each other and do a few things before or after, but when we're ready to read the scriptures, we say a short prayer, asking the Lord to bless us and then we read. Recently, she said to me, "This is so great." We finish, and she'll say, "I'm not going to say this again, Ann. You'll just laugh at me if I say it, I know." And I'll say, "What?" and she'll say, "This is so great." And I'll say, "Yes, you did say that yesterday, you know." That was even after reading Leviticus.

Cathy Thomas, who also teaches part-time in the BYU Religion Department, and I have studied Greek together. I do the same thing to her. We get finished with studying, reading the New Testament, I haltingly, she really reading in Greek, helping me, teaching me as we go. I say, "I feel wonderful, but I was so tired when we started. What happens that, although we've studied so hard for this last hour or two hours, I feel great? What's happened to me?" I don't know what it is; I don't know how to explain it exactly, but I feel better afterwards. I feel as rested as if I'd had a long nap.

I'd suggest occasionally reading other English translations besides the King James Version. If we sometimes read another translation, we may see things we completely missed before. We all have a tendency to avoid seeing the familiar. We come to familiar scriptures, and they run off us like water off a duck. We read, "Choose you this day whom ye will serve; . . . but as for me in my house, we will serve the Lord." (Joshua 24:15.) We say, "Oh yes, I know that," and go across it. But if we read it in another translation, it's just different enough that we *think* when we come to it, and we hear it and see it in a way that we may not have seen it before. I'd suggest as another English translation the New International Version. I've found that particular translation is very close to the Hebrew and Greek translations, but it's also different enough to shake us a bit, so that we have to think about what we're reading.

We should also read the words of those who have seen the Lord or who have established a secure relationship with Him. There is such power in their words. Their words have been preserved for this very purpose so that we can feel that power. They are His witnesses. Courageous Abinadi declared just before he was to die, "He is the light and the life of the world; yea, a light that is endless, that can never be darkened;

yea, and also a life which is endless, that there can be no more death." (Mosiah 16:9.) And Joseph Smith, who like so many other prophets first saw the heavens opened as a young and innocent lad, reported:

"I saw a pillar of light exactly over my head, above the brightness of the sun, which descended gradually until it fell upon me.

" . . . When the light rested upon me I saw two Personages, whose brightness and glory defy all description, standing above me in the air. One of them spake unto me, calling me by my name and said, pointing to the other — 'This is My Beloved Son. Hear Him!' " (Joseph Smith—History 1:16–17.)

I love those words because they carry with them the power of the experience of the man, a chosen servant of the Lord, fourteen years of age, to whom God and His Son appeared. When I read that, the Lord has the opportunity, the Spirit has the opportunity, to testify of its truth. That's why I loved to quote it to people when I was a missionary. In Isaiah 43:10–11 we read, "Ye are my witnesses, saith the Lord. . . . I, even I, am the Lord; and beside me there is no saviour." We also can become the witnesses of whom He speaks.

We must truly repent, truly forgive

We will find the Lord if we prepare ourselves to feel comfortable in His presence. No unclean thing can enter the Lord's presence. We must truly repent, truly forgive: two sides of the same coin. We must purify our own lives without procrastinating or finding excuses to avoid this mighty change. Hugh Nibley has said, "The wicked can always find someone wickeder than they. It is a shabby substitute for repentance to point to someone wickeder than you are. It will give you a virtuous feeling. It will surely block up the way to your own repentance."[6] We often say, "Well, I'm not as bad as so and so," and that somehow makes us feel better. We do block the way to our own repentance by finding people wickeder than ourselves. In J. Richard Clarke's classic devotional on repentance delivered at BYU in 1984, he quoted Elder Orson F. Whitney, who said:

"Repentance is not that superficial sorrow felt by the wrongdoer when 'caught in the act'—a sorrow not for the sin, but for sin's detection. Chagrin is not repentance. Mortification and shame alone bring no change of heart toward right feeling and right living. Even remorse is not all there is to repentance. In highest meaning and fullest measure, repentance is equivalent to reformation; the beginning of the reformatory process being a resolve to 'sin no more.' "[7]

I love what we learn from the scriptures, "Resist the devil and he will flee from you." Sin no more, leave your sins. Bishop Clarke continued by quoting Elder Nephi Jensen:

"Faith unto repentance is the great eternal saving principle. Faith unto repentance cleanses the mind, purifies the heart, chastens the affections, nerves the will with resolute strength to conquer evil, and ennobles and perfects character."[8]

Bishop Clarke warned us that repentance is no trifling thing. He called it "an arduous journey from darkness to light"[9]; of course, God is in the light. Our journey is toward Him. President Kimball taught us, "Repentance is the Lord's law of growth, his principle of development, and his plan for happiness."[10] It is the normal daily process we should be going through in order to be happy.

Tshuv is the Hebrew word for repentance, which means "to return, to turn back." Remember when the Lord said, "Return unto me, and I will return unto you." (Malachi 3:7.) "Draw nigh to God, and he will draw nigh to you." (James 4:8.) Those are not just tautologies saying, "Well, if I'm close, you'll be close." The Lord meant that we should leave our sins in favor of His presence, so that we could come into His presence. We must *forsake* our sins. It was Lamoni's father, the king in the Book of Mormon who understood and exclaimed in his first prayer, "I will give away all my sins to know thee." (Alma 22:18.) I wonder if that won't be true for each one of us? If we want to know the Lord, ultimately we will have to give away all our sins. I'm not saying we can't know Him until we've given them all away, but we need to be in that process if we want to meet Him.

We must trust in the Atonement. Our only real affirmation

of the Atonement is our own repentance. Otherwise, we mock God. President Kimball also said, "God is good. He is eager to forgive. He wants us to perfect ourselves and maintain control of ourselves. He does not want Satan and others to control our lives."[11] We don't want other people to control our lives. God doesn't want Satan and other wicked people to lead us into doing things that are not good. "We must learn that keeping our Heavenly Father's commandments represents the *only* path to total control of ourselves, the only way to find joy, truth, and fulfillment in this life and in eternity."[12] In the video *The Faith of an Observer,* a documentary about Hugh Nibley, that splendid man said with the accumulated wisdom of his seventy-five years, "There are only two things we can do with distinction in this life: repent and forgive." I would suggest that we cannot understand the one without experiencing the other.

Dennis Rasmussen in his wonderful little book, *The Lord's Question,* taught me this: "To hallow my life, [God] taught me to endure sorrow rather than cause it, to restrain anger rather than heed it, to bear injustice rather than inflict it. 'Resist not evil,' [Jesus] said in the Sermon on the Mount. (Matthew 5:39.) Evil multiplies by the response it seeks to provoke, and when I return evil for evil, I engender corruption myself. The chain of evil is broken for good when a pure and loving heart absorbs a hurt and forbears to hurt in return. The forgiveness of Christ bears no grudge. The love of Christ allows no offense to endure. The compassion of Christ embraces all things and draws them toward himself. Deep within every child of God the light of Christ resides, guiding, comforting, purifying the heart that turns to him."[13]

What a privilege we have to forgive those who offend us or even sin against us. I love Carol Lynn Pearson's poem "The Forgiving":[14]

> Forgive?
> Will I forgive,
> You cry.
> But
> What is the gift,
> The favor?

You would lift
Me from
My poor place
To stand beside
The Savior.
You would have
Me see with
His eyes,
Smile,
And with Him
Reach out to
Salve
A sorrowing heart —
For one small
Moment
To share in
Christ's great art.

Will I forgive,
You cry.
Oh,
May I —
May I?

Sometimes I say out loud to myself, "Oh, may I, may I?" What an attitude about forgiveness. God tells us that He will forgive whom He will forgive. (D&C 64:10.) I think He meant that He is ready to forgive all of us when we repent; however, He reminds us that we must "forgive all men." I would add, if we want to be like Him. He is willing to forgive all of us. A dear friend taught me that we learn to forgive by changing ourselves. Joseph Smith instructed, "The nearer we get to our Heavenly Father, the more we are disposed to look with compassion on perishing souls; we feel that we want to take them upon our shoulders, and cast their sins behind our backs."[15] I think that's a great barometer to test ourselves to see how close we are getting to God. The closer we are to our Heavenly Father, the more we have these feelings of compassion and desire to forgive and forget.

He will find us if we will be who we are

We are each unique; we are each different from everyone else. We should respect that uniqueness and be ourselves. Socrates said, "The ignorance which causes vice and immorality is not ignorance of moral principles or laws, but ignorance of self." Carl Rogers commented on a curious paradox: "when I accept myself as I am, then I change."[16] We must first be honest with ourselves; we can fool many people much of the time, but in this one relationship, God knows us better than we know ourselves. We can't trick Him.

We try to hide, though. A short time ago in my afternoon Old Testament class a strapping ex-football player walked into the class with a big soft drink in his hand (this is 3:00 in the afternoon), sat down behind a young woman and positioned his head right behind her head. Thinking that then he wasn't seen, he began to drink, the big cup coming up behind her head and going back down, coming up behind her head and going back down. I think sometimes we behave the same way — like children who hide their heads and think they are invisible to others. That's how Mike acted with his drink. He was in full view to me. I knew what he was doing. And sometimes it was all I could do not to laugh — it struck me so funny that he was hiding behind her head with that big cup. What a waste of time it is to make excuses, to rationalize, to defend ourselves to God. Remember, as He was sending Samuel the prophet to find David among his family, the Lord said to him, "The Lord looketh on the heart." (1 Samuel 16:7.) The Hebrew says "le lev," which means "to the heart." God looks *to* the heart. He looks to it and into it, not just on it.

Our cousin Jack Adamson once wrote some lines in a prayer of dedication that have continued to mean much to me: "We ask for a greater freedom, that inner freedom that comes from an honest searching of ourselves. Let us be the first to know our own corruptions and evasions and surrenders.... Be to us, God of our Fathers, the fire and the rain; stretch and shrink us. Send us sweetness and pain. And give us the courage to be vulnerable. What we are not, let us not pretend to be. What

161

we are, let us discover and express."[17] We each have acquired layers of mortality made up of earthly habits, but beneath these, our spirits are sons and daughters of God. As my friend in Hawaii put it so well:

"We must understand that each of us has a pedigree of divinity. We are daughters of a perfect God. That realization alone gives worth to each of us. We must continue to build ourselves and love ourselves enough that when challenges face us, we will use these opportunities to grow rather than to fall. Every woman carries within herself the makings of a successful social being. Joy, strength, and our own future are all within us, and not out there someplace. We make the difference."

James Allen wrote:

"Man is made or unmade by himself; in the armoury of thought he forges the weapons by which he destroys himself; he also fashions the tools with which he builds for himself heavenly mansions of joy and strength and peace. . . .

"Of all the beautiful truths pertaining to the soul which have been restored and brought to life in this age, none is more gladdening or fruitful of divine promise and confidence than this — that man is the master of thought, the moulder of character, and the maker and shaper of condition, environment, and destiny."[18]

We need to catch the vision of ourselves, of the powers within us. Sometimes we delude ourselves into thinking someone else is responsible for our sins. We see ourselves as a victim. The message of free agency is that "I am not a victim." We are responsible for our choices. We can change.

I love this scripture hidden away in the little book of Micah. Micah was lonely in a very wicked generation and in the midst of his proclaiming what was going to happen to that generation, he said:

"Therefore I will look unto the Lord: I will wait for the God of my salvation: my God will hear me.

"Rejoice not against me, O mine enemy: when I fall, I shall arise; when I sit in darkness, the Lord shall be a light unto me." (Micah 7:7–8.)

In *our* darkest moments, is the Lord a light unto us? We

all have darkest moments, but if, in those moments, there is still that light — it may not be a very big light — but if there's a light, and it's the Lord, and we feel that, we can see it. "When I sit in darkness, the Lord shall be a light unto me."

Eliza R. Snow saw the vision, which she states so powerfully: "[We are] women of God, — women fulfilling high and responsible positions."[19] We walk the earth among wondrous princes and princesses whose potential, like our own, is beyond our comprehension. But God knows who I am and who you really are. Sometimes it may seem as if He is the only one who knows who we really are. Often, we ourselves forget who we are. We must find out from Him about ourselves. In 1 Samuel 16:7, we read, " . . . the Lord seeth not as man seeth; for man looketh on the outward appearance, but the Lord looketh to the heart." By deliberately using our agency to heighten our awareness of God, we become more conscious of Him. We can try to maintain eternal perspective to see, more nearly, through His eyes, hear through His ears. When I'm having a struggle, I often pray, "Heavenly Father, help me see this one thing the way you see it. I know I can't take in everything, but please just help me see it the way you're seeing it. Help me see this person the way you see him or her."

We will find Him if we call out to Him

Pray; talk to the Lord; reach upward; bare your soul to Him. Pray for those you love, and for those you hate. Pray for your enemies. Pray for forgiveness. Tell Him what you dare not speak aloud to anyone else. Pray for yourself. One morning on the deck of our cabin in the mountains we knelt in morning prayer with a wonderful couple who are our dear friends. One of them led us in prayer, and as he did, my soul was enlarged and my understanding enlightened when he said, "If we have offended thee, in any way, we ask thy pardon. Help us to live consistent with the covenants we have made." He prayed other things, but these two ideas were burned into my heart. In what ways do I offend the Lord? Do I live each day consistent with the covenants I have made with my Heavenly Father? Am I truly grateful? My daughter Mindy told me recently of a prayer she had offered: "Thank you for all the things we forget to thank you for all the time." Then she enumerated them: "I have clothes that fit me now that I'm pregnant. People used to have to wear whatever they had."

It is so easy to *speak* the truth. I often plead with the Lord to help me to *live* the truths that I so easily speak. After the pleading, we must learn to listen. Sometimes, before the "Amen" is said, the answer comes. We start praying, and we pray and pray, and in some of the spaces between, we receive the answer. Sometimes the answer is disguised in the words of the four-year-old who repeats a memorized line in the Primary program, or in a quiet conversation with a friend, or in the words of a faintly remembered patriarch whose blessing has yellowed. Or sometimes it may even come as I drive alone in the car, heading for the paint store, intruding upon my remodeling plans with such power that I cannot deny its source. Sometimes answers may come even before the questions or the pleading. I must learn to store the truth for future reference.

I love the iconography in ancient paintings of a man representing God with his right hand outstretched through the clouds. Later, after Nicea, people forgot that we are truly made in God's image and substituted in their paintings only an outstretched hand which appears to be parting a veil of clouds. I love this image because it represents to me the many times in scripture when the Lord pleads, "My hand is stretched out still." I also identify it with the temple. After all we can do, there is grace. How monumentally important it is that Moses saw God and even more for us that Joseph Smith saw the Father and the Son. Joseph found out for himself and for all of us that our prayers are directed and answered by exalted Persons. They are real—they are not the abstractions men impose on us in our day. Can I ever be grateful enough to Joseph Smith for putting me in touch with the true God, creator of this earth, whose plan included a Savior who has borne my griefs and has carried my sorrows and healed me with his wounds—the promised Messiah, my personal Redeemer?

We will find Him if we trust Him

God can be trusted. He lives. I am a teacher, and it is my pleasure to teach the Old Testament. It is pure joy to show my students that threading its way through that marvelous work is the absolute certainty of a living God who loves and pleads with His children to trust Him. There is indeed a cloud of witnesses.

The Lord chooses many metaphors to teach His children this trust. He compares Himself to a shepherd, responsible for all his sheep; to a father, whose son is Israel whom He rescues from slavery with an offer of freedom; to a potter who cannot change the substance of the clay, but who wishes to shape it masterfully; to a refiner of silver who after the dross has been burned away looks for his own reflection in the finished work.

Dare the encounter with God. It is up to each of us. We must choose. God does indeed stand with His arms out-stretched, waiting, and a voice within us demands that we ascend. Such an encounter has its risks and its costs because, once we know, we become responsible. But, once we know, all His options are open to us. That is one of the unique teachings of the Restoration. His course is not easy, even now. He weeps or rejoices over us just as we do over our children. Our constant questioning, "Where art thou, Lord?" is mirrored in His final question to us, just as He called for this earth's first children in the garden. "Adam, Eve, where art thou?" (Genesis 3:9.) The day will come when I myself, the me whose heart He can read, will be the only answer that will be given.

My daughter Emily has written:

"Obedience to the commandments teaches us who we really are and what we really want and, at the same time, obedience enables us to know God and Jesus Christ whom He has sent, to understand their will for us and to choose once again with both body and spirit this time to sustain their plan. It is a choice that we make over and over, all day, every day; and each right choice adds to our knowledge of the truth. If we are faithful, the time will come when we will stand before our God in His glory and see ourselves as we truly are. Then at last, we will comprehend all truth as we exclaim, 'Oh, I see, I'm just like you.' "

In 1 John 3:1–3, we read:

"Behold, what manner of love the Father hath bestowed upon us, that we should be called the [children] of God: therefore the world knoweth us not, because it knew him not.

"Beloved, now are we the [children] of God, and it doth not yet appear what we shall be: but we know that, when he shall appear, we shall be like him; for we shall see him as he is.

"And every [one] that hath this hope in him purifieth himself, even as he is pure."

This is my witness. I know that God lives. I know that Jesus Christ atoned for my sins. It makes it much easier to repent when I know that the Atonement is real. I know that Joseph Smith was a man of integrity and when he said he saw God, he did. I love the Book of Mormon. I don't know how it could happen. I've tried to translate, and in six months nobody could translate a book like the Book of Mormon alone. I know that it is true and that God intends us to have it in our hands to guide and teach us. I love the living prophets. I know that Ezra Taft Benson has been called of God to lead us. I will do what he tells me to do to the very best of my ability. Then the Lord will see that I really want to know Him. I pray that we each will be blessed in our quests to find the Lord. I hope I've been able to paint a picture for you or open a window for you, that you can see Him more clearly.

Notes

1. Abraham Joshua Heschel, *Israel: An Echo of Eternity* (New York: Farrar, Straus and Giroux, 1969), pp. 225–226.
2. I have translated some of the biblical quotations directly from the Greek or from the Hebrew, so the wording may differ somewhat from the King James Version.
3. Joseph Young, "Appendix," *History of the Organization of the Seventies* (Salt Lake City: Deseret News Steam Printing Establishment, 1878), pp. 14–15.

4. Lex de Azevedo, "Put 'No Trespassing' Signs on Your Mind," *Church News,* 11 Sept. 1982, p. 10.
5. Ibid.
6. Hugh Nibley, "Great Are the Words of Isaiah," Sydney B. Sperry Symposium, 28 Jan. 1978; transcribed by author from tape in her possession.
7. Roy W. Doxey, *Latter-day Prophets and the Doctrine and Covenants,* (Salt Lake City: Deseret Book Co., 1964), 2:257, quoted in J. Richard Clarke, "The Healing Power of Christ," *Brigham Young University 1983–84 Fireside and Devotional Speeches,* ed. Cynthia M. Gardner and Karen Seely (Provo, Utah: University Publications, 1984), p. 101.
8. Nephi Jensen, *The World's Greatest Need* (Salt Lake City, Utah: Deseret News Press, 1950), p. 63; quoted in Clarke, "The Healing Power of Christ," p. 101.
9. Clarke, p. 101.
10. Spencer W. Kimball, "The Gospel of Repentance," *Ensign,* Oct. 1982, p. 2.
11. Ibid.
12. Ibid.
13. Dennis Rasmussen, *The Lord's Question* (Provo, Utah: Keter Foundation, 1985), pp. 63–64.
14. Carol Lynn Pearson, "The Forgiving," in *Beginnings* (Provo, Utah: Trilogy Arts, 1967), p. 35; reprinted by permission of the author.
15. Joseph Fielding Smith, ed., *Teachings of the Prophet Joseph Smith* (Salt Lake City, Utah: Deseret Book Co., 1976), p. 241.
16. Carl R. Rogers, *On Becoming a Person* (Boston: Houghton Mifflin Co., 1961), p. 17.
17. Jack Adamson, Prayer of Dedication for the University of Utah Art and Architecture Center, 29 Sept. 1971.
18. James Allen, *As a Man Thinketh* (Salt Lake City, Utah: Bookcraft, 1964), p. 13.
19. Eliza R. Snow address, "Great Indignation Meeting," *Deseret News Weekly,* 19 Jan. 1870.

STRUGGLING WITH ADVERSITY

The gospel of Jesus Christ is not insurance against pain. It is resource in event of pain, and when the pain comes... rejoice that you have resource to deal with your pain.

—CARLFRED BRODERICK

The Uses of Adversity

CARLFRED BRODERICK

*W*hile I was a stake president, the event occurred that I want to use as the keynote to my remarks. I was sitting on the stand at a combined meeting of the stake Primary board and stake Young Women's board where they were jointly inducting from the Primary into the Young Women's organization the eleven-year-old girls who that year had made the big step. They had a lovely program. It was one of those fantastic, beautiful presentations — based on the Wizard of Oz, or a take-off on the Wizard of Oz, where Dorothy, an eleven-year-old girl, was coming down the yellow brick road together with the tin woodman, the cowardly lion, and the scarecrow. They were singing altered lyrics about the gospel. And Oz, which was one wall of the cultural hall, looked very much like the Los Angeles temple. They really took off down that road. There were no weeds on that road; there were no munchkins; there were no misplaced tiles; there was no wicked witch of the west. That was one antiseptic yellow brick road, and it was very, very clear that once they got to Oz, they had it made. It was all sewed up.

Following that beautiful presentation with all the snappy tunes and skipping and so on, came a sister who I swear was sent over from Hollywood central casting. (I do not believe

Carlfred Broderick, professor of sociology and head of the marriage and family therapy program at the University of Southern California, received his B.A. from Harvard and his Ph.D. from Cornell University. He is a popular lecturer and the author of numerous books, including Couples, Marriage and the Family *(a college text), and* The Therapeutic Triangle *(a text for marriage counselors). He has served as president of the National Council on Family Relations, Southern California Association of Marriage and Family Counselors, and the Association of Mormon Counselors and Psychotherapists. He has been a bishop, stake president, and temple ordinance worker. He and his wife, Kathleen, are the parents of eight children.*

she was in my stake; I never saw her before in my life.) She looked as if she had come right off the cover of a fashion magazine — every hair in place, with a photogenic returned missionary husband who looked like he came out of central casting and two or three, or heaven knows how many, photogenic children all of whom came out of central casting or Kleenex ads or whatever. She enthused over her temple marriage and how wonderful life was with her charming husband and her perfect children and that the young women too could look like her and have a husband like him and children like them if they would stick to the yellow brick road and live in Oz. It was a lovely, sort of tear-jerking, event.

After the event was nearly over, the stake Primary president, who was conducting, made a grave strategic error. She turned to me and, pro forma, said, "President Broderick, is there anything you would like to add to this lovely evening?"

I said, "Yes, there is," and I don't think she has ever forgiven me. What I said was this, "Girls, this has been a beautiful program. I commend the gospel with all of its auxiliaries and the temple to you, but I do not want you to believe for one minute that if you keep all the commandments and live as close to the Lord as you can and do everything right and fight off the entire priests quorum one by one and wait chastely for your missionary to return and pay your tithing and attend your meetings, accept calls from the bishop, and have a temple marriage, I do not want you to believe that bad things will not happen to you. And when that happens, I do not want you to say that God was not true. Or, to say, 'They promised me in Primary, they promised me when I was a Mia Maid, they promised me from the pulpit that if I were very, very good, I would be blessed. But the boy I want doesn't know I exist, or the missionary I've waited for and kept chaste so we both could go to the temple turned out to be a flake,' or far worse things than any of the above. Sad things — children who are sick or developmentally handicapped, husbands who are not faithful, illnesses that can cripple, or violence, betrayals, hurts, deaths, losses — when those things happen, do not say God is not keeping His promises to me. The gospel of Jesus Christ is not insurance against pain. It is resource in event of pain, and when that pain comes (and it will come because we came here on earth to have pain among other things), when it comes, rejoice that you have resource to deal with your pain."

Now, I do not want to suggest for a moment, nor do I believe, that God visits us with all that pain. I think that may occur in individual cases, but I think we fought a war in heaven for the privilege of coming to a place that was unjust. That was the idea of coming to earth — that it was unjust, that there would be pain and grief and sorrow. As Eve so eloquently said, it is better that we should suffer. Now, her perspective may not be shared by all. But, I am persuaded that she had rare insight, more than her husband, into the necessity of pain, although none of us welcome it.

I remember one time thinking such thoughts, such grand thoughts, and realizing that I dealt as a therapist with many people who suffered far, far more pain than I ever suffered and feeling guilty at having been spared some of the pain that my friends had experienced. Shortly after this, I developed a toothache. I'm a great chicken — I hate pain at all times. An apocryphal story was told of my mother who, as she took me to kindergarten, told the teacher I was very sensitive and, if I didn't behave, to hit the child next to me. Although that's not a true story, it truly represents my sentiments. I'll learn from others, although I don't want pain myself. So when I had this toothache, I thought here is a golden opportunity to embrace this existential experience and to join in this pain — open myself to this pain and experience it. I told myself I'm just going to sit in this pain and take it into myself and grow from it. That lasted forty-five minutes, at which time I called my dentist, "I want some pain medicine." The forty-five minutes it took between the time I took the medicine and the time the pain went away was the hardest part because I showed no moral stature, all I wanted was to get rid of that pain.

So I do not want you to think that I believe anything good about pain. I hate pain. I hate injustice. I hate loss. I hate all the things we all hate. None of us love those things. Nor, as I say, do I think God takes pleasure in the pain that comes to us. But, we came to a world where we are not protected from those things. I want to talk to you not in behalf of pain—heaven forbid—nor do I think that all pain is for the best. I'm certain that's not true. I'm certain pain destroys and embitters far more often than it ennobles. I'm sure injustice is destructive of good things in the world far more often than people rise above it. I'm certain that in this unjust awful world, there are far more victims that do not profit from their experience than those who do. So I do not want you to think I'm saying that pain is good for you. Pain is terrible.

I want to talk rather about when pain unbidden and unwanted and unjustly comes—to you or to those that you love or to these eleven-year-old girls as they get along in their lives. I want to discuss how to encounter that pain in such a way that it does not destroy you; how to find profit in that awful and unrewarding experience. I want to share with you some stories, mostly not my own, although I'm in all of them, but the pain is mainly someone else's. Some of the pain is my own. All of it is real, and all of it taught me. What I want is not to lecture to you or to sermonize you, but to share with you some lessons I have learned through pain, my own and others', that are valuable to me and, in the end, to share with you what I think I have learned from those incremental experiences.

The first two stories were extraordinarily instructive to me. They both came through opportunities I had as a stake president to give blessings. Often the Lord has taught me through blessings; as I've had my hands on someone's head, He's taught me things I did not know and sometimes didn't want to know. The first one was a case of a sister whom I'd known for years and who, in my judgment, had made some very poor life choices. She had married a handsome, charming young man who initially wasn't a member of the Church but joined the Church for her. She waited a year to marry him and then went to the temple. It was the last time he ever went to the temple. I knew he was a flake from the beginning. Out of my wisdom, it didn't surprise me that he soon returned to many of his pre-Church habits—most of the transgressions in the book that you can think of and some that I might not have.

174

There was great pain for this woman. A good, good woman, she kept in the Church; she kept in the kingdom; she suffered enormous pain because her husband went back to gambling and drinking and other things that were unhappy and unwholesome. But, the greater pain came when her children, having these two models before them, began to follow him. He would say things like, "Well, you can go to church with your mother and sit through three hours of you know what, or you can come to the racetrack with me, and we'll have good stuff to eat and drink and have a great time." It was a tough choice, and very often the children chose to go with him. They gradually seemed to adopt his life-style, values, and attitude toward the Church and toward sacred things. Although she never wavered from her own faith and faithfulness and her commitment to her Heavenly Father, her family was slipping away from her.

As she asked me for a blessing to sustain her in what to do with this awful situation in which she found herself, my thoughts were, "Didn't you ask for this? You married a guy who really didn't have any depth to him and raised your kids too permissively. You should have fought harder to keep them in church rather than letting them run off to racetracks." I had all those judgments in my head. I laid my hands on her head, and the Lord told her of His love and His tender concern for her. He acknowledged that He had given her (and that she had volunteered for) a far, far harder task than He would like. (And, as He put in my mind, a harder task than I had had. I have eight good kids, the last of whom just went to the temple. All would have been good if they had been orphans.) She, however, had signed up for hard children, for children who had rebellious spirits but who were valuable; for a hard husband who had a rebellious spirit but who was valuable. The Lord alluded to events in her life that I hadn't known about, but which she confirmed afterwards: twice Heavenly Father had given her the choice between life and death, whether to come home and be relieved of her responsibilities, which weren't going very well, or whether to stay to see if she could work them through. Twice on death's bed she had sent the messenger away and gone back to that hard task. She stayed with it.

I repented. I realized I was in the presence of one of the Lord's great noble spirits, who had chosen not a safe place behind the lines pushing out the ordinance to the people in the front lines as I was doing, but somebody who chose to live out in the trenches where the Lord's work was being done, where there was risk, where you could be hurt, where you could lose, where you could be destroyed by your love. That's the way she had chosen to labor. Then I thought, "I am unworthy to lay my hands on her head; if our sexes were reversed, she should have had her hands on mine."

Now she is doing well; one of her sons finally went on a mission. He had a bishop who took hold of him and shook him and got him to go. He went to one of those missions where people line up to be baptized when you get off the plane. He had a wonderful mission; they all but made an icon of him. He had miracles under his hands. He came back hotter than a firecracker for missions. He wouldn't leave alone his younger brother, who was planning on playing football in college instead of going on a mission, until he also went on a mission. The younger boy looked up to his brother; nobody could have turned that second kid around except his older brother. The younger went on a harder mission. He happened to have a language skill that he developed, and he turned out to be the best one at the language. He caught fire; he had spiritual experiences, and he came back red hot.

Those two boys started working with their sisters, who are harder cases; they haven't come all the way around yet. One of them looks better. One of them married a non-member, and her husband did a terrible thing — he met the missionaries and joined the Church and started putting pressure on his wife to become active. She said, "I married you because you were out of the Church." I don't know — even dad may repent, who knows? You know, she may yet win them all.

I know that she risked her life for service. In a blessing the Lord said to her, "When you're in my employ, the wages are from me, not from those you serve."

In the second case I had a woman who came to me who was an incest victim—the victim of a terrible family. She was abused physically. Her mother was neurotic and stayed in bed all the time to get her daughter to do all the work, including taking care of the husband's needs when he was drunk. The daughter had been abused in about every way there was to be abused—psychologically, physically, sexually. Besides that she had to do all the housework.

She was not a member of the Church at that time, although this happens to members of the Church also. In high school she met a young man who was a Latter-day Saint and who started taking her to church with him. Eventually they married. He was gentle and kind and patient because she didn't come with very many positive attitudes toward men, marital intimacy, or many other things. But he was long-suffering and patient and loved her. They raised some boys.

Despite this, she had recurring bouts of depression and very negative feelings about herself because she had been taught by the people most important in her early life what a rotten person she was. It was hard for her to overcome that self-image. I worked with her to try to build her self-image. One day she said to me, "You're a stake president." She wasn't in my stake, but she said, "You're a stake president; you explain to me the justice of it." She said, "I go to church, and I can hardly stand it. When I see little girls being hugged and kissed and taken to church and appropriately loved by their fathers and mothers, I just have to get up and leave. I say, 'Heavenly Father, what was so terrible about me that, when I was that age, I didn't get any of that? What did that little girl do in the premortal existence that I didn't do so she is loved, so she is safe? Her daddy gives her priesthood blessings when she's sick. Her mother loves her and supports her and teaches her. What did I do? Can you tell me that God is just if He sends that little girl to that family and me to my family?" She said, "It's a good thing I had boys. I don't think I could have stood to raise girls and have their father love them because I'm so envious."

I would not have known how to answer her in my own capacity because that is manifestly unjust. Where here or in

177

eternity is the justice in an innocent child's suffering in that way? But the Lord inspired me to tell her, and I believe with all my heart that it applies to many in the kingdom, that she was a valiant Christlike spirit who volunteered (with, I told her, perhaps too much spiritual pride) to come to earth and suffer innocently to purify a lineage. She volunteered to absorb the poisoning of sin, anger, anguish, and violence, to take it into herself and not to pass it on; to purify a lineage so that downstream from her it ran pure and clean, full of love and the Spirit of the Lord and self-worth. I believed truly that her calling was to be a savior on Mount Zion: that is, to be Savior-like, like the Savior to suffer innocently that others might not suffer. She voluntarily took such a task with the promise she would not be left alone and abandoned, but He would send one to take her by the hand and be her companion out into the light. I viewed that woman in a different way also, again realizing I was in the presence of one of the great ones and unworthy to have my hands on her head.

I think we do not understand the nature of ourselves. I think we do not understand who we are. Some people call the temple ordinances the "mysteries" of the kingdom. When I went to the temple, I thought I was going to learn which star was Kolob, where the Ten Tribes were, and other such information. But those aren't the mysteries of the kingdom; the mysteries of the kingdom are who we are, and who God is, and what our relationship to Him is. Those are the mysteries of the kingdom. You can tell somebody in plain English, but they still don't know in their hearts who they really are.

I was in a foreign country giving a workshop for others in my profession. The workshop was over, and I was just exhausted. My plane left at 7:30 P.M. back to the States, and it was now 4:00 P.M. I was right across the street from the airport in a motel. I thought, "This is nap time. I am going, in the middle of the day with the sun out, to take a nap." So I called the desk and said, "I want to be awakened at 6:00, not 6:00 in the morning but 6:00 in the evening; I'm taking a nap." I put down the receiver, undressed and curled into bed and thought how deliciously wicked it was to be sleeping in the middle of the day. I had just snuggled down when the telephone rang. It was the mission president, who also was a general authority whom I had never met, but who had read in the paper that I was there. He had a problem with one of his sister missionaries. Although he'd been working with her, she had a ticket to go home on the same flight I was on. He'd labored with her and given her blessings. She'd only been out six weeks, but she was going home and nothing he was able to say changed her mind. The mission president said, "She said she had your text in college, and I told her you were here. I asked her if she would see you, and she said she would." He said, "You're it."

I protested, "It's your job; it's not my job. You're a general authority — I'm just a stake president and out of my territory at that."

He said to me, "We'll send the car for you."

This sister and I sat down together. She had her purse clutched and her ticket prominently displayed on it. She looked at me a bit defiantly, and I said, "The president tells me you're headed for home."

She answered, "Yes, and you can't talk me out of it either."

I said, "Why?"

She told me why.

It was an awful story. She did grow up in a Mormon family in Idaho — a farm family, a rural, poor family. She had been sexually abused, not just by her father, but by all her male relatives. She was terribly abused. Incidentally, I want to tell those of you who teach girls this, she had tried to tell a couple of times, and people wouldn't believe her. When she was ten years old, they had a lesson in Sunday school on honoring your father and mother. After class was over, she said to her teacher, "But, what if your father or your mother wants to do something that isn't right?"

The teacher said, "Oh, my dear, that would never happen. Your father and your mother would never want anything that wasn't right for you."

Finally, when she was fourteen, her Mia Maid teacher believed her and convinced the bishop it was so. The bishop took her out of that home into his own home where she

179

finished her high school years; he sent her to college, and then she went on a mission. Her father's "patriarchal blessing" when she left his home was this, "Well, aren't we fine folk now? Gonna go live with the bishop and all those holy joes over on the other side of town. Well, let me just tell you something, girl, and don't you never forget it. They can't make a silk purse out of a sow's ear." That's what she decided on her mission. She decided she didn't belong there with all those silk purses. She was having sexual feelings for the missionaries because when you're only four or five when you first get exposed to regular sex, it isn't easy. You don't have the adult's or the teenager's sense of proportion and sense of reality and sense of the world to put it into proportion. So here were all these attractive young men, and she'd never had the opportunity to develop in her life the kinds of protections in her heart and in her mind that other people in more blessed and protected circumstances have. She was having feelings that she believed were unworthy and told herself, "My daddy was right. You can take a girl out of a family and send her to college, you can send her on a mission, but you can't change what she is — a sow's ear."

So she was going home to throw herself away because she didn't belong out here pretending to be someone she wasn't. I said to her, "Before you came on your mission, you went to the temple, didn't you? You were anointed to become a queen, weren't you, a princess in your Heavenly Father's house? That's no way to treat a princess. There may be — I can't imagine it — but there may be some justification in their backgrounds for the way those men treated you when you were young. I don't know; I can't imagine any. But, I'm confident of this, the Lord will not easily forgive you if you treat His daughter that way. You're going to throw her away, a princess of our Heavenly Father? Then what are you going to say to Him when He says, 'How have you handled the stewardship that I gave you of this glorious personage who lived with me, who is my daughter, who is a royal personage of dignity and of honor? I sent her down to the earth, and how have you brought her back to me?' " She with the eloquence of her age and circumstances started to cry, but she stayed.

I saw her in Provo two or three years later when I was there speaking. She asked if I remembered her, and I did, which was a miracle in its own right because I forget my own children's names; I can't get them all straight. I remembered her and her name and said, "How are you doing?" She answered, "I'm growing just as fast as I can. I thought you'd want to know." She understood who she was. I told her that I felt her stewardship was to get that daughter of our Heavenly Father home, home to Heavenly Father, home where she belonged. That's the mystery of the kingdom, that's the mystery of godliness — that we are our Father's children.

Now I'm going to tell you three other stories. One of them concerns a sister I used to home teach years ago. She was something. President Benson was president of the Quorum of the Twelve and used to send out the schedules specifying when stakes had their conferences. For several years in a row we always had our stake conference on Mother's Day. It was nice because you saved money on carnations, but this lady was outraged. She couldn't see why it always had to be our stake on Mother's Day. She wanted the carnations and the respect for women. So she finally wrote a stern letter to President Benson calling him to repentance for not observing the importance of motherhood. She said the priesthood leaders talked a good fight, but where were they when it really counted on Mother's Day? And he changed the date of our stake conference. So you get some feel for this woman — a good woman, but not shy.

Anyway, I was her home teacher and her stake president. She was also one of those sisters who felt that if you just have a cold, it's all right to have your husband give you a blessing, but if it's anything more serious, you need at least the bishop. Stake presidents are better. If there's a general authority in the area, that's the best. She wanted real sparks — none of this home-grown stuff.

They had two or three girls, and she'd had troubles with her deliveries, which were caesarean. Her doctor told her that she had nearly died the last time. He said, "Your uterus is so thin that when I was working there, I could see my hand through it. It is not going to sustain another pregnancy. If you want to die, get pregnant again. Is that very clear? Will you let me take it out?" She said, "No." He said, "It's no good except to kill you." She said, "Don't take it." So he said, "All right, but I want you to know that if you have another pregnancy, you're dead."

Well, that lasted about four years. I accused her of having gone to see *Saturday's Warrior* one time too many. She decided they had a little boy up there waiting to come to their family. Her husband said, "Oh, no, you don't. You think you're going to get pregnant and leave me to raise those girls without you. No way; I'm not going to do that. The doctor told you, and that's sensible, and that's it."

"But I just feel there's still one up there for us."

"No way. We are not going to take any risks with your life. I'm not up to raising three daughters alone. I'm sorry; 'no' is the answer."

"Well, when President Broderick comes, let's have him give me a blessing."

Well, he got to me first, of course, and I couldn't have agreed with him more. I didn't want that on my hands. That's what we have doctors for. So I was not very moved by this woman's ambition to have one more child and said, "Now, look, Sister so-and-so, you can't do this." But this lady is not an easy person to say no to. So her husband and I laid our hands on her head, and I heard myself telling this lady, "Sure, go right ahead and have a baby. No problem. You'll have no problem in the pregnancy; it'll be just fine. You'll have a fine big boy, nurse him, and everything will just be terrific." I could not believe I was saying it. Her husband was looking at me in horror. I left immediately.

But it happened just like the blessing said. It was just one of those stories where the Lord gives you the answer. She got pregnant. The doctor shook his head, but when the baby was delivered, it was fine. The uterus was fine; the baby was terrific. One little hitch—only it wasn't a little hitch; it was a big hitch.

In the hospital somehow she had contracted a blood disease, Haverman's disease. I'd never heard of it before, and I've not heard of it since, but it's vividly etched in my memory. She broke out in spots all over. They're very irritable, like having the skin off your hand or off your back. She had at one point two hundred spots all over her body. She couldn't lie down or sit down or be comfortable anywhere, and they looked awful. It looked like she ought to wear a veil to cover these big red, size-of-a-fifty-cent-piece blotches all over her body. There was a medication she could take to relieve the symptoms. While it doesn't cure the disease, it does make the symptoms go away and allows you to live and function normally. But she couldn't nurse her baby if she took it.

"You promised in the blessing," she said, "that I could nurse this baby."

I said, "It was a throw-away line. What are you talking about?"

She said, "You promised, the Lord promised I could nurse this baby. I can't nurse him and take medication so you have to do something about this."

I said, "Look, get a bottle. Your husband can get up in the middle of the night. It'll be terrific. Take the medication; you're home free — the baby's fine. Rejoice, you've got a beautiful boy."

She would not have any of that. She wanted another blessing to take away this disease so she could nurse this baby. I wished I were not her home teacher, not her stake president. But I put my hands on her head, and I heard myself telling her that her disease would go away and she would be able to nurse this baby. Then I left for New York — not just because of that. I had a meeting in New York, but I did not want to be there hour by hour to see how this worked out.

I gave the blessing on a Sunday evening. Wednesday at 2:00 in the morning, I got a telephone call while I was in a deep sleep. I was president of this national organization and worrying about the next night when I was to give my presidential address. It was hard to sleep, but I was doing my best. The call woke me, and she said, "You promised me these spots would go away, but they're worse. I visited the doctor today,

183

and he says they're worse. Nothing's going well. You promised. I've done everything I know to do. I've been on the telephone all day to people that I might have offended, even in my childhood. 'Please, please, if there's anything I've done to offend you, please forgive me.' I'm trying to think of anything I've ever done in my life and to set it right. But my spots haven't gone away. Why?"

"I don't have any idea why," I said.

She retorted, "Well, don't you think you ought to have an idea. You gave me that blessing."

I felt terrible. I did something I've never done before or since—I stayed up the rest of the night, what there was of it, praying. I said, "Lord, this woman's faith hangs on the blessing she received at my hands. I felt your Spirit at the time. If I was wrong, don't penalize her. Cover me." (And I started thinking of the people I should be calling.)

But she didn't call again, and I thought maybe it's all right. I got home Saturday night late, flying all day from New York, exhausted from the trip. I walked into the house, and there was a note that said, "No matter what time you arrive, call sister so-and-so." I didn't dare not do it, so I phoned her. She said, "You get on over here." Is that any way to talk to a stake president?

It was two o'clock in the morning, but I went over. She was bitter and empty. She said, "I want you to know that I have no faith left. I felt the Spirit of the Lord, the same Spirit when you gave me that blessing, that I've felt in sacrament meetings, in testimony meetings, when I read the scriptures, and in prayer. I felt that same Spirit, and here's my testimony." She raised her hands, which were covered with spots. "Well," she said, "what have you got to say?"

"Nothing."

"Don't you think you owe me an explanation?"

I said, "I have no explanation. I prayed all night. I don't have any idea why. I feel awful that I've been the instrument of your loss of faith. I cannot think of a worse thing that could have happened, that I could have spent my priesthood on, than to destroy your faith."

184

"Don't you think you owe me an explanation?"

"I tell you I have no explanation."

"You and the Lord—don't you think you owe me an explanation?"

"I'm not giving you any more blessings."

She said, "I think you owe me that, don't you?"

I never did anything with less grace in my life than when I laid my hands on her head. The Lord spoke to her, not of her disease and not of nursing babies, but of His love for her— that she was His daughter, that He cared for her, that He had died for her. He said that He would have died if she had been the only one. He would have suffered at Calvary for her sins, if hers had been the only ones. He didn't say one word about healing her.

The next day was fast Sunday. She came to church although she had said she never would again. With the spots she looked awful. It was not easy; she was not an overly proud woman, but it was not easy for her to appear in public looking as she did. She got up in testimony meeting, and her spots were worse than ever. She told the story and at the end she said, "I do not know why I have these spots, why my breasts have dried, but I do know this." And she bore a powerful witness of the Savior's love for her. That afternoon the spots went away and the milk came in, but not until she understood the mysteries of the kingdom, which don't have much to do with spots or milk or even with blessings, but have a lot to do with who we are and who our Father is, who our Savior is, and the relationship among the three of us.

I'm going to tell just two more stories. My mother, I trust, did not have a typical Mormon woman's life. She married three times, but she got better at it as she went along. I've been grateful to her that she didn't stop until she got a good man. He wasn't a member of the Church when she married him, but he eventually did join the Church and became a bishop— a very good man. I'm sealed to him, and I love him. I wear his ring. He wanted me to have it because in his family when somebody died, people quarreled over the tea cups. He wanted me before he died to have the ring so no one would quarrel over it, and I could have it. I wear it with love.

He died, in some ways, in a bad way, a hard way. He was a strong man — a man who'd been a sickly youth, but he'd done some of the Charles Atlas exercises. I used to love to hear him tell about how eventually he'd turned the table on the bullies. I was one who always ran away from bullies, walked to the other side of the street and went home the other way, but I loved to hear his stories about how he'd finally gotten strong enough to take them on and beat them at their own game. I had a lot of vicarious satisfaction from his stories.

But at the end his lungs filled up with fiber so he had only five percent of his lungs to breathe with. With only five percent of the oxygen that he needed to metabolize his food, he just got weaker and weaker. His bones showed everywhere on his body. This big, beefy, all-solid-muscle man got to the point where all of his muscle had been eaten alive. I could easily carry him in my arms, although I'm not a strong man physically. He became petulant and childish because he could hardly breathe. He was constantly asphyxiated. He could hardly eat or go to the bathroom because he didn't have the oxygen to close his mouth that long. What a strain to see this strong, good man waste away.

A week before he died I asked him for a father's blessing. He could reach over only one hand because he couldn't find a position where he could breathe and get both hands together. He gave me a blessing; I'd never had one in my life before. With one hand, he gave me a father's blessing, which I treasure. Then I asked him — and it was more talking than he had done for a long time in one space — I asked, "Vic, what have you learned from this six months of wasting away?"

He said, "Patience; I was never patient. The Lord has taught me patience. I wanted to die six months ago, and He left me. I've had to wait upon Him. You know those stories I used to tell?"

"Yes, the ones I liked so well."

"Son, those aren't good stories; they're full of revenge. They're not loving stories. I repent of them."

That man did not waste those six months. How many of us would have gotten bitter at God? "Why don't you take me? I've done everything; all I want to do is come home." That man spent those months being refined. I know he's presiding today over his family. We've done genealogy for his forebears and sent them up to him to work on in the spirit world. I know he presides over them today, and I know he's a better president of his familial branch in the spirit world than he was a bishop, and he was a good bishop. But, I know he was refined by his pain, by his adversity. He needed to go through that suffering. He could have been embittered; he could have been destroyed. His faith could have soured and left him, but he chose to learn from his pain. I do not want you to think that it was the pain that was good. It was the man that was good and that made the pain work for him, as indeed our Savior did.

Last Easter a friend, after having brought two boys, then four and two, into the world had a baby daughter. While she was in the hospital, her husband wanted to come to see the baby, but he had those little children at home. So his home teacher was kind enough to say, "Hey, bring the kids over. We've got a bunch of kids at our house. Bring the two kids over; my wife'll watch them." (That's not quite what King Benjamin said about service, but it's one step off.) "You go and see your baby."

So he did. While he was in the hospital seeing his new baby, his two-year-old got away from that woman's care and drowned in the pool. Through CPR she was able to bring him back to his heart beating and his lungs working but never to real functioning. For two months he lay in a hospital bed, breathing, with his heart beating on machines that helped. His little knees somehow (I don't understand the mechanics of this) bent backwards. His feet bent backwards. I don't know why. In the rigidity of his coma he became deformed. He had been a perfectly whole, wonderful child, but now it was hard for me to go visit him. I would go and sit beside him, looking at his mother who was rubbing him and singing to him. It was hard.

The ward fasted every Sunday for a month for that child.

They kept a twenty-four-hour vigil so that there'd be somebody he knew there when their faith made him whole. He was blessed by the stake patriarch, by the stake president, by a visiting general authority who was kind enough to add that additional duty to his busy schedule. In all those blessings the mother took hope. I will not say that she was promised flatly, but she took hope by what was said, that the child would live, that she would raise him in this life, and that he would perform many gracious acts and achievements. She would not even tolerate anyone's raising the possibility that he would not get better because she felt that everyone's faith had to be whole and focused.

I never saw so many people at the hospital—dozens of people kept vigil, fasted, and prayed for this child. After two months it became clear the child was wasting away and was not going to get better. His mother was the last to finally acknowledge what everyone else came to see—he was not going to live. It was costing, I forget how many, thousands of dollars a day. So they finally decided to do the gracious thing and let him return to his Father. It was the hardest thing they ever did. They prayed, fasted, consulted with priesthood leaders and finally, finally, decided the only thing to do was to pull the tubes. His mother said, "I can't stand it. I don't want to kill that little boy again. How many times is he going to die?"

So his grandmother went and held him in her arms when they pulled the tubes, but he didn't die. He lived another two weeks. I cannot express to you how spiritually exhausted everybody was when he finally died. The family had spent days and nights for weeks with him. Everybody had scarcely slept in two and a half months. Just a week before that baby died, the newborn got a temperature of 105 and was taken to the hospital and diagnosed with spinal meningitis. It was a misdiagnosis, but they put the baby in the room just right down from the other baby.

Her husband said, "Honey, let me go bless the baby."

She said, "You get your priesthood hands off my baby." She didn't want God to take that baby too. She said, "God's got all the babies he wants. Why does he want my baby? God doesn't need him on a mission—don't tell me that." People are not always helpful with the things they say. "God needs him worse than I need him—don't tell me that. He's got billions of babies, and I only have one; I have one two-year-old. Don't tell me he has a mission that can't wait fifty or sixty years more on the other side. There's lots of work for him here. We'll keep him busy."

At the graveside the grandmother gave the opening prayer, and the grandfather dedicated the grave. In a somewhat unusual choice, both the boy's parents spoke. Can you imagine that? What they said was this: "We trust our faith will never again be tried as it has on this occasion. The things we have faith in have come down to a short list, but that list is immovable. We do not have faith that God must do what we entreat Him to do." Earlier she had cried out to God, "I asked for a fish, and I got a serpent. I asked for a loaf, and I got a rock. Is that what the scriptures promise?"

But after it was all over, at her little son's graveside, she was able to say, "I am content that God be God. I will not try to instruct Him on His duties or on His obligations toward me or toward any of His children. I know He lives and loves us, that He is God. He's not unmindful of us. We do not suffer out of His view. He does not inflict pain upon us, but He sustains us in our pain. I am his daughter; my son is also His son; we belong to Him, and we are safe with Him. I used to think we were safe from grief and pain here because of our faith. I know now that is not true, but we are safe in His love. We are protected in the most ultimate sense of all—we have a safe home forever. That is my witness."

And that is my witness to you, that God lives, and He does not live less though you have injustice and adversity and pain and unkindness and violence and betrayal. God is in His heaven. We chose to come to an unjust world and suffer. But God is God, and He loves us. His son died for us. There is for each of us, because of who we are and who He is and who we are together, hope. There is hope. The uses of adversity are whatever use we put them to—for you and for me, for the parents of the little boy, for the lady with Haverman's disease, and for the incest victims, for my dad, for all of us — the uses of adversity are the uses we put them to. May they hone us and purify us and teach us and not destroy us, because of who we are and who God is and what our relationship to Him is, is my fervent prayer.

Communities of Love

SHARI E. PACK

*J*ust as my own dear parents yearned and prayed for the birth of their children, my husband and I have also prayed for the birth of each of our children. As each child was born, it has been for me like opening a very special present, a gift from our Father in Heaven, a precious surprise of inestimable worth whose value grows with time. I have sometimes wondered, as this tiny soul has been placed in my arms, if at birth those spirits who have associated with the new baby before mortality have mixed feelings such as we do at death, rejoicing for the loved one's chance for progression beyond mortality but mourning the loss of the loved one's presence for a time.

Death is for all of us a separation of an undetermined length. From our point of view here, death is so final. No matter how we miss the one who has died, we cannot contact them. My husband and I have experienced the death of a child twice in our life together. The first time we were rather young. Our third child, a son, was born one beautiful balmy evening in Hawaii in the Kahuku Hospital amid the sugar cane. I remember how easy the birth had been and how nonchalant I was about everything. I had another beautiful boy—it had almost been too easy. His heart defect did not show, and when he died, it was so quick and final. But we live in communities of love. The first is our family, and the other that we become aware of very soon and that will help us all our life, if we let it, is the Church. At the graveside funeral our good bishop in his talk promised us that we would be blessed with other children. His words were an answer to our prayers. And indeed his

Shari E. Pack, homemaker and music teacher, received a degree in vocal music from Brigham Young University—Hawaii. She has taught voice and harp at Ricks College and has served as choir leader in her ward. She and her husband, David, are the parents of thirteen children, eleven of whom are living.

promise was fulfilled. Within two and a half years we had two wiggly, special boys: as a dear Polynesian sister of faith said to me, "The Lord took one away and gave you two."

Many times it has come to me that we can be the answer to someone's prayer by what we do or say. We can be a great force for good without our knowing, if we are trying to serve the Lord. The bishop's promise and the Polynesian sister's words of faith were such forces for good.

Our second experience with the death of a child came just a few years ago in Idaho where we now live. Our oldest son, seventeen years old, collapsed and died after running in a long distance race. Evidently his heart could not take the stress of long running. He had been such a choice young man. This son, this gift from our Heavenly Father, had grown in value to us over time, and we did not want to let him go. My good husband's priesthood healing blessing for our son in the hospital, as the doctors were working frantically to bring him back, was answered with a quiet "No." And then we began to search for answers from the scriptures and the prophets. What a community of love is found in the Church writings and the gospel of Jesus Christ. We were taught that the priesthood blessing was right, but that our son had been appointed unto death and was to join his brother in the next world of spirits.

So many people answered my prayers for understanding and comfort during this period. These people did not know they were answering my prayer; they were only being a part of this community of love in the Church. One gray afternoon I was driving home. It had been raining slightly, and as I drove up the wet hill, I noticed a sister walking to her home. The Spirit whispered to me, "Pick her up." I really didn't know her very well; but, after a brief argument with myself, I turned my car around, went back to where she was, and offered her a ride. What a sweet feeling she gave me in those five minutes as I drove her home. She told me of a recent fast meeting in her ward, during which a young man had borne his testimony and had talked about our son who had died and the work that he would be doing in the spirit world. This young man had prayed for understanding and received inspiration that there was an eternal purpose for our son's death. How grateful I was for her words that reinforced what I had thought and felt.

Several months later I was participating in a musical program in another city. I have often found that when I have accepted opportunities to participate in meetings I would not ordinarily attend, such participation aids me; I learn something I would not otherwise have learned, or something is brought into my life that I would have missed. After the program an older man came up to me. He had read my name in the program and asked if I were related to ---------, and he gave the name of our son. "Yes," I said. "I am his mother. Did you know him?" He said, "I did not meet him when he was alive, and yet I feel as if I know him very well." He took off his coat and laid it on the edge of the pulpit and talked about our son for a long time. He explained that he worked for the county with the assignment to prepare the dead bodies and assist in the examination of them. He had experienced an unusual feeling as he had been asked to work with our son's body. He sensed that this young man was righteous, and he felt he knew all about him. He wanted me to know that our son's body had been treated with great respect and care. I treasured those words and pondered them, recognizing them as part of the community of love, and another example of answered prayer through other people's words and actions.

In the Doctrine and Covenants a scripture has become important to me.

"Wherefore, fear not even unto death; for in this world your joy is not full, but in me your joy is full.

"Therefore, care not for the body, neither the life of the body; but care for the soul, and for the life of the soul.

"And seek the face of the Lord always, that in patience ye may possess your souls, and ye shall have eternal life." (D&C 101:36-38.)

I have thought about these words, to "seek the face of the Lord *always* that in *patience* ye may possess your souls, and have eternal life." (Italics added.) For me this translates into striving each day to become better, to be worthy to seek the face of the Lord. Each new day gives us many opportunities;

how wonderful it would be to live so that we could be the answer to someone's prayer. I am glad that we are taught weekly in our meetings and are reminded continually of the things that will help us in our life, such as daily prayer and daily study, for I believe that it is through our daily actions that we are seeking "the face of the Lord." Another key word in that scripture for me is "patience," since perfection is built slowly as we go on from grace to grace. We are all striving to be on the straight and narrow path that leads to eternal life, but we each are in different places along the route. As we help each other along the way, we also help ourselves, for we really cannot be exalted alone.

There is an additional example of how my prayers were answered by others in the communities of love that surround us all. A year after the death of which I have spoken, I was asked to come to the cemetery for a special graveside service for a woman I did not know, who had spent her life working to establish and maintain a hospital in Hawaii. Her family had brought her body back to Idaho and wanted me to sing "Aloha Oe" as a final good-bye to this beloved sister at her graveside service. In reality it seems that I came to learn and feel as well as to sing. As we waited around the grave, I saw members of the family and friends arrive and mingle quietly, and yet so happy to see each other among the grave markers and granite tombstones. I could feel with them what a pleasure it was to be together after the periods of separation, and I thought about the resurrection—how much more joyous would be their greetings and radiant faces if they were there to bring someone forth from the grave and not to bury them. There was a beautiful feeling of love in the cemetery among those special people. It taught me to look forward to the promises of the resurrection, that we all will be brought forth from the grave. It is almost impossible to imagine such a joyous time!

The words of a new hymn describe better what I feel:

> Savior, may I learn to love thee,
> Walk the path that thou has shown,
> Pause to help and lift another,

Finding strength beyond my own.
. . . .
I would be my brother's keeper;
I would learn the healer's art.
To the wounded and the weary
I would show a gentle heart.
Savior, may I love my brother
As I know thou lovest me,
Find in thee my strength, my beacon,
For thy servant I would be.
Savior, may I love my brother—
Lord, I would follow thee.[1]

I am grateful for the love and the answers to prayer that I have experienced in my life. I am grateful for the promised resurrection. I pray that we may always seek the face of the Lord in our lives and live so that we can be the answer to another's prayer.

Note

1. Susan Evans McCloud, "Lord, I Would Follow Thee," *Hymns* (Salt Lake City: The Church of Jesus Christ of Latter-day Saints, 1985), no. 220; used by permission.

Worse Is Better

SIGNE HALE GILLUM

J began my "great balancing act" about eight years ago. Our family's life was relatively smooth and uneventful, except for the birth of nine of our children, the eighth and ninth being twins. Our business was beginning to show signs of success, we were building our dream home, the children were bright and healthy, we were active in the community, school, and church, and were raising two Navajo daughters.

Then, in January 1978, the roof fell in on our world. I was eight and one half months pregnant with our tenth child, when my husband slipped into unconsciousness one morning. The doctors soon discovered that three of my husband's main arteries to the heart were 60 to 90 percent closed, and he would need bypass surgery to stay alive. Everything happened so fast that I didn't have time to think or plan anything. I hadn't even packed a bag and ended up staying at the hospital for the next four weeks. The doctors didn't want me to travel the thirty miles each way from home to the hospital because I could deliver any minute.

Three days after my husband passed out, he had triple bypass surgery. The operation went beautifully. In fact, the doctor said the angels were in attendance. My husband had every expectation for a long, healthy life. He seemed to be recuperating normally, but ten days later, while still in the hospital, he had a stroke. I don't know why I didn't crumble

Signe Hale Gillum, a graduate of Brigham Young University in music education and member of the Utah Valley Symphony, worked for four years as departmental assistant in the history/religion reference section of the Harold B. Lee Library at BYU. She co-chairs with her husband the Springville, Utah, Historical Preservation Commission. She has been a stake missionary, ward music director, and teacher in the auxiliaries. Her marriage to Gary P. Gillum after the death of her first husband created a family of seventeen children, her eleven and his six.

right then and there, but I didn't. It seemed that I knew I had to do whatever had to be done, even though I didn't know what that was. I do know that two very important things helped: my knowledge of the Savior and tremendous family support, both from my husband's family and my own.

Two weeks after my husband's stroke, I delivered our third son. My husband didn't realize the birth had occurred until several weeks afterwards. After leaving the hospital, I continued to visit my husband for the next six weeks while he was in rehabilitation. He was ready to come home three months later.

Then the trials *really* began. The stroke was disastrous to my husband. I hadn't known up to that time that he had a very low self-image. When we met at BYU, he was a "big man on campus" —yearbook editor and photographer and well-respected and liked. During our marriage, he was always in control, very much the patriarch. I was a new member of the Church and very anxious to be a model Mormon wife and mother. I went about raising children, helping in the business, and learning the gospel. It was a good life. But it's better now, and let me tell you why it's better.

As my husband's personality altered, he became increasingly demanding; his temper was violent, he began using terrible language, and his judgment was very poor. He also became severely depressed and was suicidal for about four years following his stroke. On top of that, his diabetes was completely out of control, which caused further emotional and physical damage.

Three months after my husband came home, we lost our business. He had been in and out of the hospital several times for his depression. Shortly thereafter we also lost our home and moved to Provo, to a nice, but smaller, home. We were surviving but drowning in debt. I began to feel trapped in an impossible situation. I cried until I couldn't cry anymore and prayed until all I could do was groan. On the outside I appeared strong and in control (everyone asked, "How do you do it?"), but on the inside, I was a mess.

After about a year of incredible verbal abuse to me and our children, my husband was convinced by the bishop and the doctors to get psychiatric help. We went together and over the next few years "wore out" four different doctors. If my husband wasn't helped, I certainly was. I learned a lot and, gradually, I began to pull myself together.

After much thought and prayer, and advice and help from family, I decided to look for work. I didn't know what I could do, but I could type and I did have a degree, so I began looking. I was very fortunate to find the very good job I have now. It has helped me learn how to talk to people, to see life from different perspectives, and to really appreciate home.

I learned to talk to people, to neighbors, the bishop, friends and family. When the neighbors came to help me clean house, we shared our experiences. I appreciate those times. I discovered that many people have very similar problems — parents who have had strokes, family members on the verge of divorce, and loved ones facing death or terrible illnesses. It was so good to talk, to share ideas on how to cope, and to help each other by just listening and understanding.

We cultivated our already-established family traditions — making gingerbread houses and taking them to friends and neighbors at Christmastime, visiting friends and making new friends at nursing homes. Our children transferred the skills of compassion they learned at the nursing homes to their daily coping with their father, and even though he never got well, there were many times that he responded positively. Gradually, the children and I were able to feel calm and in control, even when he responded negatively. Each of the children, even the little ones, began to see things in an eternal perspective. Having expensive toys and clothes no longer mattered to them; unthoughtful children calling them names didn't bother them; their studies at school became more important; and getting along with each other became top priority.

I learned to exercise. I began to walk and do aerobics. My mind cleared up; I felt better about everything, and I had more energy.

I learned that the main ingredient was a good attitude — not a Pollyanna attitude, but a positive, realistic one, looking at all the beautiful things around me but recognizing the problems and dealing with them in a positive way.

I discovered I *was* strong and had been all along, but I hadn't realized it. I found out I was intelligent and capable of making decisions. I learned to do the bookkeeping; it took seven years, but we are now out of debt.

One of the nicest things I have learned is the "soft touch." If someone I love is out of control and shouting at me, I just reach out and lightly touch his or her arm and force myself not to yell back. It's impossible to be angry with that person, when I have done that simple thing. At least, it really works for me.

I learned not to envy others or their accomplishments. It was incredible to discover that my friends, the eloquent, highly educated ones, the famous ones, the accomplished ones, all had serious problems, problems I am very glad I don't have.

I have learned there is not just one right way to do something, that my way may not be the way someone else may do it, but, if it works for me, it's okay.

I have learned to be less discouraged and to pick myself up and try again, over and over and over again.

I have learned how important it is to completely submit myself to the Lord. My favorite scripture has come to be Psalm 46:10, "Be still, and know that I am God." This means to me to be calm, that God is in control, and everything will be all right. I just have to do my best and be patient. I have learned to talk to the Lord every moment, in all situations, not just on my knees morning and night, but any time. I pray when I'm typing, or driving, or walking from one place to another, or playing my violin—even when I'm disciplining children! The Lord is always there, and I know it. The biggest trick is to really listen and understand His answers. But I know that whatever happens is a means for me and mine to grow.

I have learned that one of the best ways to forget or at least minimize my own problems is to serve someone else. It is rejuvenating to do something nice for someone.

I have learned not to waste my time thinking about Satan. He has no power over me, only to instill fear in me. People have the power of God to overcome their problems, and we should rejoice, because God finds us worthy and capable of great things.

Coping with our situation has had its price, however. Being a musician, I hunger to give my children music lessons, but I don't have time to teach them myself and can't afford private lessons. But music is still in our home, and the children have learned to appreciate all kinds of good music and to discern the good from the bad. It's very gratifying to me to tiptoe past their bedroom doors and hear them listening to good music while they are doing homework or just visiting with each other.

Home evenings, as a structured time, have been mostly abandoned, because my husband hasn't the ability to lead or contribute in a positive way. Instead, I try to make every moment a family home evening, either with several children together (around the dinner table), or one-on-one. I think they are learning the gospel just as well that way.

A big price for me is our messy house. Much of the time our house isn't very clean. I used to despair, but I began to realize we're doing our best under the circumstances. The children and I have drawn very close to each other; we have learned to talk openly and to express our feelings and frustrations, and to have fun with each other. We just try to be happy and loving, and that is very important to me.

Through all of these experiences, I have learned much. Many of the problems are still with me, but by learning to see more clearly and using new skills, I have been enabled to cope better. I know that as Heavenly Father's children, if we not only endure our trials but learn from them, we will conquer them and become capable of great things.

UNDERSTANDING OUR WORLD

We need to lengthen our stride, learn everything we possibly can, and develop our talents so we can serve God's children in the best possible way.... As we become prepared and empowered, the Lord can pluck us out of His scabbard and use us wherever and whenever He needs us.

—IDA SMITH

LDS Women: At Home and Beyond

IDA SMITH

*W*omen at home and beyond is a topic of current interest. I would like to explore with you what it might mean for us collectively or individually in our rapidly changing society. These ideas are gleaned from my own personal observations and from working with women for many years and are not intended in any way to be a pronouncement to the women of the Church. Rather, they are intended to stimulate thoughtful contemplation surrounding some very difficult issues for women today. I share these with you for what they might be worth and pray that what is said will be helpful as you—and your own personal revelator, the Holy Ghost—plot the course of your destiny.

Some of you will identify with some things, and some with others. We all do not fit just one mold. Some of you are married and at home full-time with husband and children. Some are married and working to subsidize the family income in order to put children through school or to support them on missions. Some are divorced and working to support yourselves and perhaps your children. Some are older and widowed with empty nests; others are young and widowed with children still at home. Some of you have never married, but many—of all ages—still hope to be. Some have serious financial worries, while others are financially secure and will probably never have to worry about where their next meal or their next

Ida Smith, founding director of the Women's Research Institute at Brigham Young University, is currently coordinator of Student/ Alumni Programs at BYU. She received her B.A. from the University of Utah and is pursuing a Ph.D. with the Union Graduate School. Previously she worked for fifteen years as office manager with the National Association of Manufacturers. A popular and widely traveled lecturer, she has served in various Church capacities including ward and stake Young Women presidencies, Gospel Doctrine and Relief Society teacher, and member of a BYU Relief Society stake board.

month's rent will come from. There is no set of answers to fit all of the above situations, because they have different sets of questions.

I feel a need for us to be honest with ourselves, with our families, and with each other. I saw a fascinating educational film recently entitled *The Abilene Paradox*, which deals with this issue of being honest with ourselves and others. The film depicts four individuals (two couples) who end up traveling a fair distance on a hot summer afternoon to have dinner in Abilene. They later discover that none of them wanted to go. They all went because they thought everyone else wanted to go, and no one wanted to play the spoilsport. Being honest with ourselves and admitting our own needs must be central to the plotting of our destinies, because if we cannot be true to ourselves, we will ultimately find it impossible to be true to anyone else.

Our lives are filled with paradoxes and hard questions. One of the most often asked questions I hear is: how can I prepare for a career (i.e., to acquire a marketable skill in order to care for myself and perhaps, if necessary, care for dependent children as well) and at the same time prepare to be a wife and mother in the home? And I want to ask: can you be the wife and mother you need to be in this era of the world and not acquire a marketable skill? Sister Camilla Kimball stated it best:

"I would hope that every girl and woman here has the desire and ambition to qualify in two vocations — that of home-making, and that of preparing to earn a living outside the home, if and when the occasion requires. An unmarried woman is always happier if she has a vocation in which she can be socially of service and financially independent. . . . Any married woman may become a widow without warning. Property may vanish as readily as a husband may die. Thus, any woman may be under the necessity of earning her own living and helping to support dependent children. If she has been trained for the duties and emergencies of life which may come to her, she will be much happier and have a greater sense of security."[1]

Some of the ideas I am going to present may be frightening — or seem threatening — to some. I plead with you to stay with me and not read selectively what I write. As we think about the admonition to be at home and some of the implications of "going beyond," we must consider how we define "home." Is a "home" to you as a chador might be to a woman of Islam: a veil to be worn at all times and forever, the leaving of which is to be seen as creating an offense to your society as serious as a Muslim woman's removing her veil might be to hers? Is a home, then, to be a woman's prison? Is she to be labeled deviant should she desire, or try, or need to leave? What does it do to a woman psychologically to feel that she is "taking off her veil" if it becomes necessary — for whatever reason — to venture beyond the walls of her own home?

Do we define home narrowly as the four-walled structure in which we live? Or do we more broadly think of home with the many facets listed in a dictionary which move from a "personal dwelling place," to the "city, state or country" in which we were born or reared, to a "restful congenial place where one is comfortable and likes to be"? Let us take a look for a moment at what a home has been historically.

A home two hundred years ago was a manufacturing and producing center where children were regarded as extra hands rather than as additional mouths to feed, and husband and wife were considered business partners, both of whose activities were considered economically essential to the survival of the family.

Home, historically, has been a center of learning. Many of our great leaders, such as Abraham Lincoln, received their educations at home — in humble homes — rather than in the hallowed ivy-covered walls of a university. Homes were social and community centers long before buildings were built specifically for those purposes. Home was a base from which to make things happen; the results of these efforts would influence the family, city, state, nation, and even the world. Some of the most important religious movements in history, including the restoration of the LDS Church, began in someone's home. Indeed, the lion's share of the teaching of the gospel in our day takes place in homes. One of our most famous homes, the

Beehive House in Salt Lake City, was the center of activity for much that transpired in the early Church in Utah. During the years the Beehive House was home for Brigham Young, it resembled Grand Central Station as virtually every dignitary who passed through Salt Lake City was entertained there. President Young brought the world to his family, and the family was enriched thereby.

The spread of the gospel in ancient times as now has been quickened or slowed to the extent of the members' willingness to open their homes to missionaries and non-members. Martha set the example: she enriched not only her guests and her brother's and sister's lives, but her own as well as she listened to the gospel in her own home from the Savior himself.

Joseph and Emma Smith had people from all walks of life pour through their home, many of whom stayed for extended periods of time, and went away the better for the experience. Their home was a place where connections were made and growth was encouraged. Perhaps in our efforts to maintain our homes as havens from a hostile world, we sometimes exclude rather than expand to include what is noble, exciting, or worthwhile in the world. Where better to learn about and become prepared for the outside world than within the walls of one's own home? If we are to feel comfortable (at home) in a variety of places, be they the halls of legislatures, offices of business, courts of law, or classrooms, where better to gain knowledge and self-confidence than within the walls of our own homes?

I was fortunate to grow up in a home where our parents brought the world to us in wonderful ways. Our house in Honolulu was host for thousands from every conceivable walk of life: social, religious, governmental, and educational circles. Some of my best childhood memories are of being allowed to sit on the fringes and listen to the grownups visit (we were seen and not heard on those occasions). We listened to individuals renowned in their own spheres, Church authorities, professors in a variety of fields from all over the country— visitors who would never have been in our home were it not for our parents' dual involvement outside it. Unfortunately, Mother never kept track of all the people who stayed at, let alone visited, our house in Honolulu. But during the thirty years we lived there, the number was in the thousands. I was very glad that my parents were not absorbed with material things and that having a very modest home and possessions did not deter them from inviting anyone to come into it.

Both our parents were teachers. As children we were convinced that it was necessary for us to be poor so that Mother would have to teach. We were convinced that the Lord recognized that all those little non-LDS children needed her love and guidance, too! I never thought of her as a "working mother." I thought of her as a mother and a teacher—both worthy vocations, one inside the home and one outside it. We learned a lot through her experiences as she, as well as my father, brought colleagues and students home.

In the early sixties Father did two exchanges with professors in New York, and our family lived on Long Island. One of those years Mother taught at a Jewish yeshiva. She brought the rabbi home one evening, not for dinner, since he ate only kosher and our kitchen was not equipped to cook kosher, but for a long visit with the family. He taught the children much about his religion and the Jewish culture. Mother always felt that life would be very dull if you did not reach out to those around you—and so she and my father always did.

On another occasion in New York my father invited four of his students to dinner: one Greek, one Russian, one Jewish, and one black. All came but the Russian. It was 1960, and the civil rights movement was making headlines. The Jewish student described what he thought the blacks were experiencing, the black described what the blacks were, in fact, experiencing, the Greek tried to mediate, and my siblings will never forget it! That experience forever colored my sister's view of the civil rights movement, giving her insights she might never have had otherwise. And that connection was made in the home.

On another occasion in Hawaii Father invited a black professor to dinner. The one-on-one experience with this fine man forever destroyed the "black stereotype" in the minds of my brothers and sisters. How many of us are guilty of not bringing members of other churches or races into our homes for fear they will somehow contaminate us — instead of thinking how such contacts and connections can broaden and enrich our family's experiences? Or how many of us do not bring strangers in because we doubt our own abilities to deal with what is outside our prior experience and, therefore, outside our comfort zones? Mother's comfort zone was critically stretched the night we had ninety people at a fireside in Honolulu. She feared our house on wooden stilts would not be able to sustain the weight!

A home is a place where people learn to connect: first with Mother and Father, then with siblings, aunts, uncles, and cousins, widening the concentric circles until we feel connected as the family of God, which includes us all. At issue here is the question: will we accept full adulthood within the family of God, and if we do, what does that mean? What does it mean to establish a home? When the Lord said, "Organize yourselves; prepare every needful thing, and establish a house, even a house of prayer, a house of fasting, a house of faith, a house of learning, a house of glory, a house of order, a house of God" (D&C 109:8), did He not intend that description for our own homes as well as for the building of a temple?

The importance of building a home in which all who live therein can thrive and grow cannot be overemphasized. And in the scheme of things there is no question that women have a vitally important place there. Problems begin to arise for women when we fail to distinguish between what it means to be at home and what it means to be mentally housebound.

First, let us examine some of the reasons we stay at home in addition to child-rearing responsibilities: is it not safe there? Do we not feel secure and know that we will be taken care of there? (Any of you who have been through a divorce and consequently forced out of the home to be a breadwinner have learned that that sense of security can be illusory.) There may be less pressure to change there. Familiar chores fill the day and with this routine comes a sense of belonging. If you have done what is expected of you, you feel you have a right to be happy. That is why feelings of malaise are so disquieting. How often I have heard women complain: "I have a wonderful husband, lovely children, money to spare. I have no 'right' or 'reason' to be depressed—so what is wrong with me?" The facts are that women are twice as likely to suffer depression as are men, and doctors tend to prescribe more drugs for women than for men suffering from depression. The greatest drug abuse in Utah—and perhaps elsewhere—continues to be with prescription drugs. According to the *Deseret News*, Utah has the highest per capita drug prescription rate in the country, and the highest abuse is among women ages thirty-five to fifty who are at home full time.[2] Any woman who must have downers to get to sleep at night, uppers to get out of bed in the morning, and something else in between just to get through the day is demonstrating neither a positive self-esteem nor control over her life.

Medical research shows overwhelming evidence that both positive self-esteem and good health are related to the degree of control a person feels over events in his or her life. Women who do feel they are in control of their lives rarely need to abuse drugs to help them function. Eating disorders—anorexia and bulimia—are other serious problems for women, which also grow out of problems of low self-esteem and issues of control. We tend to be happy in large part to the degree we feel we have control of our own lives. A bird in a gilded cage—no matter how opulent the cage—is still in prison. A gorgeous spacious house on a hill can be a prison to the woman who is confined there if she sees it as the *only* proper place for her to be. If the door of the bird cage were opened, many a bird might very well stay, but knowing she had the option to spread her wings and fly occasionally would in all likelihood make her staying a happier experience. So, too, with the woman who stays at home because she *wants* to, not because she *has* to.

It is crucial for a woman's mental health that she have victories of her own, accomplishments for which she alone is responsible. If she lives only through the accomplishments of her husband or her children, she runs the risk of either becoming a nag or feeling that if *they* fail, *she* is a failure. We all at one time or another make a big mistake in thinking we are, or can be, responsible for the happiness of others. No person can make another person happy. Abraham Lincoln once said that a man is just about as happy as he decides to be. We need to be concerned about our own happiness. Happy people shed their own sunlight, warming others as they warm themselves. They give of themselves freely, dispensing joy to those around them; blessed is the home that has such people in it. But no individual can make another happy unless that person is already inclined to be happy. Women who feel that *they* are responsible for the happiness of their husband and children have placed themselves in a no-win situation. If family members are in a mode of daring their mother to make them happy, no matter how much she does for them, it will never be enough. Many abused mothers and battered wives have had to learn this lesson the hard way. Children need to be reared to understand that they are not only responsible for their own things and their own rooms, but for their own moods and their own happiness as well. Husbands need to understand that principle too, as children will learn responsibility by modeling responsible parents.

Often women seeing their own children having problems will entrench themselves in the home in the belief that pulling up the drawbridge and backing off from all outside activities will somehow "fix" their children's problems when, in fact, perspectives and insights they might gain from working with others in the Church and in the community might offer them the very things they need in order to deal with problems at home in a more effective way.

Too often, also, many of us put on our veils and feel justified in shunning our responsibilities and withholding contributions (i.e., hiding our light under a bushel) to the community by using "my place is in the home" as an excuse not to be involved with or responsible for anything that happens outside it. There are others who feel so secure and comfortable at home they want someone else — anyone else — to deal with any trouble or unpleasantness that might arise in the community. If so-called "adult" bookstores and movies abound in your community, you need to be concerned about it. If there are drugs in your children's school, or if there are antichrist or atheistic ideas being taught to your children, you need to be concerned about them. If satanism is taking root in your community (and it is in some Utah communities), you had better be concerned about it. Paraphrasing Edmund Burke, all that is necessary for evil to triumph is that good men — and good women — do nothing. The best way for you to protect your home might be to take off your veil and spend a few volunteer hours in your local school, hospital, or shelter for the homeless, or to monitor school board and city council meetings or sessions of the state legislature. You may determine that you can best serve your child and affect the climate in which he is growing up by running for an office in one of these bodies yourself. If you wait to engage the battle until it has reached your own door, you may very well be too late.

Family concerns and issues do not stop at the front door of our houses. To show we care, sometimes we will have to do things outside the home. Mothers with small children may not have the freedom to do what they might later when the children are older or in school, but they still have options, such as using the telephone or exercising the power of the pen. If your imagination has atrophied to the point where you cannot even imagine an activity outside the home, perhaps you are doing not only yourself and your family a disservice but your community and the world as well.

Being "housebound" is a state of mind, not just a physical state. *There is nothing wrong with being at home.* But if you are at home because you feel there is no other choice, you are denying God's greatest gift to His children: agency.

If we could only grasp the enormity and significance of this gift, we would do everything in our power to sustain and defend it. The Lord evidently felt strongly enough about our right to exercise agency that He prepared a land and a government founded on the principle that all men are created equal and are endowed by their creator with certain inalienable rights. Two hundred years after the Revolution we have taken those words so for granted that we forget how much the principles of equality must have chafed England's King George III,

211

who believed some (England-born Englishmen) were more equal than others (the new "Americans"), and who, believing in the divine right of kings, ruled in England because "God had ordained it." As long as King George held his view of the world and the new Americans clung to their beliefs, war was inevitable. Because our government was founded on the principle of free agency with man being endowed at birth with rights from God, the restored gospel has survived.

We deny the gift of agency to whatever extent we live our lives in an externally controlled world, where rules for all our actions come from outside ourselves. We skew our own growth if we spend our lives trying to live up to someone else's expectations and plans for us rather than listening to and following the Spirit's directives to us personally. From the beginning of the restoration we have been exhorted by our leaders to seek and follow the Spirit for guidance in our own lives. Speaking in the Tabernacle on January 12, 1862, Brigham Young said:

"I am more afraid that this people have so much confidence in their leaders that they will not inquire for themselves of God whether they are led by Him. I am fearful they settle down in a state of blind self-security, trusting their eternal destiny in the hands of their leaders with a reckless confidence that in itself would thwart the purposes of God in their salvation, and weaken that influence they could give to their leaders, did they know for themselves, by the revelations of Jesus, that they are led in the right way. Let every man and woman know, by the whispering of the Spirit of God to themselves, whether their leaders are walking in the path the Lord dictates, or not. This has been my exhortation continually. . . .

"Break not the spirit of any person, but guide it to feel that it is its greatest delight and highest ambition to be controlled by the revelations of Jesus Christ; then the will of man becomes godlike . . . [and] God shall reign within us to will and do of his good pleasure.

"Let all persons be fervent in prayer, until they know the things of God for themselves and become certain that they are walking in the path that leads to everlasting life; then will envy, the child of ignorance, vanish, and there will be no disposition in any man to place himself above another: for such a feeling meets no countenance in the order of heaven."[3]

At an April general conference in our own time President Ezra Taft Benson stated similarly:

"Usually the Lord gives us the overall objectives to be accomplished and some guidelines to follow, but he expects us to work out most of the details and methods. The methods and procedures are usually developed through study and prayer and by living so that we can obtain and follow the promptings of the Spirit. Less spiritually advanced people, such as those in the days of Moses, had to be commanded in many things. Today those spiritually alert look at the objectives, check the guidelines laid down by the Lord and his prophets, and then prayerfully act — without having to be commanded 'in all things.' This attitude prepares men for godhood."[4]

This is not to say that following the Spirit may not sometimes seem risky or dangerous, causing us or others discomfort. A passerby watching Nephi from a side street the night he separated Laban's head from his body might not have thought, "There goes a future prophet about his Father's business." And yet not only was Manasseh's posterity blessed because of Nephi's obedience to the Spirit, but Ephraim's and the whole of the house of Israel's as well. Mary Fielding Smith incurred the displeasure of her wagon master by deciding to come West when she did, but she was following the voice of the Spirit to her and came despite the displeasure. Her descendants, numbering in the thousands, are the beneficiaries of her obedience to its promptings.

Ann Littlefield was told by the Spirit to leave her abusive husband in England and bring her children to Zion in Utah. She did so at great personal sacrifice to herself, having to go against conventional wisdom in order to follow the Spirit's prompting for her. Because of her courage, hundreds of her own descendants have enjoyed the blessings of the restored gospel, and thousands more have been brought to a similar knowledge through the missionary labors of her posterity. If Mary Fielding Smith had not had the courage of her convictions, my father might not have been raised in the Church, and if

Ann Littlefield had not been similarly strong, a host of my mother's cousins would not have been members either. If anything, the Lord needs even stronger women now than He did a hundred and forty years ago to help bring the wagons across the plains. We are headed toward the winding up scene. The world is being polarized. Women strong enough to lay claim to being daughters of Rebecca are needed as never before: first, to *listen* to the spirit of revelation to themselves, and then to take courage in their knowledge and convictions to follow it.

We can live our lives with "I should" and "I ought" rather than "I want," but that does not exemplify a use of agency. We are taught in the gospel of Jesus Christ that to achieve godhood and become like our Father and Mother in Heaven means to grow in righteousness to the point that our desires and actions have become aligned with Theirs, that we do what we do, not because we have to or because we are commanded to, but because we want to, because that is our choice! That ideal state cannot be reached without our exercising agency.

No two of us are alike. We have not had identical backgrounds, our current experiences vary enormously, our timetables are not the same. It is important that we not compare ourselves with others, which often causes us to see ourselves in a negative light. Also, we must constantly guard against the temptation to assume that where there is a difference, there must also automatically be a defect. Too often we not only berate ourselves, but each other as well, saying, "If you were really a righteous woman, you would/wouldn't be doing what you're doing!" If we are honestly doing what we feel we must do for ourselves and our loved ones, and are doing so because that is our choice, ratified by the Spirit, we have the right to feel good about ourselves and to be free of feelings of guilt. There is a world of difference between *being* guilty and *feeling* guilty, and women are far too prone to allow themselves to feel guilty when they are not living up to someone else's expectations of what they should or should not be doing. My youngest sister started college the fall my father died. When Mother returned to Honolulu after the funeral, she returned to an empty house. It took a while before she stopped feeling she had to go home right after school every day. She felt guilty about not going home to prepare dinner and had to remind herself there was no one at home waiting for her, no one but herself to prepare dinner for when she got there. It took a while for her to let the guilty muscles atrophy and to learn to readjust her life to an empty nest: one devoid of husband as well as children.

I learned a great lesson from watching my mother in her travels after my father died. She traveled to see and be with her children and to go to school for a year at BYU. Mother has a marvelous way of sinking her roots to China no matter where she goes, and in a very short time she is truly "at home" wherever she is. Home does not have to be a geographic location, but can be anywhere you allow yourself to feel comfortable — i.e., any place you extend yourself to make connections. If you confine yourself to a physical spot rather than to a frame of mind, you are truly limiting your capacity to exercise agency.

An important aspect of agency is responsibility; the two are opposite ends of the same stick. We cannot — should not even try to — pick up one end without also picking up the other. Thus, if we choose to marry and choose to have children, we have taken upon ourselves responsibilities to that husband and those children as the second and third most important of our priorities. Our first priority must always be ourselves and our relationship with God. If that core relationship is good, we will somehow manage to accomplish what we must regardless of our circumstances. If we allow anything else to be at the core — be it husband, children, church, or whatever — our labors will be more difficult. Putting oneself first is not selfish if our aim in perfecting ourselves is to become a perfect shaft in the Lord's quiver so that we might be ready to answer the call whenever and wherever He needs us. Having a family may very well curtail our involvement in other activities for varying periods of our lives. That is going to influence where our bodies can be physically, but it should not imprison our minds nor curtail our concerns nor inhibit the influence we can exert on a world with which our children will have to deal even if we do not.

The Lord prepared the world as a place for Adam and Eve and their posterity to grow and develop so that we may all return "home." In the 88th section of the Doctrine and Covenants the Lord outlines some of the things we must learn in order to eventually be at home with Him. We need to lengthen our stride, learn everything we possibly can, and develop our talents so we can serve God's children in the best possible way whenever and wherever we are called upon to do so. Spencer W. Kimball said:

"The basic decisions needed for us to move forward, as a people, must be made by the individual members of the Church. The major strides which must be made by the Church will follow upon the major strides to be made by us as individuals.

"We have paused on some plateaus long enough. Let us resume our journey forward and upward. Let us quietly put an end to our reluctance to reach out to others—whether in our own families, wards, or neighborhoods."[5]

Mother Teresa, a native of Bavaria, has made her home among the poor of India, and people all over the world have been blessed as she has extended herself to suffering members of the family of God. Golda Meir was not a far out liberationist. She was, rather, a woman who extended her motherly instincts to establish a home for her Jewish brothers and sisters in Israel. Florence Nightingale forever changed the course of nursing with what started out as an extension of home care.

This is not to say that these well-known women are in *any way* superior to the woman who has spent her life at home full time with her children. Their life experiences have simply been different. We need to take care not to imply a defect with the difference.

We have been criticized in the past that too few full-time homemakers have been highlighted at Women's Conference, that all the women who have been asked to speak have done things outside the home with the implication being that the former are the obedient ones and the latter are not following the proper, prescribed plan. Perhaps the latter simply see their role as "homemaker" extending to individuals and families that live beyond the four walls of their own houses. Would we really want to eliminate all female school teachers? Every grade school teacher I had was a woman. I can remember all of their names where I find it difficult to remember the names of teachers since. Imagine what would happen to the status of our health care if all the nurses quit and went home? Or to the entire economy if all the secretaries packed it in?

Where, then, should LDS women be "at home"? President Spencer W. Kimball taught that women's role was to preach the gospel, to be a righteous example not just in the home but in the world. Indeed he said that:

"Much of the major growth that is coming to the Church in the last days will come because many of the good women of the world (in whom there is often such an inner sense of spirituality) will be drawn to the Church in large numbers. This will happen to the degree that the women of the Church reflect righteousness and articulateness in their lives and to the degree that the women of the Church are seen as distinct and different — in happy ways — from the women of the world."[6]

The Prophet Joseph Smith told the women in the newly formed Relief Society in 1842 that knowledge, intelligence, and the gifts of the Spirit would flow down to them henceforth, and that from that time forward they were to be responsible for their own sins. Their eternal salvation was not to be in the hands of their fathers, nor of their husbands, but in their own wise use of agency.[7]

If Mormon women are going to make a difference in this world, they need to make their presence known. Women have often been referred to as the world's civilizers. Examples abound. The wild-wild West was civilized as the female population grew beyond the saloons and into homes. It was women just like you who, in the last century, led the fight for child labor laws. Women just like you who were concerned with temperance. Women just like you who have led the battles to curb domestic violence of every kind. It was women like you in my former community of Palo Alto who led the fight, and

won, to have prostitution fronting as massage parlors eliminated from our town. It was in fact our Relief Society president
who spearheaded that movement.

Not long ago there was a newspaper story of a young
woman who made the boys' team in high school basketball.
No comparable program existed for the girls. When the boys
were asked how they were adjusting to having a girl around,
one said that it had caused them to clean up their language. I
hear the same kind of comment made by businessmen who
have had women break into their previously all-male ranks.
They clean up their language, and the off-color stories start to
diminish. We hear that women should not be subjected to
"rough situations," and yet their very presence can have an
upgrading and civilizing effect. There is a message here of the
power of positive female influence that should be noted, not
ignored. If women expect to help civilize the world, some of
us are going to have to be in it.

Latter-day Saint women who have set a standard of service
for us are legion: from an Emmeline B. Wells, Relief Society
general president, editor of the *Woman's Exponent* (forerunner of the *Relief Society Magazine*), and promoter/sup-
porter of women's rights, to a Belle S. Spafford, also general
president of the Relief Society, as president of the National
Council of Women, to an Ardeth Kapp, who with no children
of her own has become mother to hundreds of thousands as
president of the Young Women of the Church, to a Christine
Durham, mother of four and justice on the Utah State Supreme
Court, to your local PTA or Primary worker who is at home
with her own children as well as serving others as she is called
upon to do so or as she perceives a need.

For more than a hundred and fifty years LDS women have
set a standard for leadership and caring. I feel many of them
must have read about the "virtuous woman" in Proverbs who
managed somehow to do it all: she was working from early
morning to late at night. She had her own garment business,
making and selling clothing; she was in the real estate business;
she planted her own vineyard; she succored the poor and took
care of the needy; she was vocal and was known for her wisdom;

and her children and husband rose up and called her blessed. I should think so! (Proverbs 31:10–31.) I, for one, find that superwoman model extremely difficult to follow and really don't like to hear women encouraged to "go thou and do likewise." It makes me tired just to read about it!

As we rise to meet a proper standard for us, it is important to remember that it was not Satan who put Jesus where he could be tempted, but rather the Spirit. The Joseph Smith Translation states that the *Spirit* took Jesus to the top of the mountain and to the pinnacle of the temple and then left Him to allow the devil to come and tempt Him. (JST, Matthew 4:1–10.) We need to allow ourselves to be led by the Spirit and be placed where the Lord knows we need to be. It is only by listening to the Spirit and following its promptings that we will develop the muscles we need to reaffirm here the choices we made in the pre-existence that qualified us for our mortal experience. It is important to remember also that the Lord's primary desire for His children is to bring to pass the immortality and eternal life of man and woman. That is to say, His primary goal is to empower us to become like Him. If we are to be workers in our Father's business, we must first of all prepare ourselves. That means we must stop waiting for somebody else to make things happen for us or to tell us what to do, and begin to see ourselves as being capable of becoming empowered by our Father in Heaven to act for ourselves.

I believe that President Romney had both men and women in mind when he said:

"Doctrine and Covenants 29:34–35 tells us there is no such thing as a temporal commandment, that all commandments are spiritual. It also tells us that man is to be 'an agent unto himself.' Man cannot be an agent unto himself if he is not self-reliant. Herein we see that independence and self-reliance are critical keys to our spiritual growth. Whenever we get into a situation which threatens our self-reliance, we will find our freedom threatened as well. If we increase our dependence, we will find an immediate decrease in our freedom to act.

"Thus far, we should have learned that self-reliance is a prerequisite to the complete freedom to act."[8]

As we become prepared and empowered, the Lord can pluck us out of His scabbard and use us wherever and whenever He needs us. A few years back my sister, then living in another state, felt impressed to volunteer for the crisis line. She was told by the counselors that all she needed was to care; they could teach her what to do. The requirement was that when she was "on duty," she had to stay at home and keep her telephone free. She suggested that other women in her stake might get involved as a natural extension of compassionate service, and the Relief Society presidents favored such participation. The advisor to the Relief Society discouraged their involvement; however, the Spirit continued to prick my sister to become involved, and so she did. At one of the monthly crisis center training meetings someone made derogatory remarks about the Church and the behavior of its male members. My sister spoke up and defended the Church and the men in it. She could have defended neither the Church nor its male members had she not been involved in the crisis program and present at that meeting. We need to learn confidence in following the Spirit, and to have faith that our brethren, after recovering from the initial shock of our acting on our own, will see fit to support us in our righteous endeavors.

Another example that has touched me recently is Jihan Sadat, a very impressive woman who has done much to further the cause of women and children in Egypt. She didn't come to her present status suddenly. She married at age fifteen, had four children fairly quickly, and lived a very traditional life. For years she took care of the house and children and stayed aloof from her husband's affairs. Her first serious ventures out of the home came during and just after the Six Days' War when she did volunteer work in the hospitals. Later she left home to work in villages and suburbs devastated by poverty. By then her husband was president of the Egyptian Parliament, and his understanding and tolerance of her new activities outside the home came very slowly. In the process, however, she became his confidante. They grew together, working for each other's causes, sharing each other's lives. She truly became a companion and a help-meet for her husband. Through her influence on him and through her own efforts since his assassination, she has done much to improve the status of women and children in her country. She didn't plan to step outside the home; she simply broadened her concerns and, therefore, redefined her home as the whole of Egypt.

Again, her kind of service should not be compared to the value of a woman who serves by shopping for a sick friend or who reads to and plays with her children or who cares for an aging parent. All are valuable. The differences should not imply a defect. We should not judge ourselves or each other on what we see with our mortal eyes. God in His infinite wisdom will judge us, and as with the widow's mite, each act of private care and human kindness will weigh heavily on the scales of eternal justice.

According to the apostle Paul, we need to be both hungry and filled.[9] Home, therefore, should be a place of refuge; it also needs to be a place where we are pricked to grow, to reach out, to connect. Yet, in order to grow, we must leave our comfort zones. We are faced with a paradox: on the one hand we need to be at home wherever we find ourselves; yet, on the other hand, we need to be so committed to growth toward our eternal home that we will never feel completely at home until we get there.

It is important that you understand that I am *not* advocating a single course of action here for anyone. Nor am I advocating that a woman abandon her responsibilities at home. What I am saying is that it is important for you to view realistically the vast changes that have taken place in women's lives in our lifetime and be flexible to the individual changes that will take place in your own. I hope that you will see yourselves and others in expanded ways, and then do what you can, when you can, the best you can, and that you support each other in your differences as well as in your similarities, and that you expand your vision of what home is. President Joseph Fielding Smith frequently paid honor to our Mother Eve for her courage in making the choice that led the way to our having this vital mortal experience, without which we could not progress to become like — or live eternally with — our Heavenly Parents.

She moved out of her comfortable and beautiful Eden and took on the lone and dreary world for our sake. The world is our, as it was Eve's, God-given home. We have only, as did Eve, to move in.

Notes

1. Camilla Kimball, "A Woman's Preparation," *Ensign,* Mar. 1977, p. 59.
2. "Hospital Offers Treatment for Women with Prescription-Drug Dependencies," *Deseret News,* 6 Sept. 1987.
3. Brigham Young, "Eternal Punishment—'Mormonism,' &c.," in *Journal of Discourses,* 26 vols. (Liverpool: Latter-day Saints Book Depot, 1853–86), 9:150.
4. Ezra Taft Benson, in Conference Report, Apr. 1965, p. 121.
5. Spencer W. Kimball, "Let Us Move Forward and Upward," *Ensign,* May 1979, p. 82.
6. Spencer W. Kimball, "The Role of Righteous Women," *Ensign,* Nov. 1979, p. 104.
7. See Joseph Smith, *Teachings of the Prophet Joseph Smith,* sel. Joseph Fielding Smith (Salt Lake City, Utah: Deseret Book Co., 1976), pp. 227, 229.
8. Marion G. Romney, "The Celestial Nature of Self-Reliance," *Ensign,* June 1984, pp. 5–6.
9. See Philippians 4:12.

Family Structure and Its Influence on Family Dynamics

STEPHEN J. BAHR

*F*amilies come in a variety of forms. Some have two parents, others only one. In some families both parents are employed in the labor force, while others depend on one parent for economic support. Families differ greatly in size, sex composition, and spacing of children. These basic differences in family structure influence interaction among family members.

Family Size, Spacing, and Birth Order

One important aspect of family structure is the size of the family. Growing up as an only child is much different from growing up with one or more siblings. A child with five siblings has a very different environment than a child with only one sibling. Also, birth order and the length of time between births may affect a child. Having a sibling five years older is much different than having a sibling a year older, and being the youngest of three children is quite different from being the oldest of three. How much effect does family size, spacing, and birth order have on the development of children?

First, let us examine what we know about only children. There is a popular stereotype that the only child is alone, unhappy, and maladjusted. There is no evidence to support

Stephen J. Bahr received his Ph.D. in sociology from Washington State University. He is a professor of sociology at BYU where he also heads the Family and Demographic Research Institute. He has served as associate editor of the Journal of Family Issues *and has previously served as president of the Utah Council on Family Relations and associate editor of the* Journal of Marriage and the Family. *His Church callings have included stake high councilor, stake physical activities director, teacher, and scoutmaster. He and his wife, Carol, have six children.*

this stereotype. Glenn and Hoppe (1984) estimated the effect of being an only child on eight dimensions of psychological well-being. They found that, although the differences were relatively small, only children scored higher than others on all eight dimensions. Mott and Haurin (1982) found no unique advantage to being an only child in terms of intelligence, educational progression, career, family, or social-psychological outcomes. Their data did suggest that being an only child was preferable to coming from a large family. According to Kidwell (1978) only children perceive greater parental affection than firstborns, and Blake (1981) maintained that only children do not suffer from lack of siblings. On the other hand, Bell and Avery (1985) noted that only children regard parents as more intrusive than do children with siblings. Overall, there appear to be some advantages and disadvantages to being an only child, but the overall effect on children is very small (Bell and Avery, 1985).

Popular wisdom in the press and among professionals is that large families are bad for children. Many assume that the more children there are, the less parents are able to provide personal and economic resources to help each child develop. Because parental resources are finite, the greater the number of children, the fewer interpersonal and material resources there are for each child. This has been termed the "dilution model" by Blake (1981).

There is some evidence to support the "dilution model." Blake (1981, 1985) noted that children from large families tend to have less ability, lower grades, and lower levels of educational achievement. In a review of existing research Heer (1985) concluded that family size is related to educational attainment, although it has relatively small effects on occupational status and earnings. In a provocative article titled "Dumber by the Dozen," Zajonc (1975) maintained that intelligence declines with family size. To have smart children, Zajonc suggested that parents have few children and space them far apart. According to Rahav (1982) delinquents tend to come from larger families because parental involvement and control are reduced as family size increases.

Economic well-being is negatively associated with family size. As the number of children in a family increases, the family standard of living tends to decrease (Espenshade et al., 1983). Delayed childbearing along with small family size may have long-term economic benefits, according to Hofferth (1984).

Kidwell (1981) observed that adolescents perceived their parents to be more punitive and less supportive as family size increased. As space between siblings increased, perceptions of punitiveness decreased and perceptions of supportiveness increased. Kidwell (1981, 1982) also reported that middleborns, compared to firstborns or laterborns, had lower self-esteem and perceived their parents to be more punitive and less reasonable and supportive.

Other research, however, suggests that the apparent effects of family size, spacing, and birth order may be artifacts of other variables. Heer (1985) identified methodological limitations that may have affected results of many studies. Price et al. (1984) have shown that the formulas used by Zajonc (1975) are logically invalid and that his model's ability to predict intelligence is a mathematical artifact. Mare and Chen (1986) maintained that some of Blake's (1981, 1985) results may be artifactual. Mednick et al. (1985) investigated the relationship of family size and birth order with seventeen measures of children's intellectual, psychosocial, and physical growth. The effects of family size and birth order were weak. Family size was related to only one measure of intellectual performance and to none of the psychosocial variables. Galbraith (1982, 1983) demonstrated that individual differences in intelligence were not related significantly to family size, birth order, or spacing. In a comprehensive review of existing research on birth order, Ernst and Angst (1983) concluded that birth order has little or no influence on personality. Finally, Bell and Avery (1985) found that the effects of family size, birth order, and spacing on parent-adolescent relationships were small.

Given the conflicting results, what can be concluded about the effects on family dynamics of family size, spacing, and birth order? Recent research that has controlled for other relevant variables indicates that the effects are small. It has not been demonstrated that children from large families tend to be inferior or superior to those from small families, or that close spacing of births is better or worse than wide spacing, or that there is a disadvantage or advantage to being a first or last born. Additional research is needed to resolve the currently inconsistent findings.

Sex Composition

Another important structural determinant of family interaction is sex composition. The family I grew up in illustrates this well. There were five boys and one girl in our family, the girl being the youngest.

In American society there has been a tendency to divide family labor according to gender. Females are more likely to be assigned household tasks such as cooking, sewing, and cleaning, while males are more likely to do outside work. In our family, however, there were no girls available to whom household tasks were assigned, since my sister was too young to help initially. My mother was not about to let us sit around while she did all the household work. As a consequence, we all had to help with household tasks, which were not defined as "woman's work," but simply as family work that needed to be done. Having no girls available affected the family division of labor and our attitudes toward household work.

Dual-Earner Families

Another important element in family structure is the employment status of the parents. One of the major social changes during the past fifty years has been the increase in labor force participation among married women. In 1940 only 9 percent of mothers were employed compared to 57 percent in 1980 (Hoffman, 1984). As the proportion of mothers who are employed has increased, some have expressed concern for its possible effects on children. How does the employment of the mother affect children?

From World War II to the present there have been numerous studies exploring the possible effects of the employment of mothers on their children. Most of the studies have found that the employment of the mother, by itself, has little effect on children. It depends on the mother, the child, and the situation.

This is illustrated by the experiences of three adolescents. Jane said that when her mother went to work her family situation improved. Her mother liked working and always had interesting things to talk about. Jane's mother seemed to be happier and have higher self-esteem when she worked. She became more confident and informed. And, her working enabled the family to be more financially secure. Jane was able to get clothes and do other things she wanted (like take piano lessons) that she had not been able to do before her mother became employed. Jane said her mother spent just as much time with the children after she went to work; in addition, the quality of the time improved.

Conversely, Linda hated it when her mother went to work. Before she began working, Linda's mother spent much time doing things with her children. After becoming employed, however, her mother usually came home from work tired emotionally and physically and, thus, no longer felt like doing things with the children. She not only spent less time with them, but the time she did spend was lower in quality. Linda felt neglected, and her relationship with her mother deteriorated somewhat because of her mother's employment.

A third adolescent, Ken, resented his mother's calling as Relief Society president. His mother was not employed, but she might as well have been. She was seldom there after school, and Ken felt as if his mother put everything into her church responsibilities and did not have time or attention for him.

These three examples show how employment of the mother may have positive or negative consequences, depending on the situation. Whether a mother is employed or not, the critical factor is the quality of the parent-child interaction. Employment may help, hinder, or have no effect on that interaction. Also, church and community involvements may have negative effects on children in some circumstances. Just because a woman is not employed does not make her a better mother. A mother may be physically in the home but give precious little time and attention to her children. This fact was noted by another adolescent, Jed, who said when his mother went to work it did not affect him one way or the other because he didn't have a very close relationship with her anyway. Her working made little difference in the amount of time and attention he received from her.

The research on employed mothers is consistent with the above examples. Most of the research has failed to identify differences between the children of employed and non-employed women. Children of employed mothers do just as well in school as children whose mothers stay at home. In fact, in lower class families, there is some evidence that children do better in school if the mother is employed (Moore and Sawhill, 1984). Several studies have found that when the mother is employed the children, particularly daughters, tend to develop less traditional sex role attitudes and value female achievement (Hoffman, 1974, 1984; Lamb, 1984; Moore and Sawhill, 1984). Children of employed women may become somewhat more responsible and independent, and fathers sometimes do more child care and housekeeping if the mother is employed (Hoffman, 1984; Moore and Sawhill, 1984).

Over the years one of the concerns has been whether very young children develop adequate attachment to their mother when she is employed. Although some scholars have found no significant effects of maternal employment on infant-mother attachment, several recent studies suggest that the likelihood of insecure attachment increases when the mother is employed (Lamb, 1984). Nevertheless, Lamb (1984) and Sroufe and Ward (1984) maintain that maternal employment does not necessarily have an adverse impact on infant-mother attachment, and that the quality of the infant-mother interaction is the critical variable.

In summary, the mother's employment may increase independence and responsibility in children and make their sex role attitudes less traditional. In some cases fathers may become more involved in child care and housekeeping. Among infants, maternal employment may in some cases interfere with infant-mother attachment. Nevertheless, the major conclusion from research is that the effects of maternal employment on children *depend* on a variety of factors, including motives for employment, salary, satisfaction with job, flexibility of hours, attitudes of husband, adequacy of child care, age of children, help with housework, and socioeconomic status (Moore and Sawhill, 1984).

It is the situation and meaning of employment that makes the difference, not employment per se. If a mother is dissatisfied with staying home, she may become a more adequate mother if she works. Women who are dissatisfied with staying home and stay home only out of "duty" tend to do poorly as mothers (Sroufe and Ward, 1984). On the other hand, if a woman's job leaves her tired and unresponsive to her children, her employment may be harmful to the children. The research is conclusive in showing that the quality of parent-child interaction is the critical factor, not whether or not a mother is employed.

Single-Parent Families

One of the dramatic changes in family structure during the past twenty years has been the increase in single-parent homes. In 1970 about 85 percent of children were living in a two-parent home, compared to only 74 percent of children in 1984 (U.S. Bureau of the Census, 1985). More than half of all children will live in a single-parent home at some point before they reach age eighteen (Bumpass, 1984a; Hofferth, 1985; Furstenberg and Nord, 1982). Hofferth (1985) estimates that white children born in 1980 will spend 25 percent of their childhood in a single-parent home, while black children will spend 44 percent of their childhood in a single-parent home. A large majority of children are in single-parent homes as the result of divorce, and most children in single-parent homes live with their mother.

What effect does living in a single-parent home have on children? Some maintain that it has negative consequences for children, while others counter that it is not the single-parent-hood that hurts children, but inadequate parenting. Let's look at the evidence.

When children from single-parent homes are compared with children from two-parent homes, it appears that children from single-parent homes are not as well adjusted. Adolescents from single-parent homes take more health risks, such as intemperate drinking and not fastening seat belts (Saucier and Ambert, 1983). They tend to start dating earlier and are more likely to have premarital sex, which is related to pregnancy and out-of-wedlock childbearing (Coleman et al., 1985; Newcomer and Udry, 1987). Further, they are more susceptible to pressure from friends to engage in deviant behavior (Steinberg, 1987).

Children, and particularly boys, from single-parent homes have poorer social adjustment and do not perform as well academically as children from intact homes (Guidubaldi et al., 1986; Hodges et al., 1984). Differences in social and academic adjustment are evident even after six years (Guidubaldi et al., 1986).

Kellam et al. (1977) found that children's social and psychological adjustments were related to family structure. They examined the adjustment of school age children who lived in four different types of families: (1) two natural parents, (2) mother-grandmother, (3) mother-stepfather, and (4) mother alone. Children in mother-alone homes were at greatest risk for maladjustment, while children who lived with both natural parents had the best adjustment. Children in mother-grandmother homes did almost as well as children from intact homes, however, while children in stepparent homes did almost as poorly as children in mother-alone homes. Kellam et al. (1977) concluded that remarriage may not help adjustment, and that mother aloneness was more important than father absence.

Children from single-parent homes evaluate their parents more negatively than do children from two-parent homes (Parish and Kappes, 1980). Fathers, who usually are the noncustodial parent in divorce, are rated particularly poorly by their children. Amato (1987) reported that children rated their mothers similarly in support and punishment regardless of family type. Children in one-parent homes, however, rated their fathers as less supportive and controlling than did children from intact homes.

Glenn and Kramer (1985) suggest that the negative effects of divorce may be long lasting. They found that young adults whose parents had divorced rated their happiness and life satisfaction somewhat lower than adults whose parents had not divorced.

Although the above evidence suggests that single-parent homes may place children at risk, there is considerable evidence that it is the quality of parent-child interaction rather than number of parents that is important for children. When viewed cross-culturally, the one-parent family is not necessarily pathological or inferior (Bilge and Kaufman, 1983). Lamb (1978) maintains that divorce is not necessarily harmful to children's personality development if the parents are willing and able to care for a child.

Recent research suggests that some of the reported differences between children from single-parent and two-parent homes may be spurious because relevant variables have not been controlled (Blechman, 1982; Kanoy and Cunningham, 1984). For example, differences between children from divorced and intact families were reduced substantially when income was controlled (Guidubaldi et al., 1986). Goldstein (1982) found that when parental education and income were controlled, father absence was not related to academic performance. A review of the literature by Wells and Rankin (1985) revealed that the relationship between broken homes and delinquency was weak.

Several scholars have found that it is the amount of parental conflict rather than disruption per se that affects child adjustment. Emery (1982) concluded that much of the association between divorce and child behavior problems may be explained by parental conflict. Lucpnitz (1978) maintained that the stress of divorce on children was due more to the turmoil involved in parental conflict than living in a one-parent home. Long (1986) found that self-esteem of daughters was related to parental discord but not to family structure. Parental discord appeared to lower self-esteem while parental separation did not. Other research is consistent with these conclusions (Nye, 1957; Hess and Camara, 1979).

What may be concluded about the effects on children of living in a one-parent home? It appears that living in a one-parent home is not, by itself, detrimental to children; however, children in single-parent homes may be at risk for several reasons. First, parental conflict is often associated with divorce, and severe parental conflict has been shown to be detrimental to children.

Second, raising children is not easy, and having two parents may decrease parental stress and increase the quality of parental monitoring. Kellam et al. (1977) observed that the aloneness of the mother was more important than the absence of the father. Role overload is a common complaint of single parents (Bahr, 1982).

Third, economic problems are associated with marital disruption. Women usually get custody of the children, and a high proportion have only marginal incomes. As noted above, when income is controlled, the negative effects of single parenthood diminish; but the fact is that a large majority of single parents and their children have very low incomes (Weitzman, 1985). Divorce itself may not hurt children, but divorce reduces women's income, and a low income negatively affects children.

Finally, marital disruption may decrease an adult's capacity to parent. Wallerstein (1985) suggests that marital disruption is often followed by less sensitivity, less talk, less play, less supportiveness, and less overall parent-child interaction. This may not be a necessary result of divorce, but Wallerstein found that it is fairly common.

Remarriage

A common occurrence among single-parent families is remarriage. About three-fourths of all divorced persons eventually remarry (Glick, 1984). In 20 percent of currently married couples at least one spouse has been previously divorced. Given that half of current marriages will end in divorce and three-fourths of divorced persons will remarry, we can expect that more than one-third (.5 X .75 = .375) of all persons who marry will experience a remarriage.

Are remarried people as happy as people in first marriages? Does the stress associated with divorce make it difficult for individuals to succeed in a second marriage? Available evidence suggests that remarried persons tend to be as happy and well adjusted as persons in first marriages. Fine et al. (1986) compared individuals in first marriages and remarriages on several measures of well-being, including anxiety, depression, marital satisfaction, and child problems. They found no differences between individuals in first marriages and remarriages on any of the dimensions.

Buehler et al. (1986) made comparisons among four remarriage groups: (1) neither former spouse had remarried; (2) only husband had remarried; (3) only wife had remarried; (4) both former spouses had remarried. They compared the four groups on self-esteem, parental satisfaction, divorce-related stress, and economic well-being. There were no differences among the four groups on any of the variables except economic well-being. Women who had remarried had higher economic well-being than women who had not remarried. Furthermore, women who had remarried, but whose former husband had not remarried, tended to have higher economic well-being than women in the group in which both spouses had remarried. This suggests that remarrying improves the economic situation for women. On the other hand, when the husband remarries, it tends to hurt the economic status of the former wife.

Longitudinal research by Day and Bahr (1986) is consistent with the findings of Buehler et al. (1987). Per capita income of women increased substantially upon remarriage, while the per capita income of men decreased substantially upon remarriage.

Weingarten (1980) found the individuals in remarriages were similar to individuals in first marriages with regard to marital adjustment, parental adjustment, and overall well-being. Albrecht (1979) observed high levels of marital satisfaction among his sample of remarried persons. Using three national surveys, Glenn and Weaver (1977) found no differences in the marital satisfaction of men in first marriages and remarriages. Women in first marriages had somewhat higher marital satisfaction than women in remarriages, although the differences were not large.

The major problems encountered by remarried couples concern children and money (Ihinger-Tallman and Pasley, 1987). In that sense they are no different from individuals in first marriages. Stepparenting and visitation may make child-rearing stressful, while distributing resources to both one's former and current marriage is bound to create conflicts.

There is also some evidence that boundary maintenance may be a problem. By boundary maintenance we mean clear definitions of what a family is and whom it includes. Among remarried couples there may be some ambiguity regarding who is the family, since there is a blending of individuals from previous marriages (Ihinger-Tallman and Pasley, 1987).

Another problem of remarried families is loyalty conflicts. Children may feel disloyal to one parent if they side with the other during a conflict. There may also be feelings of loyalty involved in interactions between stepparent and stepchild.

What can be concluded from these studies? Taken together, the research is remarkably consistent in showing few differences between first marriages and remarriages in marital satisfaction and overall well-being; however, the blending of individuals from previous marriages may create some stress.

About one-sixth of all children in the United States live in a remarried family (Cherlin and McCarthy, 1985). About half of all children whose mother divorces will experience the remarriage of their mother within five years (Bumpass, 1984b).

In children's literature stepparents are often viewed in a negative light. For example, the stepmother mistreated Cinderella. How do children feel about stepparents and how do they adjust to remarriages? Fine (1986) compared the views of college students from intact, single-parent, and stepparent homes. He found that stepparents, particularly stepmothers, were viewed less positively among all three groups; however, students from single-parent and remarried families did not view stepmothers as negatively as students from intact families. Fine's research suggests that exposure to stepparents may decrease negative stereotypes and increase appreciation for stepparents.

Available evidence suggests that living in a remarried family is difficult for children. As noted earlier, Kellam et al. (1977) found that children in mother/stepfather families were similar to children in mother alone families and had significantly lower social adjustment and psychological well-being than children in mother/grandmother or mother/father families.

The research by White and Booth (1985) showed that children are a significant stress among remarried couples. Because of the stress, teenagers living in stepfamilies tend to leave the home somewhat earlier than teenagers living with two natural parents. There is also evidence that rates of child abuse are substantially higher in remarried families than in two-natural-parent homes (Wilson and Daly, 1985).

Overall, children in remarried families tend to have somewhat poorer adjustment than children in first marriages. The relationship between stepparent and stepchild is often somewhat strained (Ihinger-Tallman and Pasley, 1987).

Summary and Conclusions

I have made six major points in this paper. Let me summarize them briefly. First, recent research indicates that the effects of family size, spacing, and birth order on the intellectual and social competence of children are relatively small. Second, age and sex composition of the family influences our attitudes and the way family tasks are assigned. Third, the effects of the mother's employment are complex and may be positive, negative, or neutral, depending on the family situation. Increased money and father-child interaction may be benefits. Decreased mother-child interaction is a possible cost. Employment of the mother does not necessarily result in poorer mother-child interaction. Fourth, living in a single-parent home may increase the risk of maladjustment in children because parental conflict, role overload, diminished parenting, and economic problems often accompany single parenthood. Fifth, there are few differences between first marriages and remarriages in marital satisfaction and overall well-being of the partners. Finally, children in remarried families tend to have somewhat poorer adjustment than children in first marriages.

When applying these findings to actual decisions, one should keep in mind that findings from social research are based on general trends and may not always apply to a particular individual or family. In addition, scientifically based conclusions are always tentative and may need to be modified as new evidence becomes available. The research on family size provides a good example of how conclusions change as new evidence accumulates. Until a few years ago, the scientific evidence overwhelmingly showed that large families were harmful to children intellectually and socially. Recent studies have shown that previous research did not adequately control for relevant background variables and that, with appropriate controls, family size has little effect on the overall well-being of children.

The above findings have implications for families, particularly LDS families. The image portrayed in public media is that large families are detrimental to children. The research shows that this is not necessarily the case, and the effects of family size and birth order have been shown to be small. It seems that the critical factor in family interaction is the quality of the relationship between husband and wife and parent and child, and not the number of children that exist. It is also well to remember that in the sociological sense, large families are relatively small groups. On the other hand, the existing research has not examined all facets of family size and how it may affect family interaction. There is no question that raising children takes a tremendous amount of money, organization, and energy, and larger numbers of children increase the money, energy, and organization that parents must contribute. From personal experience I know that it is much more difficult to put four pre-schoolers to bed than one. Parental time, energy, and money are finite resources, and it seems unwise to assume that family size has no effect just because the research has not demonstrated strong effects.

Similarly, the decision to have two parents who are employed is complex and depends on the situation. In some cases, the effect may clearly be negative, while in others, it may have great beneficial effects for children and parents. In still others, the overall effect may be neutral. Each family must decide what is best for them, given their particular situation, personalities, and needs. The examples presented in this chapter show that in some situations mother's employment could clearly hurt the children. In other situations, it appeared to be very beneficial for the children. The research clearly shows that it is incorrect to make a general statement regarding the employment of the mother that applies to all families.

The findings on single-parent families have important implications for the increasing number of single-parent families in our society. Living in a single-parent home may increase the risk of maladjustment in children because parental conflict, role overload, diminished parenting, and economic problems often accompany single-parenthood. Therefore, it is important that single parents receive social and economic support to decrease role overload and economic distress. Separated and divorced parents should be encouraged to keep their children out of their conflicts. Intense parental conflict has been shown to be one of the major risks of a divorce for children. Furthermore, single parents need to be more sensitive and supportive of their children. Diminished parenting is a chief hazard for children of divorce, but it is not inevitable. When single parents are warm, sensitive, and available, their children tend to have normal social and cognitive development (Crouter et al., 1984).

Finally, it is important that couples who remarry take into account the effects of their remarriage on their children. Living in a remarried family is not easy for minor children and may be stressful to the parent but it is particularly so to the children.

References

Albrecht, Stan L. 1979. "Correlates of Marital Happiness among the Remarried." *Journal of Marriage and the Family* 41: 857–67.

Amato, Paul R. 1987. "Family Processes in One-Parent, Stepparent, and Intact Families: The Child's Point of View." *Journal of Marriage and the Family* 49: 327–37.

Bahr, Stephen J. 1982. "The Pains and Joys of Divorce: A Survey of Mormons." *Family Perspective* 16 (4): 191–200.

Bell, Nancy J., and Arthur W. Avery. 1985. "Family Structure and Parent-Adolescent Relationships: Does Family Structure Really Make a Difference?" *Journal of Marriage and the Family* 47: 503–8.

Bilge, Barbara, and Gladis Kaufman. 1983. "Children of Divorce and One-Parent Families: Cross-Cultural Perspectives." *Family Relations* 32: 59–71.

Blake, Judith. 1985. "Number of Siblings and Educational Mobility." *American Sociological Review* 50: 84–94.

Blake, Judith. 1981. "Family Size and the Quality of Children." *Demography* 18 (4): 421–42.

Blechman, Elaine A. 1982. "Are Children with One Parent at Psychological Risk? A Methodological Review." *Journal of Marriage and the Family* 44: 179–95.

Buehler, Cheryl, M. Janice Hogan, Beatrice Robinson, and Robert J. Levy. 1986. "Remarriage Following Divorce: Stressors and Well-Being of Custodial and Noncustodial Parents." *Journal of Family Issues* 7 (4): 405–20.

Bumpass, Larry L. 1984a. "Some Characteristics of Children's Second Families." *The American Journal of Sociology* 90 (3): 608–23.

Bumpass, Larry L. 1984b. "Children and Marital Disruption: A Replication and Update." *Demography* 21 (1): 71–82.

Cherlin, Andrew, and James McCarthy. 1985. "Remarried Couple Households: Data from the June 1980 Current Population Survey." *Journal of Marriage and the Family* 47: 23–30.

Coleman, Marilyn, Lawrence H. Ganong, and Patricia Ellis. 1985. "Family Structure and Dating Behavior of Adolescents." *Adolescence* 20: 537–43.

Crouter, Ann C., Jay Belsky, and Graham B. Spanier. 1984. "The Family Context of Child Development: Divorce and Maternal Employment." *Annals of Child Development* 1: 201–38.

Day, Randal D., and Stephen J. Bahr. 1986. "Income Changes Following Divorce and Remarriage." *Journal of Divorce* 9 (3): 75–88.

Emery, Robert E. 1982. "Interparental Conflict and the Children of Discord and Divorce." *Psychological Bulletin* 92 (2): 310–30.

Ernst, Cecile, and Jules Angst. 1983. *Birth Order: Its Influence on Personality.* New York: Springer-Verlag.

Espenshade, Thomas J., Gloria Kamenske, and Boone A. Turchi. "Family Size and Economic Welfare." *Family Planning Perspectives* 15 (6): 289–94.

Fine, Mark A. 1986. "Perceptions of Stepparents: Variation in Stereotypes As a Function of Current Family Structure." *Journal of Marriage and the Family* 48: 537–43.

Furstenberg, Frank F., Jr., and C. W. Nord. 1982. "The Life Course of Children of Divorce: Marital Disruption and Parental Contact." *Family Planning Perspectives* 14: 211–12.

Galbraith, Richard C. 1983. "Individual Differences in Intelligence: A Reappraisal of the Confluence Model." *Intelligence* 7: 185–94.

Galbraith, Richard C. 1982. "Sibling Spacing and Intellectual Development: A Closer Look at the Confluence Models." *Developmental Psychology* 18 (2): 151–73.

Glenn, Norval D., and Sue Keir Hoppe. 1984. "Only Children As Adults: Psychological Well-Being." *Journal of Family Issues* 5: 363–82.

Glenn, Norval D., and Kathryn B. Kramer. 1985. "The Psychological Well-Being of Adult Children of Divorce." *Journal of Marriage and the Family* 47: 905–12.

Glenn, Norval D., and Charles N. Weaver. 1977. "The Marital Happiness of Remarried Divorced Persons." *Journal of Marriage and the Family* 39: 331–37.

Glick, Paul C. 1984. "Marriage, Divorce, and Living Arrangements." *Journal of Family Issues* 5 (1): 7–26.

Goldstein, Harris S. 1982. "Fathers' Absence and Cognitive Development of 12- to 17-Year-Olds." *Psychological Reports* 51: 843–48.

Guidubaldi, John, Joseph D. Perry, and Bonnie K. Nastasi. 1986. "Long-Term Impact of Divorce on Children: A Report of a Two- and Three-Year Follow-up of a National Sample." Paper presented at the 63rd annual meeting of the American Orthopsychiatric Association, Chicago, April.

Heer, David M. 1985. "Effects of Sibling Number on Child Outcome." *Annual Review of Sociology* 11: 27–47.

Hess, Robert D., and Kathleen A. Camara. 1979. "Post-Divorce Family Relationships As Mediating Factors in the Consequences of Divorce for Children." *Journal of Social Issues* 35: 79–96.

Hofferth, Sandra L. 1985. "Updating Children's Life Course." *Journal of Marriage and the Family* 47 (1): 93–115.

Hofferth, Sandra L. 1984. "Long-Term Economic Consequences for Women of Delayed Childbearing and Reduced Family Size." *Demography* 21 (2): 141–55.

Hoffman, Lois Wladis. 1984. "Work, Family, and the Socialization of the Child." Pp. 223–82 in R. D. Parke, R. N. Emde, H. P. McAdoo, and G. P. Sackett (eds.), *Review of Child Development Research: Volume 7, The Family*. Chicago: University of Chicago Press.

Hoffman, Lois Wladis. 1974. "Effects on Child." Pp. 126–66 in Lois W. Hoffman and F. Ivan Nye (eds.), *Working Mothers*. San Francisco: Jossey-Bass Publishers.

Ihinger-Tallman, Marilyn, and Kay Pasley. 1987. *Remarriage*. Beverly Hills: Sage Publications.

Kanoy, Korrel W., and Jo Lynn Cunningham. 1984. "Consensus or Confusion in Research on Children and Divorce: Conceptual and Methodological Issues." *Journal of Divorce* 7 (4): 45–71.

Kellam, Sheppard, Margaret E. Ensminger, and R. Jay Turner. 1977. "Family

Structure and the Mental Health of Children." *Archives of General Psychiatry* 34: 1012–22.

Kidwell, Jeannie S. 1982. "The Neglected Birth Order: Middleborns." *Journal of Marriage and the Family* 44: 225–35.

Kidwell, Jeannie S. 1981. "Number of Siblings, Sibling Spacing, Sex, and Birth Order: Their Effects on Perceived Parent-Adolescent Relationships." *Journal of Marriage and the Family* 43: 315–32.

Kidwell, Jeannie S. 1978. "Adolescents' Perceptions of Parental Affect: An Investigation of Only Children vs. Firstborns and the Effect of Spacing." *Journal of Population* 1: 148–66.

Lamb, Michael E. 1984. "Fathers, Mothers, and Child Care in the 1980s: Family Influences on Child Development." Pp. 61–88 in Kathryn M. Borman, Daisy Quarm, and Sarah Gideonse (eds.), *Women in the Workplace: Effects on Families.* Norwood, N.J.: Ablex Publishing Corporation.

Long, Barbara H. 1986. "Parental Discord vs. Family Structure: Effects of Divorce on the Self-Esteem of Daughters." *Journal of Youth & Adolescence* 15: 19–27.

Luepnitz, Deborah Anna. 1978. "Children of Divorce: A Review of the Psychological Literature." *Law and Human Behavior* 2: 167–79.

Mare, Robert D., and Meichu D. Chen. 1986. "Further Evidence on Sibship Size and Educational Stratification." *American Sociological Review* 51: 403–12.

Mednick, Birgitte R., Robert L. Baker, and Dennis Hocevar. 1985. "Family Size and Birth Order Correlates of Intellectual, Psychosocial, and Physical Growth." *Merrill-Palmer Quarterly* 31 (1): 67–84.

Moore, Kristin A., and Isabel V. Sawhill. 1984. "Implication of Women's Employment for Home and Family Life." Pp. 153–71 in Patricia Voydanoff (ed.), *Work & Family.* Palo Alto, Calif.: Mayfield Publishing Co.

Mott, Frank L., and R. Jean Haurin. 1982. "Being an Only Child: Effects on Educational Progression and Career Orientation." *Journal of Family Issues* 3: 575–93.

Newcomer, Susan, and J. Richard Udry. 1987. "Parental Marital Status Effects on Adolescent Sexual Behavior." *Journal of Marriage and the Family* 49: 235–40.

Nye, F. Ivan. 1957. "Child Adjustment in Broken and in Unhappy Unbroken Homes." *Marriage and Family Living* 19 (November): 356–61.

Parish, Thomas S., and Bruno M. Kappes. 1980. "Impact of Father Loss on the Family." *Social Behavior and Personality* 8 (1): 107–12.

Price, Gary Glen, Daniel J. Walsh, and William R. Vilberg. 1984. "The Confluence Model's Good Predictions of Mental Age Beg the Question." *Psychological Bulletin* 96 (1): 195–200.

Rahav, Giora. 1982. "Family Size and Delinquency." *Sociology and Social Research* 66 (1): 42–51.

Saucier, Jean-Francois, and Anne-Marie Ambert. 1983. "Parental Marital Status and Adolescents' Health-Risk Behavior." *Adolescence* 18: 403–11.

Sroufe, L. Alan, and Mary J. Ward. 1984. "The Importance of Early Care." Pp. 35–60 in Kathryn M. Borman, Daisy Quarm, and Sarah Gideonse (eds.), *Women in the Workplace: Effects on Families.* Norwood, N.J.: Ablex Publishing Corporation.

Steinberg, Laurence. 1987. "Single Parents, Stepparents, and the Susceptibility of Adolescents to Antisocial Peer Pressure." *Child Development* 58: 269–75.

U.S. Bureau of the Census. 1985. *Statistical Abstract of the United States: 1986* (106th ed.). Washington, D.C.: U.S. Government Printing Office.

Wallerstein, Judith S. 1985. "The Overburdened Child: Some Long-Term Consequences of Divorce." *Social Work* 30 (2): 116–23.

Weingarten, Helen. 1980. "Remarriage and Well-Being." *Journal of Family Issues* 1 (4): 533–59.

Weitzman, Lenore J. 1985. *The Divorce Revolution.* New York: The Free Press.

Wells, L. Edward, and Joseph H. Rankin. 1985. "Broken Homes and Juvenile Delinquency: An Empirical Review." *Criminal Justice Abstracts* 17 (2): 249–72.

White, Lynn K., and Alan Booth. 1985. "The Quality and Stability of Remarriages: The Role of Stepchildren." *American Sociological Review* 50: 689–98.

Wilson, Margo, and Martin Daly. 1985. "Risk of Maltreatment of Children Living with Step-Parents." To appear in R. Gelles & J. Lancaster (eds.), *Biosocial Perspectives on Child Abuse.* New York: Aldine.

Zajonc, Robert B. 1975. "Dumber by the Dozen." *Psychology Today* (January): 37–43.

Money, Values, and Family Dynamics

*W*hy a discussion about money and values? Because values provide direction for efforts to acquire and use money. In other words, values influence what we *will* do and what we *will not* do relative to the acquisition and use of money.

Money is a tool which facilitates economic exchange. According to the traditional economic definition, money is a store of value (expressed in terms of the goods and services it can command), a measure of value (expressed in relationships between goods and services), and a means of exchange (easing the transfer of goods and services from one owner to another). It becomes value-laden only as we, individually or collectively, choose to attach meaning to it. That meaning is dependent on our value system and the role money plays in our own behavior and in our efforts to control the behavior of others.

One of the major societal changes that occur through time is a sometimes slow, sometimes rapid, but always inexorable alteration in the relative alignment of the values, or fundamental beliefs, held by people. This change has been more noticeable in recent years. Considering the major impact this change has had on various segments of personal and social life, it would be unrealistic to ignore its influence on how we view and use money.

Kay P. Edwards, professor of family sciences at Brigham Young University and former chair of that department, received her Ph.D. from Cornell University. A noted scholar and published writer in her field, she teaches courses in family asset transfers, the family and the law, and financial planning. Dr. Edwards is also a chartered financial consultant and a chartered life underwriter. In addition to service in the auxiliaries, she has been a member of the Gospel Doctrine writing committee for the Church.

Values Defined

Rokeach[1] recognized that it is difficult to separate values from attitudes. He defined a value as a single belief that guides actions and judgments, across specific objects and situations and beyond immediate goals, to more ultimate end-states of existence. Such beliefs that might affect how money is used include honesty, security, and achievement. These beliefs are values because they influence behavior and judgments in many situations and toward many objects other than just money and its use.

Attitudes, on the other hand, were defined by Rokeach as several beliefs (based on fact and evaluation) that focus on a specific object or situation. When we go into the marketplace to make a purchase with money, we have beliefs about where we should shop, how we should be treated by the salespeople, which brands are the "best," what constitutes an acceptable price range for us, and so on.

Because of the close relationship between beliefs that function as values and beliefs that function as attitudes, Rokeach chose to combine these two concepts and talk about the *value-attitude system.* He suggested that each of us has two value-attitude systems that operate simultaneously and influence our behavior — one focusing on end-states of existence we think are personally and socially preferable, e.g., comfort, happiness, security, and the other focusing on specific modes of conduct we think are personally and socially preferable, e.g., honesty, obedience, ambition. Once these value-attitude systems are internalized, according to Rokeach's hypothesis, they become a standard for (1) guiding our own actions; (2) developing and maintaining attitudes toward objects and situations; (3) justifying one's own and others' actions and attitudes; (4) morally judging ourselves and others; (5) making comparisons between ourselves and others; and (6) influencing the values, attitudes, and actions of at least some other persons. This last use is illustrated in the socialization process. As parents, we draw upon our own value-attitude systems in teaching our children, hoping they will formulate systems identical to our own, or,

243

if not, at least sufficiently similar that we can continue to interact with them in a productive way.

Our value-attitude systems should not be taken lightly. They are powerful influences on our thinking about ourselves and others and on our behavior. Severe dysfunctions can occur when these deepest and most personal beliefs are violated in our behavior. For example, some people feel very real symptoms of physical illness after making a major financial commitment that conflicts with their values of security or thrift.

From these deep-seated beliefs, we develop specific goals and establish the standards for evaluating their accomplishment. We then proceed to *act, interact,* and *react* according to our determination of what is right and appropriate.

Although this has been discussed as a conscious process, in reality we are, for the most part, unaware that values and attitudes are developing. From the moment an infant is born, the process of inculcating him or her with value-attitude systems, goal selection, and prescribed and proscribed behaviors begins. Imagine the opportunity for misunderstanding, conflict, and dissension that exists when two people with well-established and inevitably somewhat different value-attitude systems, goal commitments, and ideas about right and wrong behavior come together as husband and wife to make decisions about the appropriate use of a finite amount of money.

Values and Behavior Related to Money

Values Related to Money. What does money mean to you? A filmstrip developed by The Learning Seed Company[2] suggests that people can be divided into four money-types, based on the value-attitudes that have a primary influence on how they use money. None of these types is right or wrong, and any one of them taken to an extreme can produce an unbalanced life-style and personality. The four types identified are those who see money as *security,* as *power,* as *a means to buy love and acceptance,* and as *freedom.*

1. Money As Security. Those people who identify money with security view it as their safety net in a hostile environment. The larger the net, the safer they feel. They pay bills promptly

and rarely use credit beyond what can be repaid in thirty days. They spend cautiously, often with a feeling of guilt or loss. Thus, consumption decisions are made carefully in order to get the most possible for the loss of each dollar. Sales and bargains are important because they add to the illusion of saving money instead of losing it. To such persons, money is for saving, not spending. People of this money-type often come from a background of insecurity, either their own or their parents'. Those with money in short supply as a result perhaps of divorce or a death and those who experienced the Great Depression often fit into this category. The fear that everyone is out to get their money is an extreme expression of the world-view held by persons who see money as security.

2. Money As Power. For the power brokers, money is a way to obtain superiority, a feeling of importance, and control over people and events. For them, money exists to clear away obstacles that stand in the way of their gaining more power. They believe that everyone has his or her price. More money does not satisfy, because they can never have enough power. For some, the struggle for power is an attempt to compensate for their own lack of self-esteem. A person doesn't have to control millions of dollars to be a power seeker. Control over the family budget, over purchasing decisions, over doling out the money to individual family members can be enough.

3. Money As a Way to Buy Love and Acceptance. Those who find it difficult to achieve love and acceptance by others can be tempted to use money to "purchase" fulfillment of these emotional needs. Parents, otherwise unable to express love and affection to their children, offer gifts and money. The children learn that money equals love, an equation that soon falls, however, from its internal contradictions. According to Belk[3], money—and to a somewhat lesser degree, goods and information—are generally inadequate substitutes for more direct interpersonal expressions of love. Those who equate love with money are often the most gullible concerning requests for money for whatever purpose. Those who feel unattractive or unlovable may use expensive gifts to attract some-

one of the opposite sex. This money-type often tries to buy *friends,* as the power broker buys *control,* or the security seeker grasps for *safety.*

4. Money As Freedom. People who see money as the path to freedom may take one of two different approaches. Some feel that a great deal of money can buy freedom, while others view freedom as being free from money itself and the pursuit of material goods. Such attitudes are manifest, respectively, in persons' seeking the ability to do what they want, go where they want, live where they desire, and, generally, to be free of restrictions sought or imposed by others, and in the vow of poverty taken by some religious groups. Money is important to this former group only as it is necessary to their doing or having what they want. This money-type expresses itself in both foolish and cautious spending. Many look forward to retirement with unrealistic and unattainable expectations of economic independence. When they reach that stage, they often find life boring and disappointing.

Each of these four money-types is based on elements of truth about money and the role it plays in life. An emergency savings account is always recommended by financial advisors; giving gifts is an enjoyable way to express love; money does buy a certain amount of power and control over our environment; and to some extent, freedom can be secured with money. If we look closely, we all will probably find elements of each type in our own attitudes toward money and the use of it, as well as in the attitudes and use of money by family members and close friends.

The challenge is to recognize unhealthy signs of these money-types and to make an effort to resolve underlying deficiencies that may cause undesirable behavior. It is important to find other ways to improve self-esteem, to shore up feelings of inadequate love and support, to provide opportunities for choice, and to be able to allow others appropriate control over their life experiences.

Values related to life-span stage. In addition to money-type differences, Belk[4] found evidence to suggest that life-span stage also influences the values of family members and their use of money.

Specifically, according to Belk, the strong interest of young children in money and material possessions seems to decline as they get older. As children enter adolescence, their concern with identity shifts from possessions to activities and their attention becomes more future-directed. The possessions that are important are those that give a sense of independence and accomplishment, such as cars and musical instruments.

Younger adults tend to regard money as a moral evil, while those who are slightly older and have joined the work force see it as a means to achieve comfort and security.

Parenthood seems to be a key life-span event that results in a shift from egoistic concern with self to an altruistic consideration of others. The values of family, happiness, friendship, love, and security seem to peak during middle age.

For older persons, keepsakes and mementos are dearly treasured, and there is a tendency to live vicariously through their children and grandchildren. The most frequently mentioned values in this group are good health and the success of their children.

The extended family is characterized by having individual members in all stages of the life-span. All of their conflicting values have to be realized from the money managed by the family.

Values related to life-style. Another aspect of values that influences money management behavior is life-style. Daniel Yankelovich[5] contends that cultural shifts in value-attitude systems and in the life-styles they produce have been occurring in recent years. His research indicates a marked change in the United States from a traditional ethic of self-denial and sacrifice to an ethic of self-fulfillment that denies people nothing. This focus on self-fulfillment comes into direct conflict with an economy that increasingly calls for restraint. Recognition that duty-to-self is not a viable guide to conduct is now pushing us toward an ethic of commitment to altruism that does not require an ever-increasing affluence or prodigal expenditures. As this new ethic takes hold, there will be a significant change in how we view money and, perhaps, a lessening of the role money plays in interpersonal conflict. A heightened recognition of and concern for the values and needs of others broadens perspective and lessens the inclination to see problems as solvable only by doing it "my" way.

Satenig St. Marie,[6] former vice-president for consumer affairs at J. C. Penney Company, described six new values that more recent Yankelovich research indicates have emerged "which alone, and in combination, are shaping *a new agenda* for the 80's." They are (1) *reciprocity,* or fairness; (2) *autonomy,* which means independence and self-reliance, that is, "standing on your own two feet"; (3) *community,* or a sharing of common interests; (4) *pluralism,* which means acceptance of diversity within our society; (5) *expressivism,* which means the importance of developing new sides of one's potential; and (6) *pragmatism,* or a practical rather than theoretical approach to life.

Associated with these shifts in ethics and values, SRI International[7] has identified nine American life-styles that when categorized into three larger groups, describe "a way of life characterized by specific values, needs, dreams, beliefs and points of view."

1. Need-Driven People: Survivors and Sustainers. People whose economic activities and orientations to money are driven by need rather than choice are known as survivors and sustainers. Incomes are usually below or slightly exceeding poverty levels; many are minorities; most are either young families (often fatherless) or individuals or old people; more are women than men. They make up about 11 percent of the population.

2. Outer-Directed People: Belongers, Emulaters, Achievers. Constituting approximately 67 percent of the population, outer-directed people form a large, diverse category of middle-class and hard-driving upper-middle class people who conduct their lives in accordance with what they imagine others will think. Their decisions about the use of money are made in response

to what they believe it says *about* them, not what it does *for* them.

3. Inner-Directed People: I-Am-Me, Experiential, Societally Conscious, Integrated. The remaining one-fifth of the population are generally post-World War II babies who grew up in affluent, "achiever" homes. They experiment with opposing values and life-styles and choose nontraditional ways of life. Decisions about money are made to satisfy their own inner priorities and pleasures, rather than responding to the norms of others.

A very small proportion of this group has sufficient resources and is able to combine the values of achievers and the societally conscious into an integrated life-style that results in individualistic spending.

In general, these various unique life-styles are developmental, and it is unlikely that someone who is need-driven can have any understanding of or feeling for the values, needs, and views of people who have reached the other stages. By the same token, few people adopt an inner-directed life-style unless they have been extensively exposed to the success of outer-directedness.

The corollary of this is that those who have experienced previous stages in the developmental sequence should have some understanding of and feeling for the values, needs, and views of people presently in those stages. Unfortunately, that is not always the case.

Values related to church membership. One advantage individuals, couples, and families who are members of The Church of Jesus Christ of Latter-day Saints have is commitment to a shared value-attitude system. The LDS philosophy toward money management is based on the value-attitudes of family, work, honesty, thrift, safety, security, and "sufficiency."[8] These values can be realized in the acquisition and use of money by following twelve guidelines: (1) teach family members early the importance of working and earning; (2) teach children to make money decisions in keeping with their capacities to comprehend; (3) teach each family member to contribute to the total family welfare; (4) teach family members that paying financial obligations promptly is part of integrity and honesty; (5) learn to manage money before it manages you; (6) learn self-discipline and self-restraint in money matters; (7) use a budget; (8) make education a continuing process; (9) work toward home ownership; (10) appropriately involve yourself in an insurance program; (11) strive to understand and cope with existing inflation (and changes in inflation); and (12) appropriately involve yourself in a food storage program.[9]

The five desirable behaviors toward money that should result from implementing the Church's value-attitude system in money management are: (1) pay an honest tithing; (2) live on less than you earn; (3) learn to distinguish between needs and wants; (4) develop and live within a budget; and (5) be honest in all your financial affairs.[10]

By implementing this shared value-attitude system in a family, the value-attitude differences among family members can more easily be reconciled and integrated. Working out value-attitude differences among family members within this shared institutional framework of economic counsel will assure financial well-being and a minimum of conflict about money in family life.

Improving Family Dynamics through Values Clarification

Money management between husband and wife should be on a partnership basis, with both parties having a voice in decisions and in policy making. Furthermore, as children reach the age of accountability, they, too, should be involved in money concerns on a limited partnership basis.[11] To accomplish this cooperative goal satisfactorily, we should analyze the conflicts and misunderstandings that arise among family members about money matters. Determining differences in value-attitude orientations toward money that are playing a part in the conflicts is an important step in resolving them.

The process of understanding our own and others' values is called values clarification. One approach to clarifying values related to the acquisition and use of money follows.

Money, Values, and Family Dynamics

Values are reflected in choices. Each family member should ask herself or himself, "If only I had more money, I would . . . "; then try to analyze herself or himself relative to her or his money-type and stage in the life-span and the nine life-style groups outlines above. What value-attitudes emerge? Then, examine the differences that exist between or among those in the family. Again, it is important not to view any particular value-attitude orientation or life-style preference as right or wrong. They are simply different; such differences among us can lead either to conflict or to a more stimulating and rewarding existence. By accommodating the diversity of values among family members, the horizons of each individual are broadened, experiences are more varied, and growth occurs in new directions.

Next, look for a solution to the money issue that will satisfy the needs of each person involved. Recognition of the source of the conflict, open and frank discussion, and compromise are required if an acceptable outcome is to be reached. Recognizing where the differences exist should lay the groundwork for the discussion and provide an opportunity to understand one another better. Reaching compromises that recognize the diversity that exists, that do not violate the integrity of *anyone* involved, and that are acceptable to *everyone* involved will reduce the conflict that managing money introduces into our lives.

Notes

1. Milton Rokeach, *Beliefs, Attitude, and Values* (San Francisco: Jossey-Bass, 1968).
2. *Money and Values*, part 1: "The Psychology of Money" (The Learning Seed Co., 1980), filmstrip.
3. Russell W. Belk, "Materialism: Trait Aspects of Living in the Material World," *Journal of Consumer Research* 12 (December 1985): 265–279.
4. Ibid.
5. Daniel Yankelovich, "New Rules in American Life: Searching for Self-Fulfillment in a World Turned Upside Down," *Psychology Today* (April 1981), pp. 35–91.

6. Satenig St. Marie, "A New Agenda, " Phi Kappa Phi address, Brigham Young University, 24 Feb. 1987.
7. "Values and Life-styles: A New Model," *FORUM* (J. C. Penney Co., Sept. 1983), pp. 4–10.
8. D&C 42:32.
9. Marvin J. Ashton, "One for the Money," *Ensign*, July 1975, pp. 72–73.
10. N. Eldon Tanner, "Constancy Amidst Change," *Ensign*, Nov. 1979, pp. 80–82.
11. Ashton, pp. 72–73.

Index

Larsen, Anna, 137
Last days: women in the, 17–19; service in the, 20–21; Church members in the, 24
Law, William, 24
Law of Consecration, 58–59, 62–63, 65–66
Lee, Harold B., 4, 118
Lence, Pearl, 13
Life, definition of, 54
Life of Adam and Eve, 91–92
Lifestyles: values related to, 247–48; American, 248–49
Lincoln, Abraham, 205, 210
Littlefield, Ann, 213–14
Lord's Question, 159
Love: destroyed by worldliness, 16–17; definition of divine, 55–57; men and women are equal in divine, 65–67; communities of, 191–92
Luther, Martin, 117
Lyman, Amy Brown, 126–27, 130–31, 134

McConkie, Bruce R., 108
McCune, Elizabeth Claridge, 130
McKay, David O., 43, 118
Male and female. *See* Female and male
"Man-honor-fight" dogma, 109
Marriage: Christian, 98; oneness in, 113–14; as school of love, 117; equality in, 117–18; examples of successful, 118–19. *See also* Remarriage; Sex
Marsh, Sarah, 124
Maturity: spiritual, 44; of Nephi, 74–77
Maxwell, Colleen, 13
Meir, Golda, 216
Money: definition of, 242; as security, 244–45; as power, 245; as a way to buy love, 245–46; as

freedom, 246; sharing management of, 250–51. *See also* Values
Mormonism, sex discrimination in, 52–53
Mother Teresa, 118, 216
Music, improving the home with good, 151–52, 200

Nature, understanding our eternal, 178
Nephi, maturity of, 74–77
Nibley, Hugh, 103–4, 159
Niebuhr, Richard R., 96
Nightingale, Florence, 216

Order: God is source of, 69; eternal level of, 70–71; of the natural world, 72; personal level of, 73–74; divine, 85
Original sin, LDS theology rejects notion of, 97

Pain: necessity of, 172–73; stories of people who experienced, 174–78, 179–81, 181–89; God sustains man in his, 189–90. *See also* Adversity
Palmer, Annie, 128
Parenthood, role of, 74, 119–20
Patience, dying man learns, 186
Patriarchal societies, women's movement condemns, 51–52
Pearson, Carol Lynn, 159–60
Peck, M. Scott, 98
Phillips, John A., 94
Plan of salvation is part of eternal order, 71
Polygamy, reasons for, 109–10
Power: equality of, 60–61; availability of God's, 80–81
Prayer: coming closer to the Lord through, 163; reality of, 164, people serving as answers to, 191–92, 193, 194

255